How The Bible INVALIDATES The Central Doctrines of CHRISTIANITY

Devon S J Morgan

ISBN 978-1-5136-9805-2 (paperback)

First published 2022 by TruthSeekers Publishing

healthtruths4u@hotmail.co.uk

CONTENTS

TRUTH

The truth is incontrovertible, malice may attack it, ignorance may deride it, but in the end, there it is. – Winston Churchill

A lie gets halfway around the world before the truth has a chance to gets its pants on. – Winston Churchill

A truth's initial commotion is directly proportional to how deeply the lie was believed. It wasn't the world being round that agitated people but that the world wasn't flat. When a well-packaged web of lies has been sold gradually to the masses over generations, the truth will seem utterly preposterous and its speaker, a RAVING lunatic. – Dresden James

The ideal tyranny is that which is ignorantly self-administered by its victims. The most perfect slaves are, therefore, those who blissfully and unawaredly enslave themselves. – Dresden James

For you to be enslaved no one needs to physically have you shackled, they just need to sell you on an idea that disempowered you and gives them the upper hand. --

In a time of universal deceit, telling the truth is a revolutionary act. – George Orwell

All truth passes through three stages. First, it is ridiculed, second, it is violently opposed, and third, it is accepted as self-evident. – Arthur Schopenhauer

As scarce as truth is, the supply has always been in excess of demand. – J Billing

Truth revels in the most intense examination, but a lie will wilt under any intense examination.

If the truth is that ugly; which it is; then we do have to be careful about the way that we tell the truth. But to say somehow that telling the truth should be avoided because people may respond badly to the truth seems bizarre to me. – Chuck Skoro, Deacon, St. Paul's Catholic Church

Each progressive spirit is opposed by a thousand mediocre minds appointed to guard the past. – Maurice Maeterlinck

No matter how logical the conclusion, if it's based on a false premise, then the conclusion is wrong.

The lack of widespread reading is our greatest challenge which results in ignorance and this is a voluntary misfortune, especially if you have access to the Internet.

The broad mass of a nation…will more easily fall victim to a big lie than to a small one. *Mein Kampf* (1925)

Despite us all knowing that all life comes from a woman, the masses believe that man existed first!

Educate a man, you educate an individual, educate a woman, you educate an entire nation. – Dr. James Emmanuel Kwegyir-Aggrey

Ignorance is humanity's worse enemy.

A man/woman who is in love with learning is a man/woman who is never without a bride/bridegroom for there is always more.

Ignorance can be a mental prison that is more secure than all the physical prisons combine.

They must find it difficult, those who have taken authority as the truth, rather than truth as authority. – Gerald Massey

No lie can live forever. – Gerald Massey

The mass of people who are bible-taught never get free from the erroneous impressions stamped on their minds in their infancy, so that their manhood or womanhood can have no intellectual fulfilment, and millions of them only attain mentally to a sort of second childhood. – Gerald Massey

This book is not a divine revelation.

All religious books claim to be a divine revelation

If there is a God who is like a person, the wisdom of any book he inspired would be astonishing in its simplicity, clarity, and the knowledge it entails would always challenge us to grow beyond our current understanding. No religious book fits this description.

Knowledge begins where faith and belief end. Belief is that uncertain state of mind which is experienced in the absence of knowledge. – The Bible of Bibles by Kersey Graves, (1870)

How fortunate we are that in our court of law what we believe is not entertained. Our courts are only interested in what we know.

If to place a man between two all-powerful beings, and have them both trying to direct his actions at once, don't make him a machine, then we have no use for the word. – The Bible of Bibles by Kersey Graves, (1870).

Most of what you know or think you know has been put there by a process similar to hypnosis. It's been placed there by the power of suggestion, inertia, Chinese whisper, the power of imagery, ignorance, and outright lies.

We tend to protect what we believe and unconsciously filter out information we don't want to receive. Most of us are programmed without being aware of it. A child learns that his needs will more likely be met if he conforms to what is expected of him. Society and institutions reach and reward conformity and obedience to authority. What this does is discourage the individual from developing the capacity to think for himself and it also discourages any serious challenge to authority. – Steven Jacobson

Many religions flourish because of the fear of everlasting punishment and the desire to live forever. The desire to live forever is built in because life is energy and energy cannot be destroyed. As far as we know humans are the only life form that can have the desire for eternal life. If the belief in these two ideas should disappear then so would many religions.

How awesome it would be if we could understand Existence outside the mysticism and anthropomorphic idea of religion.

Apart from seeing, hearing, feeling, tasting, and talking what else would you want to do except learn, and what else would you want to learn except the truth?

You are not responsible for the programming you received in childhood. As an adult, you are 100% responsible for fixing it. Unknown

DEDICATION

This book is dedicated to truth-seekers, it's not for the religious because religion is a deeply emotional commitment that convinces its adherents that they have all the answers they will ever need. Religion gives comfort, identity, belonging, and it can serve as a permanent escape from truth. The belief that all answers have been found causes a loss of intellectual curiosity, and therefore an unwillingness to question or interrogate beliefs. Beliefs have become their central viewpoint as opposed to knowing. Belief is an emotional acceptance of ideas without proof. Despite so many years of human growth and development, it seems like most people can't tell the difference between what they believe and what they know. And even if they recognise the difference, they tend not to regard it as being very important – they think it's interchangeable.

Because of the deeply emotional nature of religiosity, it often requires intellectual dishonesty to avoid the pain of cognitive dissonance. Religiosity often causes us to be in a state where we will filter out any idea that would disrupt our comfort zone and cause us to examine or challenge beliefs that give comfort or alleviate fear. Inadvertently, we search for ideas that will confirm what we already accept as truth. Ultimately, we can become wired to be hostile towards anyone or any idea that challenges who we have become. Because religiosity is the opposite of that which is real, it cannot be defended with rationality, truth, and intellect. A classic example of intellectual dishonesty was the response to a question that should destroy the belief in punishment by a Creator. The question was, "If a watch was not keeping accurate time, would you blame the watch or the maker of the watch?" It should go without saying that the standard we would hold a Creator of the universe to would be infinitely higher than a watchmaker. Also, it's on the premise that the watch was not damaged. His response was, "The watch could be faulty." This book is for those who don't believe in religion, recognise its harm, and wish for more information to help in the fight for freedom from religion. It is also a tool to prevent future generations from embracing religion, and this would be the ultimate achievement, because if enough children and those who are undecided should avoid religious indoctrination, religion will eventually, at least, lose its relevance, perhaps disappear, and we would have a better world.

***The man would be a fool who should blame a watch for not running right, knowing that the maker conferred upon it all the properties and powers it possessed. The maker of the watch alone is held responsible for all its perfection and imperfections.* (*The Bible of Bibles by* Kersey Graves, 1870).**

"Progress is born of doubt and inquiry. The Church never doubts, never inquires. To doubt is heresy, to inquire is to admit that you do not know—the Church does neither." — Robert G. Ingersoll,

PROLOGUE

A quote from Kersey Graves' book – The Bible of Bibles 1870

"If such texts are not calculated to foster the spirit of murder, and to extinguish the natural repugnance to cruelty and bloodshed in the human mind, we can conceive of no language that would have such an effect, especially when it is taken in connection with Christ's injunction, **[St. Luke 22:36-38]** "He that hath not a sword, let him sell his coat, and buy one." These injunctions to murder and slaughter have been faithfully obeyed, and the effect has been to submerge Christendom in a sea of blood. I hope the churches will never again hold the reins of government and shape the laws of the country. The reason we do not witness such horrible scenes now is that many church members have outgrown their Bible, and if there are any who have not, they are restrained by laws enacted by liberal minds of too much good feeling and good sense to permit the churches to thus cruelly persecute each other or those who conscientiously differ from them." Since Jesus, the Prince of Peace, supposedly had supernatural powers to raise the dead etc. why would his disciples need swords? Another contradiction of a doctrine of Christianity. Here are just a few Bible texts that correspond with what Kersey Graves wrote:

Exodus 32:27 And he said unto them, Thus said the Lord God of Israel, Put every man his sword by his side, and go in and out from gate to gate throughout the camp, and slay every man his brother, and every man his companion, and every man his neighbour. **Deuteronomy 21:18-21** If a man has a stubborn and rebellious son, which will not obey the voice of his father, or the voice of his mother, and that, when they have chastened him, will not hearken unto them. **19** Then shall his father and his mother lay hold on him, and bring him out unto the elders of his city, and unto the gate of his place. **20** And they shall say unto the elders of his city, our son is stubborn and rebellious, he will not obey our voice; he is a glutton and a drunkard. **21** And all the men of his city shall stone him with stones, that he die: so shalt thou put evil away from among you; and all Israel shall hear, and fear.

Kersey Graves is correct in his conclusion as to the effect Biblical endorsement of murder can have on religious adherents. In response to a question, online, as to the reason for the instruction in **Exodus 32:27**, someone answered "I believe this was a partial punishment for worshiping the golden calf, thus breaking the first commandment."

This matter-of-fact answer was given without repulsion for the mass slaughter of three thousand men who God supposedly rescued from Egypt. The 'crime' was bowing before a graven image. Since people have worshipped many gods and goddesses for the past thousands of years, we would expect this God to continue killing people for the same "crime". The person didn't see the contradiction of the extreme intolerance of a supposedly loving God whose love and mercy are supposed to endureth forever. Also, he should be curious as to why it says, "Lord God of Israel". Isn't it the same God for everybody? The story that led to the mass slaughter is extremely implausible and ridiculous. Here is a synopsis of some of the salient points. How can we believe that these stories are real and the vile actions were sanctioned by a being we regard as possessing the highest sense of justice and morality and it does not corrupt our morality, and cause psychological and emotional damage by making up tolerant to cruelty if we were convinced the action was sanctioned by God? If a child grew up admiring criminals, wouldn't the child likely become a criminal, or at least be tolerant of such behaviour?

Exodus 4:21 And the LORD said unto Moses, When thou go to return into Egypt, see that thou do all those wonders before Pharaoh, which I have put in your hand: **but I will harden his heart, that he shall not let the people go.**

He also told Moses to tell pharoah if he refuses he will kill his son.

Exodus 4:31 And the people believed: and when they heard that the LORD had visited the children of Israel, and that he had looked upon their affliction, then they bowed their heads and worshipped.

Exodus 13:15 And it came to pass, when Pharaoh would hardly let us go, that the LORD slew all the firstborn in the land of Egypt, both the firstborn of man and the firstborn of beast:

Exodus 14:22 God parted the sea for them to escape.

Exodus 14:30 God killed the Egyptians who were chasing them.

Exodus 14:31 the people saw and feared God and believed him and Moses.

Exodus 20:4 God told them not to make graven images.

Exodus 32:1 Because Moses was late coming from the mountain they asked Aaron to "Make us gods which shall go before us" and he complied without question. **[They saw God performed miracles, saved them, killed their pursuers, feared him, yet disobeyed him for such a trivial reason?]**

Exodus 32:10 God gets angry and intended to kill them.

Exodus 32:14 Moses reprimanded him, "And the Lord repented of the evil which he thought to do unto his people." **[Didn't know God could be reprimanded like this. However, he eventually committed the evil he thought of so it was temporary.]**

Exodus 32:27 Moses conveyed God's order for mass slaughter to the children of Levi

Exodus 32:28 the children of Levi killed three thousand men (God's people).

Over two hundred references were found for, "God of Israel", "Lord God of Israel", or other special relationships with God and Israel. This is a massive contradiction of what the Bible is claimed to represent, God's words for all human beings for all time. You have read the implausible story above of him having three thousand of his special people killed. However, the contradiction gets worse: **Leviticus 22:32** Neither shall ye profane my holy name, but I will be hallowed among the children of Israel: I am the LORD which hallows you,

Hollowed means made holy. So, he made them holy. But, he then smote them **(strike them sharply)** in **2 Chronicles 13:15-17**

Then the men of Judah shouted: and as the men of Judah shouted, it came to pass, that **God smote Jeroboam and all Israel before Abijah and Judah. 16** And the children of Israel fled before Judah: and **God delivered them into their hand. 17** And Abijah and his people slew them with a great slaughter: so there fell down slain of Israel **five hundred thousand chosen men. [So, he smote them and when they tried to escape he used his power to deliver some of "his holy children" to be slaughtered]**

The many references to 'the God of Israel' such as his claimed special rescue of his people out of Egypt, his mass killing of some of them, delivering them to be slaughtered, and also doing the direct opposite of venerating them and declaring them to be holy, has to mean exactly the way it appears. It is a fable about a people and their turbulent relationship with their "one and only true God". This is the way things are today in one respect, people believe in different "one and only true God". If this was not the case they would all worship together and marry each other, but they don't and most devotees would recoil at the idea.

Can people grow if they believe that "God" used to beat his children, and have five hundred thousand of them slaughtered? How would he go about striking them in the manner described? How would they survive a heavy or sharp strike from the most powerful force in the universe? At this stage in our development, we should be able to recognise mythological stories or fables.

Once we've imported into our conscious and subconscious mind beliefs that defy logic, wisdom, common sense, and disregard for the truth, we set in motion an erosion of our thinking faculty.

Common sense is based on this universal formula that is steeped in logic: All men are mortal, Socrates is a man, therefore, Socrates is mortal.

INTRODUCTION

In a world dominated by beliefs, it takes extraordinary strength to think outside of this box. We are social beings; therefore, our natural tendency is the desire to be accepted. So, to be born and be socialised (socialisation[1]) in a society where religious beliefs are strong and dominant, such a reality will test one of the core characteristics that define us as humans, the capacity to embrace the science of logic and apply it to every subject. Applying the science of logic to religion requires the most courage. In some countries, you could get killed for questioning beliefs. The science of logic is also called common sense which some regard as a misnomer, citing that common sense is not "common".

We are socialised by the culture we grew up in. If it has strong elements that are destructive and disempowering we should strive to change them. Cultures are not set in stone. The solution is to educate our minds and emotions, that is, elevate their levels of sophistication.

It's a fact that we humans have worshipped various gods or Deities from ancient times.

---

1 In sociology, socialisation is the process of **internalising** the norms and ideologies of society. It is the means by which social and cultural continuity are attained.

If the one true God wants us to know that he exists, what's stopping him? It's not possible for a God who has infinite power to fail at accomplishing such a minor task, therefore, no such God exists who wants us to know he exists.

If you ask any religious person if God, Jehovah, Yahweh, or Allah, wants us to know that he exists they would say yes, they wouldn't say no. Yet either answer exposes the fact that a Creator in the form of an organised personality (God) is an invented concept. They cannot say "No" because this would render their religion to be pointless. If they say "Yes" this is also problematic because if this is true**, belief** and **faith** would not be a requirement to accept that there is a Creator, it would be as certain as living and interacting with our biological father. In contrast, the Gods of religions are never seen and are the subject of many interpretations. In Bible stories, or what is known as "Biblical times", there are many tales of God speaking to humans. However, no such communication has happened in our time, hence the myriad of different religions and beliefs. Surely, if God exists and wanted us to know that he is the only God, it would be the easiest thing for him to do. If there was an all-wise God who wanted us to recognise only him, the obvious thing that he would do is eliminate the current confusion by communicating with humanity, not individuals, in such a manner that leaves no doubt.

Hebrews 11:1 "Now faith is the substance of things hoped for, the evidence of things not seen." **If you need faith then you don't have evidence, and if you have evidence you don't need faith. It's better to have evidence, it's more reliable.**

The contradiction of God being mysterious but wanting us to know that he exists

One of the most notable interactions that the Bible claims took place between God and man tells a story that is a contradiction of a common theme in Christianity, that is, "No one has ever seen God's face". This story should leave no doubt that it is claiming God came to earth and spoke to a man named Abraham up close and personal who recognised him, and therefore, he would have seen his face. The purpose of outlining this story is to illustrate scriptural contradictions, and the length believers will go to deny that there are contradictions. The existence of many Biblical contradictions is proof that religion is rooted in manmade dogma – an infinitely intelligent being would not inspire contradictions. So, if religious texts are filled with manmade dogma, then man invented religion and God. This is because belief in a God is subjected to the descriptions and rules[2] attributed to that God in books written by man, such as God's name and temperament, etc. that are in religious texts. Without such texts, we would be left with our imagination to interpret reality as people did in earlier civilisations. **For example, according to a historical narrative by Derek Partridge in a documentary on religion, "The naked truth":**

"Try and imagine earth in pre-historic[3] times, a place filled with a multitude of dangers, giant animals and reptiles, huge predators, earthquakes, volcanoes, tornadoes, meteors, and the subsequent fear and hostility such an unforgiving environment would breed. If you could be a time traveller, and be spirited back to these ancient times equipped with all the sophisticated modern knowledge you now have, admit it, you would be scared to death, I know I would be. Now, try to imagine what it must have been like for these ancient people, totally devoid of all the knowledge we now take for granted about the awesome forces of nature. A volcano erupts destroying everything in its path; the sky reverberates with thunder, as a vio-

[2] Example, the Ten Commandments

[3] Before writing

lent electrical storm hurled thunderbolts to earth which starts fires. Tornadoes sweep people, animals, and trees away into the sky. The earth opens up, and an earthquake swallows a village in the twinkling of an eye. Pretty scary stuff, and it still is today.

But try to think of it as if you had absolutely no understanding of these natural occurrences at all. And at night, gazing up into those fearsome skies filled with infinite numbers of stars, not to mention shooting stars, without having the remotest idea of what they were… is it no wonder that these ancient people created a myriad of all-powerful nature gods and the countless myths that surrounded them, the gods that have been worshipped, and sacrificed to, for thousands of years since. For example, **the mighty Thor,** who when angry struck his anvil with his hammer and created thunder. The same Thor from his abode in the clouds or heavens sends his lightning bolt and it caused terror in mortals on earth. If alone in the dense forest and felt fearful, and sense a presence of an unknown threat, then it had to be **the forest god Pan** from whom we got our word panic - and at night when it became cold, dark, dangerous, and downright frightening, without a convenient and comforting light switch, who else came out to rule but the fierce prince of darkness, and then came the dawn with its light, warmth, and new life, and who brought it, and in so doing defeated the prince of darkness? None other than the sun, which became known as god's **sun**, the light of the world.

**Thor
God of
Thunder**

Human beings are the only creatures capable of the process of logical thought, and imagination, and of questioning everything around them. In fact, the very evolution of humans has been dependent on our ability to seek, find answers and adopt. However, a small weakness has been known, if logical answers are not readily available, human imagination often invented or created suitably, and at least temporarily satisfying answers, such as the very basic need to have a reason to explain our existence, and the equally important need to feel that life must be for some purpose and that it cannot simply end at death, that there must be something beyond. This remains as true today as it was for ancient man. Consider again how little ancient man knew compared to us. In order to create some liveable explanations, gods and myths had to be created. All questions require answers, real or created so that we can get on with life."

In earlier times, perhaps after the times mentioned in "The Naked Truth", it was common for a person to bid farewell by saying, "May the gods be with you", and gods were based on various attributes of Nature or attributes that suited the desire of the populace such as **Ares, the god of war**. But now, most believers claim there is just one God. However, they don't believe in the same God. If they do, how do they explain, in the main, not worshipping with, or marrying each other? This would be a massive contradiction. The evidence points to a belief in a different one and only true God. But now, there is no conscious connection between these Gods and Nature, they have now given the various "one and only God" human qualities with supernatural powers – the anthropomorphic Gods. Billions of people now believe in these one and only true Gods, and it speaks to the power of socialisation.

Ares – the god of war

Sexism – evidence of the power of socialisation

The power of socialisation is self-evident when we realise that we have all been socialised into accepting many aspects of sexism as being normal. It will be a surprise to many if they realise that religion is the architect of normalizing sexism, and its power is so awesome that women are inadvertently the biggest supporters of their discrimination. So, for those who desire freedom from religion, you should endeavor to disrupt this socialisation by aiming this knowledge at current and future generations.

This book is written for two kinds of people, those who are uncertain about religion and those who are already certain that religion is false – a manmade story. For those who are certain, chances are you already realise how harmful it is and would love if it was relegated to insignificance or become obsolete. This book can be another tool to help this process. In the contents of this book, you will see that religion has targeted, killed, and oppressed women over many centuries, and the discrimination against, and oppression of women continues today. So, this is the elephant in the room – women are the unrealised secret weapon for freedom from religion. This is because women are the vast majority of those who are socialised and indoctrinated into religious beliefs, particularly in Christianity – they propped up these institutions. So, what if women start to realise that religion is manmade, the architect of sexism, therefore it is responsible for all the evils they endured in history, and by believing in it they are helping to maintain sexism and discrimination? Wouldn't this accelerate freedom from religion? The consequences of religion as it relates to women are the most profound demonstration of the destructive nature of religion.

CHAPTER ONE

An important historical contradiction – powerful evidence that man invented God – the worship of Goddesses

Our first concept of Deity

Let's examine the religious' certainty that there is a God and this being is male. Religious history throws up interesting facts that confirm that concepts of deities have shifted throughout the ages within different cultures. Current "Creators" or "Gods" are referred to as male beings. Yet, **earlier civilisations that would be closer to the "Adam and Eve, 'in the beginning' story" had significant differences in their concept of Deity.** According to Encylopedia.com:

Goddess Worship: An Overview

Mother Goddess

"The scope and antiquity of goddess worship are remarkable. Female sacred images are associated with some of the oldest archaeological evidence for religious expression and they still have efficacy in the contemporary world. Goddess images are depicted in a wide range of forms, from aniconic representations, such as abstract organs of reproduction, to fully elaborated icons decorated with the finery of a monarchy. They are linked to all major aspects of life, including birth, initiation, marriage, reproduction, and death. They display the elaborate variegation of religious experiences in different cultural contexts. A historical survey reveals goddess worship to be a continuous phenomenon, despite periodic ebbs and tides during certain critical epochs.

Goddess Worship in Upper Paleolithic[4] Cultures

Some of the earliest archaeological evidence for the human religious impulse consists of sculptured images and cave paintings of female figures excavated in hundreds of Upper Paleolithic sites throughout Europe and northern Asia, including France, Spain, Italy, Germany, Austria, Ukraine, and Siberia. **These images, carved in bone, stone, antler, and mammoth tusks, outnumber those of male figures ten to one**. They have been identified sometimes as part of an elaborate, and pervasive worship of goddesses; they are commonly known as "Venuses," after the Roman goddess of love and beauty."

Note with great interest how often the word **tradition** is used and its meaning.

Based on deductions derived from the research of historian Professor Charles Finch, the worship of God as the main Deity, instead of Goddess, started eight thousand years ago. However, the earliest representation of Deity was depicted by the ancient Egyptians. It is the image of a pregnant Hippopotamus named Ta-Urt, representing

[4] Prehistoric – old stone age before there was writing

Great Mother Earth, and the image referenced a **tradition**[5] that predated them, the ancient Egyptians. So, based on us modern humans being on earth for 200,000 years, the worship of goddesses, or female representation of Deity, could be over 190,000 years. So, the people closest to the "beginning" of modern humans, did not conceive human life to have been started by a male Deity.

> **Communities of goddess worship are ancient in India. In Rigveda, the most prominent goddess is Ushas, the goddess of dawn. In modern Hinduism, goddesses are widely revered.** Wikipedia

So, we have a choice of what we use to **understand human history during the time before writing was invented,** do we accept words from a book that is filled with contradictions, or do we accept physical evidence such as statues and carvings in stone left by ancient people? Wouldn't the people who existed closer to the time life began on earth have a more accurate understanding of what took place in the "beginning"? And if a Creator spoke to humans over 2,000 times as claimed by the Bible, how come the earliest depiction of deities was female? If there was a male Creator who created the first people who he actively communicated with, and they had many descendants who the Bible claims he communicated with, wouldn't these first people have an accurate understanding of what or who was their Creator? Yet the oldest evidence of the depiction of Deity is female, and this went on for thousands of years, and still exists today, such as the goddesses in India, namely, Devi, Durga, Lakshmi, Saraswati, Kali, Sita, Ganga, Tulsi, Kamadhenu, and Radha, and many more. **This is not a suggestion that they had evidence of a female Creator, if they did there would not be multiple goddesses.** The **theory** for goddess veneration will be explained shortly.

---

5 Synonyms: belief, legend, folklore, lore, myth, superstition, culture, symbolism etc.

The history of Hinduism and Goddess worship is one aspect of the proof that the worship of female deities is older than the worship of male deities. This is because it is considered the world's oldest religion with an age of over 4,000 years. The other half of the evidence is that female deities existed in Egypt for thousands of years before the existence of what we now have, organised religion. Organised religion is the commercialisation and corruption of ancient mythological and spiritual concepts, and much of it had to do with the veneration of the sun, Nature, and the cosmos.

Organised religion and the birth of sexism – definitive proof man invented God and religious texts

The first humans would have found themselves on this mysterious planet, and like us, wonder how they got here. So, after the first pregnancy, and seeing life come out of a woman for the first time, this would be physical and living proof of how and where life comes from. These early humans would not have understood the reproductive science of pregnancy and birth, as a result, they eventually elevated this natural act to that of a "Creator" bringing forth life, and hence the concept of the mother goddess was born. Once the contribution of the male seed was understood, it became God and Goddess – two substances that create life – yin and yang – male and female energy – one cannot produce without the other. So, the veneration of the female eventually led to the acknowledgement of duality – the principle of opposites. This is the principle of being balanced.

The opposite of being balanced is not good. It cannot be a coincidence that with the absence of the Goddess women, in the main, do not enjoy equal status as men. The song, "It's a man's world" aptly describes the dominant reality. As a result, half or more of the human population is often underutilised. Unfortunately, the reduction of the status of women in society and therefore a reduction of significant input in the affairs of humanity led to many horrific historical consequences as you will see shortly. This subject is worth an extensive look because it was so bad it should leave no doubt that it did not originate from some loving and divine source. Also, although the current existence of sexism is widely acknowledged, much of it is so normalised it has been unknowingly accepted by most women and men, in and outside of religion. And since women are the overwhelming majority in many of these churches and other religious institutions, their enlightenment is the key to the disappearance of these organisations, and the world would enjoy sweet freedom from religion. This would have a positive effect on the status of women, and on society in general.

If the Bible was the ultimate history book and the undisputed guidance from our ultimate parent, an infinitely intelligent being called God, it would not contain any scripture that discriminates against women and gave birth to sexism. Organised patriarchal religion was and is the power behind the transition from a matriarchal society (ruled by women) to our current patriarchal society. There isn't a lot known about matriarchal societies in terms of how they functioned but we do know that they preceded our current system and didn't involve the oppression and destruction of women as have transpired under our current system.

Matriarchy is a social system in which women hold the primary power positions in roles of authority. In a broader sense, it can also extend to moral authority, social privilege, and control of property.

Despite the separation of state from the church in Western countries, Christianity has a strong influence on societies and is evident in governments and the judiciary system. Even in America where the constitution prohibits governments from endorsing any religion, presidents are sworn in holding the Bible, and it's the norm to swear on the Bible or invoke, "So help me God," before testifying in court or congress. Significantly, this is called testifying under oath, and if it was found that you lied you can be imprisoned. This would suggest that there is a strong belief in the central tenets of Christianity, and **if we swear on the Bible in the name of God** we deserve punishment. And yet there is no recognition under the law to claim that the supernatural powers of the Devil or God made us commit a crime. Therefore, we can conclude that the rulers who put this in place never believed in the power of God or the Devil as forces in human affairs. It seems like the Bible was used as a tool to frighten people to be truthful in court. However, whether the rulers had a great belief in religious dogma or not, religious doctrines have shaped societies more than we may realise. For example, in Islamic countries, alcohol consumption is prohibited because The Holy Quran prohibits it. In Christendom alcohol is drank freely even though there are scriptures that prohibit it. However, as is common, the Bible has contradictions, and the biggest contradiction can be classified as a celebrity endorsement, Jesus is believed to have turned water into wine. So, how has the Bible provided the authority for sexism which has led to some of the worst atrocities in history, and the current prevalence of sexism?

Sexism in the Bible is part of the most definitive proof that man invented religious texts, God, and religion.

The prevalence of sexism in the church and women accepting it is based on the belief that it is mandated by their God. This is evidence of how powerful socialisation and religious dogma can be. Women who accept Christianity are inadvertently endorsing their oppression. According to the Bible in, **1 Timothy 2:11-14**, Let the woman learn in silence with all subjection [submissiveness]. **12.** But I suffer not a woman to teach, nor to usurp authority over the man, but to be in silence. **13.** For Adam was first formed, then Eve. **14.** And Adam was not deceived, but the woman being deceived was in the transgression.

Verses 11 and 12 are the basis on which many denominations don't allow women to have leadership roles such as elders, priests, or bishops, even though they are usually the majority in these institutions. Since there is no logical reason for **verse 13**, its purpose is to demean women, and this point is on solid ground when placed in the context that the first creation story **Genesis 1:27** claims man and woman were created at the same time, and a different story was added in **Genesis chapter 2** claiming that the man was created first as you will see in chapter three. Since both of them are necessary for life to continue, who was created first is irrelevant as to who should have authority, and the word authority is more appropriate for use in an army or a government. So, this was not inspired by an infinitely intelligent being or parent, it is manmade dogma designed to control and oppress women. Saying that Adam was created first as the basis for the man's qualification to lead and the woman to be submissive to him is as frivolous and nonsensical as a parent applying the same principle to twins, saying that the one who came out first is entitled to lead.

1 Timothy 2:14 confirms that this was a deliberate agenda. It's suggesting that because Adam wasn't directly deceived by the serpent, the woman was the only one to be blamed, she is the one that "sinned", not Adam. However, in **Genesis 2:15-17,** the second creation story, when Adam was the only one created, it says, "And the LORD God took the man, and put him into the garden of Eden to dress it and to keep it. **16** And the LORD God commanded the man, saying, Of every tree of the garden thou may freely eat: **17** But of the tree of the knowledge of good and evil, thou shalt not eat of it: for in the day that thou eat thereof thou shalt surely die." And **Genesis 3:17** says, "And unto Adam, he said, Because thou has hearkened unto the voice of thy wife, and has eaten of the tree, of which I commanded thee, saying, Thou shalt not eat of it: cursed is the ground for thy sake; in sorrow shall thou eat of it all the days of thy life."

In this narrative, he was given the order directly, and presumably, he told Eve. So, this speaks to his weakness more than hers because at least it said she resisted, while he didn't even hesitate, but the story claimed God gave him leadership authority over the woman. If this was a real story, blaming the woman for causing the man to disobey God would be unfair since the man was directly given instructions not to eat from the tree, not the woman, and yet he did not hesitate when she offered it to him as you will read shortly in **Genesis 3:1-6**. This speaks to him being weak and lacking in leadership and therefore should not qualify him for automatic leadership.

The frivolous nature of what is claimed to qualify the man for leadership was not from the mind of an intelligent being of any description. In the course of this book, you will see more evidence that the Bible gave legitimacy to sexism. The blaming of the woman has worked so well that for centuries until now it is commonly accepted dogma that "Eve" caused "original sin" and therefore responsible for humanity's "fall from grace", and therefore the state of the world. And women have suffered the consequence of this for centuries, and even now. The mythology of the temptress was born from this fiction. To make it worse, the **concept** of original sin is not in the Bible and does not include the woman being blamed. You will see the evidence in chapter three.

There are many scriptures that Christians claim confirm their belief in original sin, that is, humanity inherited the sins of Adam and Eve. However, Genesis is the only scripture in the Bible where it claims God dished out punishments for Adam and Eve's disobedience. There was no punishment of hellfire for them. The word sin was not mentioned.

In general, religion is weaponised mythology that affects all of us. However, it has disproportionately targeted women and used to diminish and reduce their value and role in societies.

Genesis 3:1-6 Now the serpent was more subtle than any beast of the field which the LORD God had made. And he said unto the woman, Yea, hath God said, Ye shall not eat of every tree of the garden? **2** And the woman said unto the serpent, we may eat of the fruit of the trees of the garden. **3** But of the fruit of the tree which is in the midst of the garden, God hath said, ye shall not eat of it, neither shall ye touch it, lest ye die. **4** And the serpent said unto the woman, ye shall not surely die. **5** For God do know that in the day ye eat thereof, then your eyes shall be opened, and ye shall be as gods, knowing good and evil. **6** And when the woman saw that the tree *was* good for food, and that it *was* pleasant to the eyes, and a tree to be desired to make *one* wise, she took of the fruit thereof, and did eat, and gave also unto her husband with her; and he did eat.

In the real world, any parent who treats their boy child better than the girl because of their genitals would be a poor, and inadequate parent. And yet this action is ascribed to a God who is supposed to have endowed us with all of our human traits. Since good parents love their children equally, those who accept this dogma, inadvertently accept that humans have higher ethical and moral standards than the God they believe in. If not, they need to explain how come we, in the main, have good parental instincts that are just and fair, but their God doesn't. Since the religious claim God gives us all our talents and abilities, they have the unenviable task of explaining why their God's parental instinct is worse than that which he supposedly gave us.

No infinitely intelligent, loving, and just God, who is supposed to be our parent, would discriminate against his daughters by declaring that women shouldn't teach. This makes no sense considering that reproductive arrangement dictates that the mother, at the outset, will have greater bonding with the child because of ten months of physical attachment, then extensive feeding, and caring of the child. So, invariably she will spend far more quality time with the offspring than the man and will be its first teacher, both cognitively and emotionally.

The scripture claims the God of religion instructed women not to teach, and to remain silent in situations when they disagree with a man. It describes a God who would be a poor shadow of an intelligent and decent human parent. Such a parent should know that this would be psychological abuse and that it would retard the psychological and emotional growth of the child into womanhood. A wise and intelligent parent wants all their children to be healthy psychologically and emotionally. This scripture is one of many that is definitive proof that man invented God, and made up the Bible and other religious books to validate their mythology and gain power over women.

How did the shift from goddess worship come about? Part of the explanation is in Dan Brown's book, The DaVinci Code:

"The church had a deceitful and troubled history. Their brutal crusade to 're-educate' the pagan and feminine-worshipping religions spanned three centuries, employing methods as inspired as they were horrific.

The Catholic Inquisition published the book that arguably could be called the most blood-soaked publication in human history. Malleus Malefic arum – or The Witches' Hammer – indoctrinated the world to 'the dangers of freethinking women' and instructed the clergy on how to locate, torture, and destroy them. Those deemed 'witches' by the Church included all female scholars, priestesses, gypsies, mystics, nature lovers, herb gatherers, and any women 'suspiciously attuned to the natural world'. Midwives also were killed for their heretical practice of using medical knowledge to ease the pain of childbirth – suffering, which the church claims was God's rightful punishment for Eve's partaking of the Apple of Knowledge, thus giving birth to the idea of original sin. During three hundred years of Witch-hunts, the Church burned at the stake an astounding five million women. The propaganda and bloodshed had worked. Today's world is living proof.

Women, once celebrated as an essential half of spiritual enlightenment, had been banished from the temples of the world. There were no female Orthodox rabbis, Catholic priests, nor Islamic clerics. The once hallowed act of Hieros Gamos – the natural sexual union between man and woman through which each became spiritually whole – had been recast as a shameful act. Holy men who had once required sexual union with their female counterparts to commune with God now feared their natural sexual urges as the work of the devil, collaborating with his favourite accomplice … woman.

The days of the goddess were over. The pendulum had swung. Mother Earth had become a man's world, and the gods of destruction and war were taking their toll. The male ego had spent two millennia running unchecked by its female counterpart … this obliteration of the sacred feminine in modern life has caused what the Hopi Native Americans called Koyaanisqatsi – 'life out of balance' – an unstable situation marked by testosterone-fuelled wars, a plethora of misogynistic societies and a growing disrespect for Mother Earth …"

No loving parent would inspire a book with instructions that discriminate against his children based on gender. How can this make sense when both genders are of equal importance for life to exist? No all-wise "God" would do this, therefore it is manmade dogma. Women's role in procreation[6] and the nurturing of children is more extensive than men's. So, what happened to women based on Bible scriptures could not be the work of a being with infinite intelligence. Therefore, it was the work of man's desire to rule and dominate by destroying the Goddess mythological principle and installing the mythological male Creator principle. Since witches are mythical

---

[6] Women provide the egg, the womb, ten months of internal nourishing, the birthing of the child, breast milk, and first cognitive and emotional development.

concepts, such stories could not originate from anywhere except the minds of mankind. Not from a loving, infinitely intelligent being, who it is claimed knows all things, and therefore would not promote fiction, especially one that had the heinous consequence of witch-hunts that primarily destroyed women. For example, in Salem, of the **nineteen** people hanged for witchcraft, **five were men**, and **fourteen were women.** Historically, the numbers dramatically favour accused women over men. This competes for the worse episode in human history. Why the bias towards women, when, in terms of evil actions we men dominate? The Bible is the cause.

In **Leviticus 20:27** it states – "A man also or woman that hath a familiar spirit[7], or that is a wizard, shall surely be put to death: they shall stone them with stones: their blood shall be upon them." However, the only story of a witch was a woman, "The witch of Endor" in, **1 Samuel 28:7-25** KJV

The belief in witches and its consequences for women

The following historical perspectives illustrate further how bad it was for women, and how horrific religious influence can be. It also proves that we humans are born almost empty of any software or guidance system, and therefore we can "inherit" almost any philosophy and attitude. Since belief in witches is a twin to belief in Satan, and Satan is a religious mythical concept, belief in witches is inseparable from religion. This is further confirmed by a witch being regarded as the "Devil's consort". So, the horrific treatment dished out to mostly women accused of being witches, over centuries, was based on something that never existed, a sheer figment of imagination. So successful was this branding of women as witches, and movies have augmented this concept, we **always** associate females with the word 'witch'.

Here are some of the reasons that someone would be accused of being a witch (16th to 18th centuries)

---

[7] A demon supposedly attending and obeying a witch

Taken from separate articles written by D.G. Hewitt and Leah Beckmann

- Just being a woman –"For thousands of years, people have believed women to be more susceptible to sins than men, and sinning is a clear indication of devil worship. In Salem, of the 19 people hanged for witchcraft, five were men and 14 were women. Historically, the numbers dramatically favor accused women over men."
- You are poor/and cannot support yourself financially.
- You are rich/financially independent – do not need the help or supervision of a man.
- You are a healer.
- **You are a midwife. Wise women used their knowledge of herbal medicine to help others give birth safely – but it left them open to accusations of witchcraft…** if a woman gave birth to a healthy baby and lived, the midwife would be accused of having used magic or making a deal with the Devil. Or if the baby or mother died, the midwife might also be blamed and accused of cursing the birth…by the late-17th century, the persecution of innocent midwives had largely stopped. As men started to take over the medical professions, including midwifery, the effectiveness of herbal remedies and natural medicines became increasingly accepted." **This is indisputable evidence of sexism.**
- You have exhibited "stubborn," "strange," or "forward" behaviour.
- **You have a reputation for being argumentative. Nobody liked or trusted an assertive woman back in the 16th and 17th centuries.**
- You 'look the part'; you have a mole, birthmark, limp or have a hunched back (usually women). **Prosecutors were always on the lookout for tell-tale 'signs of a witch'** (almost any physical imperfection or skin blemish), **especially on female bodies.**

- You have a third nipple. They thought that Satan himself would suckle on the nipple…
- You have had sex out of wedlock – women were expected to follow strict sexual rules.
- **You talk to yourself: As the Salem Witch Trials (1692/93) showed, simply muttering under your breath could be seen as a sign of black magic.**
- You have broken virtually any rule in the Bible and thus entered into a pact with the devil.
- **You don't dress smartly enough: In some witch trials, an individual's refusal to dress like everyone else was seen as something distinctly sinister** - women who were expected to follow strict dress codes.
- You are married with too few (or no) children; the Devil cursed your unholy womb with infertility. Furthermore, if your neighbours and their several children are suffering in any way, they almost certainly believe the jealous crone living next to them has hexed their home.
- **You are left-handed. According to many traditions[8], there was something 'sinister' about being left-handed, and it was seen as one obvious sign that someone was a witch.**
- You have one or more female friends. A group of women congregating without a male chaperone was deemed a "coven meeting to worship the Devil."
- **You have a cat. For centuries, people really did believe that women who lived alone with cats for company were probably in league with the Devil…**pet snakes, even pet dogs might also be seen as witches' companions and could get their owners in serious trouble.
- **Failure to quote fluently from the Bible might be seen as a sign of being possessed by evil.**
- You are very old. Older women were treated with suspicion, especially if they lived alone.

---

8 Synonyms: belief, legend, folklore, lore, myth, superstition, culture, symbolism etc.

- **Have curdled milk in your house. Many believed that witches were able to make milk go bad just by walking by.**

Since the past influenced and shape the present, the extreme barbaric treatment of women which was spawned by religion, played a role in shaping our current attitude towards women. Just like most of our changes, it was gradual, and every adjustment becomes the new norm. The irony is that even those of us who are not religious are shaped by a philosophy started by religion, and are unaware of this. We think our attitude is natural and right because we do not have a historical perspective of how socialisation shaped our behaviour.

Disproportionate derogatory words and names used against women

Here are some other examples of how bad it got for women after they were removed from religious power. Are you aware that there is a large disparity of derogatory names for women versus men? We should all be aware that words have power. For example, it is well known that if we repeatedly tell a child they are worthless there is a good chance it will hurt their future. Let's start with a question:

Why are there so many derogatory words and names used against women? In each era, different countries, and cultures have had derogatory words or expressions for women. How do we account for our 'better half' meriting such disrespect? How do we justify the wide disparity between derogatory words for women and men? Many of the following derogatory words relating to women have sexual connotations, yet men, in general, tend to be more promiscuous than women. This list is by no means exhaustive:

1. Bitch. **2.** Slut. **3.** Whore. **4.** Hussy. **5.** Town bike. **6.** Beef. **7.** Thing. **8.** Old Hag. **9.** Cow. **10.** Witch. **11.** Sketel (Caribbean term for slut). **12.** Skirt. **13.** Heifer. **14.** Floozy. **15.** Jezebel. **16.** Belly warmer. **17.** Skank (woman who dates a married man). **18.** Streetwalker. **19.** Bird. **20.**

Chick. **21.** Mule. **22.** Bimbo. **23.** Piece of ass. **24.** Harlot. **25.** Flappers (used in the 1920s). **26.** Sheng nu (leftover women – women who remain unmarried in their late twenties and beyond (China). **27.** Swamp Donkey

The following male list is much smaller as the following indicates:

1. Bastard. **2.** Jerk **3.** Asshole. **4.** Creep. Douchebag. **5.** Fag. **6.** Dog (can also be used as a term of endearment). **7.** Cunt. **8.** Prick. **9.** Scumbag. **10.** Wanker. **11.** Son of a bitch (This insult is mostly derogatory to the mother)

The disparity of derogatory names for women compared to men must be connected to the origin and past treatment of women, and in the context of the horrific nature of witch-hunts, this suggests being born from deep disrespect or perhaps hatred of women. How aware are you of the depth of this anomaly? Whatever the reason for this anomaly, just a scratch at the surface shows that it makes no kind of sense, common, or otherwise. Every subject can benefit from a historical perspective:

"According to ancient superstition, women, 'whores' or otherwise, were not permitted on board ship: they were regarded as unlucky and any unfortunate woman who found herself on board would have been thrown overboard to drown." (Catharine Arnold, *City of Sin: London and its Vices,* page 23)

- "…until recently [relatively speaking] the lives of women were not considered worth recording." (Catharine Arnold, *City of Sin: London and its Vices,* page45)
- "… the Visigoths ruled that whores must be publicly whipped and their noses split open, whilst one early Aryan form of **Christianity** practised among the German tribes saw promiscuous girls and women put to death…the conditions for 'respectable' women were little better: regarded as the property of their husbands and fathers, they were

> traded like horses and sold into wedlock for financial or political gain." (Catharine Arnold, *City of Sin: London and its Vices,* page 24).

Are you getting a sense of how powerful and far-reaching religious belief can be? An understanding of psychology tells us that if humanity were still worshipping goddesses as major deities, the extreme and poor treatment of women would not have happened.

We all know that sexism is not over unless we are in denial. The question is, how bad is it? Well, it is a lot worse than is appropriate for this book to extensively delve into. As already stated, women are the key to bringing down this grotesque and destructive human invention. Religion has been so effective in shaping behaviour that even men who don't believe in religion are unaware that our attitudes are shaped by it – it's called socialisation. It is interesting to reflect on the fact that a change in our religious belief is at the root of our current attitude and actions towards women, and yet most of the world is unaware of this, including non-believers.

We have strict anti-competition laws to promote fairness in business and yet, recently, in 2015, in England, "*The Independent*" newspaper headline read, "*Gender pay gap: Firms who pay men more than women to be "named and shamed"* by the government of England. It went on to say, "*Writing in the Times, he [Prime Minister, David Cameron] said the government was making a "really big move" by forcing companies to reveal the pay gap between the sexes.* He said: "*That will cast sunlight on the discrepancies and create the pressure we need for change, driving women's wages up.*" So, we have strict anti-competition laws but the best we can do to solve wage discrimination against women is to name and shame the offenders? This is incredible.

How deep is this sexism, then? It has to be very deep for the government to publicly acknowledge that a solution is needed, yet the absurdity of "naming and shaming" as a solution means that in reality, it is going largely unchallenged. Naming and shaming are, in effect, the 'code words' for doing nothing. Is the lack of strong action against the disparity in gender pay due to it being widely regarded, in this male-dominated society, as a small issue that is not worthy of too much fuss? What about 'gender-ageism'? Well, according to the British Broadcasting Corporation (BBC) website (23 July 2017), "Andrew Marr, [of The Andrew Marr Show] who is paid between £400,000 and £449,999 a year by the BBC, said if he was a woman he would have been removed from the TV '10 years ago. 'There's a real lack of older women on the screen,' the 57-year-old said." The online medium reported that "The salaries, **published in the corporation's annual report**, revealed two-thirds of its stars earning more than £150,000 are male, with Radio 2 DJ Chris Evans the top-paid on between £2.2m and £2.25m," while, "Claudia Winkleman, Strictly Come Dancing co-host and Radio 2 presenter… was the highest-paid female celebrity, earning between £450,000 and £500,000 last year."

Is inequality of pay tantamount to the oppression of women? Shouldn't this be illegal and at least result in a fine being imposed? Do you think oppression is too strong a word? Isn't our time our most precious commodity because we can never retrieve it? So, the woman spending her time and energy and being compensated less than a man amounts to robbery of her most precious commodity. Isn't the ultimate name for not being paid for your time and energy, slavery? So, doesn't a lesser degree of this qualify as oppression? Shouldn't the women be paid for the years of being underpaid? If you found out that you were underpaid would you sue for compensation? So, does the Prime Minister's response speak, at a minimum, to an attitude of weak empathy towards sexism as it relates to women? As a solution to this deep-seated problem, naming and shaming companies is almost as useless as men's nipples. This snippet of one of the less horrific consequences of man's invention of God and holy books should leave no doubt that there are no good consequences that can be named that come close to the long stain of blood and destruction that religion has wrought on humanity.

Western wedding culture has a practice where the bride's father walks her down the aisle and "gives her away". It's part of the evidence that there was a time in the 16th and 17th centuries when she was legally her father's property, more so than his son.

Sexism is not an accidental attitude; societies shaped it, and it was also written in law. This has been passed down from generation to generation. Here is an example from Harvard Business School:

"During most of American history, women's lives in most states were circumscribed by common law brought to North America by English colonists. These marriage and property laws, or 'coverture,' stipulated that a married woman did not have a separate legal existence from her husband. A married woman or *feme covert* was a dependent, like an underage child or a slave, and could not own property in her name or control her earnings, except under very specific circumstances."

It's a fact that goddess worship exists and used to be dominant. If combined with the fact that the church went on "a crusade to re-educate feminine-worshipping religions", and the witch hunt that follows, Bible instruction that women shouldn't teach or rule, and the significant absence of female leadership in religion is proof that this was a major object of the patriarchal religious system. The discrimination against women in the wider society called sexism has its root in the church. They have succeeded.

Other Biblical examples of female discrimination: Deuteronomy 22:13-21 - If a man falsely accused his new wife of not being a virgin he would be fined a hundred shekels and cannot divorce her. If he is proven right men shall stone her to death.

Leviticus 27:5 If the person is from five years old up to twenty years old, the valuation shall be for a male twenty shekels, and for a female ten shekels.

CHAPTER TWO

The problems of an anthropomorphic God

Applying human qualities to a deity is known as Anthropomorphism. It is defined as, "The **attribution** of a human form or personality to a god, animal or thing." This means we gave form and personality to **a concept** and called it god, and not a god declaring possession of said qualities. The obvious main attribute we ascribed to the concept of God is being male. And to qualify as a male requires having a penis. Since a penis is used for urination and sex, this anthropomorphic quality is problematic for the religious to explain, why would a spiritual being require a penis? Unless it's connected to the Virgin Mary story? The gods before the current dominant religions had wives and children.

Anthropomorphism was explained to a Christian as meaning that we have ascribed human qualities to a concept of God. He didn't understand it as meaning **we invented God**. So, to justify it he quoted the Bible saying God created us in His likeness. Since every aspect of our existence is of the highest order of science, then logically science and logic should characterise whatever and whoever they conceive God to be. Yet, the same person admonished me for applying logic to interrogate the Bible and Christianity. Since logic is inseparable from science, in the confines of what he believes, he should at least associate his God with logic. This is an example of people not having clarity as to what they believe. However, this is difficult when human unpredictable qualities such as jealousy, are ascribed to a God.

The following definition is accurate since it corresponds to many descriptions and attributes of the Biblical God:

"Anthropomorphic gods exhibited **human qualities such as beauty, wisdom, and power**, and sometimes human weaknesses such as greed, hatred, jealousy, and uncontrollable anger. Greek gods such as Zeus and Apollo were often depicted in human form exhibiting both commendable and despicable human traits." Here is an example of a despicable human trait attributed to a god:

The god Mars: According to the story, **Rhea Silvia was raped by the god of war, Mars, and gave birth to two twin sons: Romulus and Remus.**

A conundrum

Being human has distinct limitations, and an example of these limitations guarantees that we will never be responsible for the existence of another planet. So, applying human characteristics to a Creator is inadequate to explain our existence. This is because it creates a conundrum, that is, a question that exposes limitations to any being or organised personality being responsible for our existence. The religious would say God's power is unlimited, there is nothing God cannot do. They would then struggle to answer these questions: "Can God create a rock that is too heavy for him to lift, or strip himself of his powers?"

If God was infinite intelligent energy and everything is different manifestations of it, then the question becomes null and void, since the rock would be an aspect of God.

The contradiction of God not having a face but if seen will cause death

In contrast to the ancient gods (god of war etc.), the attributes bestowed on the current anthropomorphic Gods are mysterious, and often contradictory. To help adherents accept contradictions and defend even the illogical, there is a common Christianity dogma that allows credibility to be given to every scripture regardless of what they claim. It could be illogical, immoral, and impossible, but it would be deemed credible. It says, "God moves in mysterious ways", and it is based on Bible scriptures[9]. A classic example of the acceptance of contradictions is the belief that no one has ever seen God's face. So, even though it's written in the Bible that their God came to earth and converse with a person named Abraham and others, it is widely taught and believed by religious adherents that "No one has ever seen God's face."

To accept that God visited and converse with Abraham and others, and also accept that no one has seen God's face as being true is to accept two opposing claims as being true, and this is supposed to be impossible. However, religion has this effect on believers. The psychology of being committed to religious beliefs requires avoiding cognitive dissonance, that is, avoiding the pain that would be experienced if opposing ideas or beliefs are held in the mind at the same time. So, whenever any contradictions, inaccuracies, immoral concepts, or immoral stories are seen in the Bible, it has to be interpreted as being consistent, and perfect, and the big get-out clause is, "Who am I to question God?" To cover the obvious contradictions within the Abraham story, Moses story, and others regarding the seeing of God's face, those who wish to dismiss Bible contradictions on this subject, advise their fellow adherents not to accept the meaning of words or the obvious meaning of stories! Here is an example regarding Moses according to Mary Fairchild:

1. "The phrase "face of God," as used in the Bible, gives important information about God the Father, but the expression can be easily misunderstood. This misunderstanding makes the Bible seem to contradict itself on this concept.

---

[9] Romans 11:33, Ephesians 5:32, Isiah 40:28, Isiah 55:8-9 See addendum for other texts and commentaries

2. The problem begins in the book of Exodus, when the prophet Moses, speaking with God on Mount Sinai, asks God to show Moses his glory. God warns that: "...You cannot see my face, for no one may see me and live." (Exodus 33:20, NIV)
3. God then places Moses in a cleft in the rock, covers Moses with his hand until God passes by, then removes his hand so Moses may see only his back.
4. Unraveling the problem begins with a simple truth: God is spirit. He does not have a body: "God is spirit, and his worshipers must worship in the Spirit and in truth." (John 4:24, NIV)
5. The human mind cannot comprehend a being who is pure spirit, without form or material substance. Nothing in human experience is even close to such a being, so to help readers relate to God in some understandable way, the writers of the Bible used human attributes to speak of God. In the passage from Exodus above, even God used human terms to speak of himself. Throughout the Bible, we read of his face, hand, ears, eyes, mouth, and mighty arm.
6. Applying human characteristics to God is called anthropomorphism, from the Greek words *anthropos* (man, or human) and *morphe* (form). Anthropomorphism is a tool for understanding, but a flawed tool. God is not human and does not have the features of a human body, such as a face, and while he does have emotions, they are not exactly the same as human emotions."

The above narrative defies logic and common sense. It demonstrates the degree of mental and "word gymnastics" that religious adherents will perform to hold on to their beliefs. They will reshape "The undisputed word of the God" so that it seems there are no contradictions. Thinking that there are no contradictions in the Bible is necessary to maintain belief in it, and even worse is the acceptance of contradictions knowing that it has been edited many times, but asserts that despite the changes the essential message remains intact. One adherent rejects stories he thinks don't belong but still embraces the Bible. It's unclear how he ascertains which stories belong in the Bible. Once again, this mental gymnastics is done to avoid **cognitive dissonance.** People tend to seek consistency in their attitudes and perceptions. So, strong conflicting beliefs can cause feelings of unease or discomfort. To avoid this, the contradiction is glossed over. Religious beliefs are so powerful[10] that adherents have become the greatest spin doctors. To accept the truth that there are contradictions in the Bible, and therefore question the Bible's legitimacy of being the result of divine revelation, would be too painful for many, especially if they have allowed their belief to define their existence. The implications of Mary Fairchild's words are, "Don't trust your understanding of words and their meaning, the Bible cannot be wrong, and always seek an interpreter[11]." Let's start the analysis with paragraphs one and two. It links two points:

It states that the phrase "The face of God" gives important information about "God the Father". What important information? Paragraph two suggests that it is, "No one can see God's face and live."

But strangely, Ms. Fairchild described this "revelation" as a problem, and that it started because Moses asked God to "show him his glory". Why is this a problem? It's a problem because she has the unenviable task of explaining that God doesn't have a face, even though the scripture claims **he said he has a face** but Moses can't see it and live! She says he hasn't got a face or human qualities even though she states in paragraph five that "God used human terms to speak of himself". Despite this admission, she admonishes us in paragraph six not to use anthropomorphism to understand God because it is a flawed tool. So, she inadvertently claims that God used a flawed tool to describe himself! This would suggest that God is like an ordi-

---

10 Historical atrocities and suicide bombing are powerful examples of this.

11 When adherents study the Bible it's usually necessary to jump from one book to another in an often failed attempt to paint a cohesive narrative. A book inspired by an infinitely intelligent being or written by competent and highly intelligent writers would be cohesive and all knowledge easily accessible.

nary person, not all-wise, and more incompetent than an average human, on a subject that should be minor, that is, describing himself! Incredible.

Could this controversy be the reason for removing the Secrets of Enoch?

You will read further in this book that the Bible was compiled through a long process of voting books in and out until the current books were settled on. The "Secrets of Enoch" is described as, "Its value lies in the unquestioned influence which it has exerted on writers of the New Testament." This quote is from, **"The lost books of the Bible and the forgotten books of Eden."** In **chapter 22:1-2** of **Secrets of Enoch,** it states, "On the tenth Heaven, Aravoth, I saw the appearance of the Lord's face, like iron made to glow in fire, and brought out, emitting sparks, and it burns. **2**. Thus I saw the Lord's face, but the Lord's face is ineffable, marvellous and very awful, and very, very terrible." Including this book in the Bible would make it more difficult to sell "No one has seen his face and live". The quote fits the description of the **Sun**.

The book was removed even though Enoch is closely connected to the main characters in the Bible as the following will show. **Genesis 4:17** "And Cain knew his wife[12], and she conceived, and bare **Enoch**: and he builds a city, and called the name of the city, after the name of his son, Enoch."

Genealogies of Jesus in the Bible are contradictory. However, even though Luke's genealogy of Jesus doesn't correspond with Genesis', Luke's genealogy confirms they are writing the same story because they both have Methusael/Mathusala or Methuselah as the father of Lamech in their genealogy that includes Enoch.

---

12 Since the story claims Adam and Eve only had two sons, Cain and Abel, where did his wife come from? Logic says, if this is a real story she would have to be his sister, and this would be incest.

Luke 3:37 "Which was the son of Mathusala, which was the son of **Enoch**, which was the son of Jared, which was the son of Maleleel, which was the son of Cainan." There are seven more references to Enoch in Genesis.

The human brain is a logical tool, just like a computer. Religious belief generates the strongest emotions known and this has fuelled a long track record of centuries of bloodshed. When such strong emotions are shaped by beliefs, (accepting something without proof) this can be injurious to the logical brain. This is because one of our strong drivers is to be consistent, that is, to make sense. So, to avoid the perceived pain that would result from challenging that which they perceived to be God's words, religious adherents often ignore facts and defy all rules of reasoning in an attempt to be consistent. If a person is convinced of the reward of heaven, or extreme punishment if they break the rules, defying the rules of reasoning is a small price to pay to gain the perceived reward.

The concept of God being a spirit and having a face is contradictory, but to acknowledge that this is contradictory requires accepting that the Bible was not inspired by a supernatural being, commonly referred to as God, and this truth cannot be accepted since it would render their belief to be pointless. **Mary Fairchild's philosophy continues:**

"The human mind cannot comprehend a being who is pure spirit" and "Nothing in human experience is even close to such a being"

If the above is true, how did the inspired men write the Bible? It would require an elevation of their minds above human capacity for them to comprehend the message. Yet, not only can Mary Fairchild comprehend "the inspired word of God", **she can add meaning to it beyond what was written by men whose minds according to her belief, were elevated above human capacity to comprehend "pure spirit"**. So, even though her mind was not elevated by God, her ability is greater than the men whose minds must have been elevated by God – if not, how else would she be qualified to question the words attributed to God from the "inspired men"? Also, by adding meaning to that written by these men who God elevated their minds to comprehend him, she is inadvertently claiming that even though God elevated their minds to understand him, he was inadequate in giving the inspired writers an accurate description of himself, even when they quoted him.

If God wasn't inadequate in describing himself, he was inadequate in elevating their minds to understand him. Either option would disqualify the Bible from being the result of divine revelation. And all of this confusion is in aid of not discarding the Bible as manmade dogma. To conclude that he doesn't have a face even though the Bible says so, and don't acknowledge that the Bible claiming "God is spirit" is a contradiction, requires intellectual dishonesty. This is a typical knot that adherents get themselves into when they try to do the impossible, ignore contradictions, and try to make that which is illogical make sense. This is injurious to our minds and retards growth and development.

"To help readers relate to God in some understandable way, the writers of the Bible used human attributes to speak of God"

She is inadvertently implying that God described himself to the inspired men in a way that the normal human mind wouldn't understand, so they took the initiative and applied human attributes to God which is suited to our level of understanding. In the above quote, she inadvertently implied three insults to her God. One, the writers were wiser and were better communicators than God, and two, he didn't understand us enough to describe himself in a way that we would understand. She is also inadvertently claiming that his description of himself is inaccurate.

We must be fortunate that she and others can tell us not to interpret the word "face" and other human terminologies literally. Because

God is like an invisible friend that no one has ever seen, she chose to believe the scripture that says "God is spirit" because it is in harmony with the belief that no one has seen God. So she has ignored the contradiction of the claim that he has a face, and is asking us to do the same. If she didn't tell us to ignore the meaning of face we would be at the mercy of the meaning of words. And yet, despite her attitude towards us interpreting some words literally, she quoted the Bible stating, "God then places Moses in a cleft in the rock, covers Moses with his hand". Should we interpret this as meaning that God has no hands, therefore, he didn't lift him and place him in the rock's cleft, and didn't cover him with his hand? So, what happened, since we can't interpret this literally?

Do we need someone with a greater than human mind to interpret this for us? Why would an all-wise God make it so difficult for us to understand his words, especially since the consequence is supposedly extreme punishment? The answer is not mystical. The Bible was written by different men without any coordination between them, hence the many contradictions. A supernatural intelligence would not inspire words that are so poorly written that they inspire many denominations with teachings and practices that are as different as night and day. This is also true if an intelligent mortal being wrote instructions and guidance. We accomplish this every day with our education curriculum and exams. If they were written at the standard of the Bible, there would be no consistency in the passing of exams and academic success.

To accept that a God of infinite power dictated a book of such low quality is to hold this God to a very low standard.

Various Biblical human characteristics of God

In paragraph six she advises us not to apply human characteristics to God, which is known as Anthropomorphism.

"Anthropomorphism is a tool for understanding, but a flawed tool...he (God) doesn't have the features of a human body."

She has the power to cherry-pick which characteristics of God the Bible mentions that we should take literally, even though in some instances it cannot make sense without a literal interpretation. Astonishingly, she acknowledges the Bible's claim that God has emotions but her extraordinary non-human mind enables her to tell us that which he didn't communicate to the "Inspired writers". "His emotions were not "exactly the same as human emotions." How does she know this? She said this despite the Bible describing him with words such as:

Anger - Exodus 32:10 (Mentioned in over 20 scriptures)
Has regrets, grief - Genesis 6:6
Loves - John 3:16
Has loyalties - Deuteronomy 7:9
Jealous - Exodus 20:5
Feels compassion - Psalms 78:38
Vindictive (vengeance). - Hebrews 10:30
Pleased – Matthew 3:17

If these emotions are not like ours, how are we supposed to understand what they mean? How does she know this, and why has an all-wise God neglected to tell us this? This would be strange since the intention is for us mere mortals to understand, and if we were not supposed to understand, what's the point of us reading the book? Based on her statement, perhaps Mary Fairchild understands God's emotions but she is reticent in explaining it to us.

Now, here is the big fat "elephant in the room" that is another example of definitive proof that man invented Holy Books, and therefore invented God. If the accurate description of God is, "God is spirit," an all-knowing God would know that we would understand this simple concept. Therefore, why would such a God include contradictory human terminologies as descriptions, including "father"?

Mary Fairchild quoted **Exodus 33:22-23,** and in it, God is quoted as saying, "And it shall come to pass, while my glory passed by, that I will put thee in a cleft of the rock, and will cover thee with my hand while I pass by**. 23.** And I will take away my hand, and thou shalt see my back parts, but my face shall not be seen." Can this be said without using human terminologies? No! the entire narrative is about concealing himself from Moses. It would be inaccurate and unnecessary to make such a statement if there was nothing to see. Why would it be necessary to claim to have hands, back, and face, if it was inaccurate? And since a non-physical and invisible entity cannot have these physical attributes, can this be anything but a poorly written mythological story? Doesn't this fit the description of many stories we now regard as Greek mythologies? View the following in the context that **Hercules was worshipped** in Rome but **he is now universally regarded as a myth**. According to Wikipedia:

"Hercules is the Roman equivalent of the Greek divine hero Heracles, son of Zeus and the **mortal** Alcmene[13]. In classical mythology, Hercules is famous for his strength and his numerous far-ranging adventures. The Romans adapted the Greek hero's iconography and myths for their literature and art under the name Hercules. In later Western art and literature and popular culture, **Hercules** is more commonly used than **Heracles** as the name of the hero. **Hercules** is a multifaceted figure with contradictory characteristics, which enabled later artists and writers to pick and choose how to represent him."

The emboldened words in the following story highlight three things, it is a story about the God worshipped by Christians; it ascribes human qualities; and it claims Abraham spoke to God while he stood before him, first he **recognised** and ran to him, hence he looked at his face. This is true unless logic doesn't count.

[13] Alcmede was a mortal princess in Greek mythology who gave birth to Heracles/ Hercules with the god Zeus - Dated over 1000 year BC. So, Mary was not the first mortal to be impregnated by a god. But this story is not currently regarded as mythology, even though there is no evidence of her on earth.

The contradiction of Abraham seeing and recognising God

Genesis chapter 18

And the Lord **appeared** unto him in the plains of Mamre: and he sat
in the tent door in the heat of the day;

2 And **he lifts up his eyes and looked,** and, lo, three men stood by
him: and when **he saw them,** he ran to meet them from the tent
door, and bowed himself toward the ground,

3 And said, My Lord, if now I have found favour in thy sight, pass
not away, I pray thee, from thy servant:

4 Let a little water, I pray you, be fetched, and wash your feet, and
rest yourselves under the tree:

5 And I will fetch a morsel of bread, and comfort ye your hearts; after
that ye shall pass on: for therefore are ye come to your servant. **And
they said, so do, as thou hast said.**

6 And Abraham hastened into the tent unto Sarah, and said, Make
ready quickly three measures of fine meal, knead it, and make cakes
upon the hearth.

7 And Abraham ran unto the herd, and fetches a calf tender and
good, and gave it unto a young man, and he hastens to dress it.

8 And he took butter, and milk, and the calf which he had dressed,
and set it before them; and he stood by them under the tree, **and
they did eat. (This suggests that God came in the flesh and ate
food, so, Jesus was not the first one to accomplish this feat unless
he was also Jesus.** Significantly, offering to wash his feet confirms
this. He, therefore, had a face.)

9 And they said unto him, Where is Sarah thy wife? And he said, Behold, in the tent.

10 And he said, I will certainly return unto thee according to the time of life; and, lo, Sarah thy wife shall have a son. And Sarah heard it in the tent door, which was behind him.

11 Now Abraham and Sarah were old and well stricken in age; and it ceased to be with Sarah after the manner of women.

12 Therefore Sarah laughed within herself, saying, After I am waxed old shall I have pleasure, my lord being old also?

13 And the LORD said unto Abraham, Wherefore did Sarah laugh, saying, Shall I of a surety bear a child while being old? (This suggests a supernatural being because he knew that she laugh **within herself** – the word Lord is frequently used in reference to God, such as, **"The Lord thy God")**

14 Is anything too hard for the LORD? At the time appointed I will return unto thee, according to the time of life, and Sarah shall have a son. **(Another confirmation that it is claiming that it was God, as he declared that nothing was too hard for him, and it is claiming he performed a miracle by making Sarah who it said was "old and well stricken in age" have a son.)**

15 Then Sarah denied, saying, I laughed not; for she was afraid. And he said, Nay; but thou didst laugh.

16 And the men rose up from thence, and looked toward Sodom: and Abraham went with them to bring them on the way.

17 And the **LORD said, Shall I hide from Abraham that thing which I do;**

18 Seeing that Abraham shall surely become a great and mighty nation, and all the nations of the earth shall be blessed in him? [This is another confirmation that this is a story told of a God with human qualities – uncertainty about talking to a man. He is uncertain if he should let Abraham know that through his "miracle son" he shall be the father of many nations.]

19 For I know him, that he will command his children and his household after him, and they shall keep the way of the LORD, to do justice and judgment; that the LORD may bring upon Abraham that which he hath spoken of him.

20 And the LORD said, Because the cry of Sodom and Gomorrah is great, and because their sin is very grievous;

21 I will go down now, and see whether they have done altogether according to the cry of it, which is come unto me; and if not, I will know.

22 And the men turned their faces from thence and went toward Sodom: but Abraham **stood yet before** the **LORD.**

23 And Abraham **drew near,** and said, Wilt thou also destroy the righteous with the wicked?

Even if we accept the belief that the Bible is the undisputed word of God and the correct interpretation of scriptures is that man has never seen God's face, we have a major problem. How can **1 John 4:12** be true when Genesis above states that Abraham ran towards God and his companions, and bowed? **1 John 4:12** states that **"No man hath seen God at any time…"** this is another example of numerous contradictions in the Bible which is more proof that the Bible was not written by the inspiration of a perfect supernatural being. It was written by different people, which is not in question, but they were not inspired by supernatural forces. They wrote it without corresponding with each other.

Genesis 18:18 is confirmation that the Bible story is not about original sin which is a central doctrine of Christianity. According to this doctrine, Abraham, and everyone born from the lineage of Adam and Eve would be born in sin. So, it would not make sense for God to declare that "Abraham shall surely become a great and mighty nation, and all the nations of the earth shall be blessed in him." A great and mighty nation that was blessed would be a contradiction of this doctrine. **If original sin was started by Adam and Eve and it was the reason evil became an option for humanity, God would have mentioned it to them. There was no mention of sin, just death as a consequence of disobedience.**

An anthropomorphic God with rare and awful human qualities

The Christian Bible describes a God who takes a side in human disputes and helps destroy one faction in favour of the other. How many human parents are capable of taking a side in their children's dispute and killing the faction they disagree with? Many parents would not give up their children to the law even if they committed the worse of crimes, their love is unconditional. It's called parental instinct and is common among parents – it is built-in. If we go by the religious narrative, their God gave us these characteristics. How come he doesn't possess the same if we were made in his likeness? The answer is obvious when we realise that all the gods in history possessed the characteristics that the people who conceived and worship them wanted. For example, there were gods of war, and even now when nations go to war they would declare that "God" is on their side. A classic example in our time is the USA vs Iraq war. George Bush declared that God was on America's side and Saddam Hussein declared that God was on Iraq's side. It is interesting to note that all current religions regard God as the ultimate of all that is good and Satan as the ultimate of that which is evil, yet no Christian or religious nation ever declared war in the name of Satan. It is interesting to note that It is difficult to find evil acts committed by the Devil in the Bible yet God is a mass murderer who has killed millions of humans and animals.

CHAPTER THREE

The problems with the Biblical creation story, original sin, and God's identity

Genesis 1:26, And God said, let us create man in our image, after our likeness, and let them have dominion over the fish of the sea, and over the fowl of the air, and over the cattle, and over all the earth, and over every creeping thing that creeps upon the earth. Genesis 1:28 And God blessed them, and God said unto them, Be fruitful and multiply, and replenish the earth and subdue it, and have dominion over the fish of the sea, and over the fowl of the air, and over everything that moves upon the earth.

Two examples of the Bible's contradiction of Christianity's core doctrines

Here is what Genesis 1:26 is inadvertently saying that contradicts a Christian doctrine – we are perfect: if we were made in God's likeness then we are like God. And if God is always perfect, so are we. If God thought he made us perfect and we were not, it would be a case of his incompetence, and therefore, not our fault, so, it would be unjust to punish us for his incompetence.

Here is what Genesis 1:26 did not say: it did not say they were meant to worship, praise, and serve God. It says they were supposed to dominate the earth, and be fruitful and multiply. And yet, it is preached and believed that God created us to worship and praise him and if we don't we will be punished. **If this is a real story and the purpose of creation is for humanity to praise and worship God, and we will be punished if we did not, God would have said this to the first people at the outset.** Preachers need to explain why God did not mention this to the Biblical first people – Adam and Eve. Why would God want us to dominate all living things instead of peacefully co-exist with them? We are only able to dominate many of the creatures on earth because we have invented lethal weapons!

There are a few scriptures in the New Testament that it's claimed Jesus mentioned worship. Before we examine them, consider that the New Testament was written over a thousand years after Genesis was written, any dictate in it to worship after it was not mentioned by God to the first humans tells us that many books in the Bible were written independently of each other without a single coordinated supernatural source.

The first four scriptures are in John. As you will read in chapter five, John was the last of the four Gospels, and it's considered to be different from the other Gospels because it does not share their "common view". The difference is that it is the only one of the four that repeatedly ascribes divinity to Jesus, and therefore was considered the "spiritual Gospel". However, note that worship is **not mandated** or **commanded**, and there is no punishment mentioned for not worshipping! Why would God or Jesus not mention these two key Christian doctrines and they are claimed to be the ones who created the universe for worship, and subsequently mandated punishment if we don't follow their rules?

New Interntional Version

Words about worshipping God attributed to Jesus

John 4:21"Woman," Jesus replied, "believe me, a time is coming when you will worship the Father neither on this mountain nor in Jerusalem."

John 4:22 You Samaritans worship what you do not know; **we worship what we do know**, for salvation is from the Jews**. [Who is we, he worshipped his father as well?]**

John 4:23 Yet a time is coming and has now come when the true worshipers will worship the Father in the Spirit and in truth, for they are the kind of worshipers the Father seeks.

John 4:24 God is spirit, and his worshipers must worship in the Spirit and in truth."

Matthew 15:9 But in vain they do worship me, teaching for doctrines the commandments of men.

Matthew 4:10 Then said Jesus unto him, Get thee hence, **Satan**: for it is written, Thou shalt worship the Lord thy God, and him only shalt thou serve.

Hebrews 1:6 And again, when he brings in the first begotten into the world, he said, And let all the **angels** of God worship him.

The mythological story of Adam and Eve has been used to push the narrative that humanity was meant to be perfect and incapable of evil actions. This was probably born out of the inability to explain human behaviour. What's the basis of this theory? Even now, many of us find it difficult to accept that we can commit evil acts without external stimulus. Now many of us have difficulty accepting that evil actions are caused by the simple processes of dysfunctional thoughts and emotions, and for many years it was believed that madness is caused by evil spirits. We should know that our thoughts shape our world. We should also know that there is an indisputable link between the extent of our education and nurturing and the types of behaviour we engage in.

If believers are asked if God is perfect they would say yes. And yet, Bible scripture says the opposite. We humans are not perfect, therefore we make mistakes and have regrets because we are always in a state of growth and learning. A perfect being or an all-wise, all-knowing God would not make mistakes and have regrets. **A general message in Genesis is the** claim that God's creation didn't go according to plan. At a minimum, this is a case of incompetence, not perfection. The story of creation is told as if all "creation", the earth, the stars, and the universe were put together for us, and after all this extraordinary work, his first human creation, the "centre-piece" of the plan, disobeyed a single instruction.

This suggests that his desire was for them to only do that which he wanted; they were not allowed any other options and to break any rules or exercise free will. Once a rule was broken its consequence reduced the value of his human creation – they were no longer perfect and he punished them. This is where Genesis stopped the story in terms of punishment. However, Saint Augustine came along thousands of years later with a theology that was adopted and was used to provide the link for the need for a saviour. And so, the story morphed into meaning that all future generations were doomed to imperfection and would face the extreme injustice of being punished for **Adam and Eve's single act of disobedience.** The adoption of the doctrine of original sin paints the Biblical God as having a more uncompromising attitude of being unforgiving, and it exerts a greater strain on its claim that "he is love" and "his mercy endureth forever." In the Adam and Eve story, the writer characterised God as having one of we **mere mortal's** worse characteristics, not accepting responsibility for the consequences of our actions. Mature humans accept responsibility for our actions even though we did not choose to have those options. We did not choose our options, we can only choose to act on them.

All the options of a computer were installed by its maker; therefore, the maker would be responsible for all its actions. Likewise, all our capabilities, inclinations, choices, and actions are the prerogative of whatever is responsible for our existence. If "God" is responsible, he is to be blamed for us having our options, and it's like leaving a loaded gun in a house filled with people, eventually, someone will use it. If we had a say in what characteristics and abilities we should have, men would choose not to go bald, humanity would choose to be able to eat every possible food without the consequence of sickness, and diseases would not exist. It's a certainty you can think of other options we would prefer but don't have.

The Bible's creation story contradicts the science of Nature and the universe

The Bible claims that in the beginning there was just God and he existed in darkness for an unquantifiable number of years. He didn't live in any specific place until he decided to create **heaven** and the earth. The Bible claims these are the sequence of creation:

Genesis 1:3-5 3. And God said, Let there be light: and there was light. **4** And God saw the light, that it was good: and God divided the light from the darkness. **5** And God called the light Day, and the darkness he called Night. And the evening and the morning were the first day. **[It is the Sun, the moon, and stars that determine night from day, yet verse 16 below suggests the sun, moon, and stars were created, again?]**

Genesis 1:11-12

11 And God said, Let the earth bring forth grass, the herb yielding seed, and the fruit tree yielding fruit after his kind, whose seed is in itself, upon the earth: and it was so.

12 And the earth brought forth grass, and herb yielding seed after his kind, and the tree yielding fruit, whose seed was in itself, after his kind: and God saw that it was good. **[Nothing grows without the Sun. If verse 4 is referencing the Sun then a different person wrote verses 14 to 16 because the sun appears after grass grew.]**

Genesis 1:14-16

14 And God said, Let there be lights in the firmament of the heaven to
divide the day from the night, and let them be for signs, and for seasons,
and for days, and years: **15** And let them be for lights in the firmament
of the heaven to give light upon the earth: and it was so. **16** And God
made two great lights; the greater light to rule the day, and the lesser
light to rule the night: he made the stars also. [**This seems to confirm
it was written by a different writer because it claims the sun, moon,
and stars were created at this point of the sequence. So, if they were
created at this point, which lights were created in verse 4?**]

If there was a Creator the way the Bible explains it, and we accept that the earliest life form (amphibious reptiles) lived over three billion years ago, and dinosaurs over 200 million years ago then these creatures would be the priority for creation because they were the first to be sustained by nature. This point is strengthened by their being evidence that Dinosaurs existed for about 165 million years. Therefore, this was not a flash-in-the-pan existence. However, the Bible claims God said let **us (more than one)** create mankind, and the story that follows suggests we are the priority for creation coming into existence by these gods. In aid of this narrative, some religious adherents have rejected the existence of dinosaurs and the scientific estimate of the age of the earth. This is because it would interfere with their creation story. After all, some claim the earth is 6,000 years old. The Bible's creation story suggests that we are the priority, using a narrative that is misleading because it provides a timeline of seven days for life, earth, and the universe to come into existence, and all of it happened like magic.

Our reality of the estimated scientific timeline of dinosaurs and of our existence being 200,000 years makes a mockery of the Bible's creation story and their claim of 6,000 years. The creation story claims all animals were created at the same time and existed with humans. It's difficult to imagine us coexisting with dinosaurs before we invented weapons. The non-Biblical theology that there is a Creator who created the earth for our purpose, and for us to serve and worship him is directly linked to doomsday theology. By implication, the Noah story is interpreted as meaning that the existence of life on earth is only tolerable to God if we are on it and well behaved. So, this God who is claimed to be super sensitive to human behaviour and punishes for minor transgressions, is the same God who created the merciless food chain, and parasites, and is very creative in designing the most vicious and venomous creatures imaginable? Isn't this a major contradiction? As long as we accept the long existence of earlier lifeforms and dinosaurs, the Bible's creation story can only exist in our minds, not in reality.

If we interpret life using the creationist beliefs, humanity cannot offend a God who is responsible for the merciless food chain. Nor can we offend the same God who designed the black widow spider so that the females sometimes kill and eat the males after mating in a macabre and violent mating ritual that gave the insect its name. The idea that such a God would punish us for having sex because we didn't sign a piece of paper is beyond ridiculous. This same God is also claimed to object to the following, Leviticus 19:27 "Do not cut the hair at the sides of your head or clip off the edges of your beard." Deuteronomy 22:11 "Thou shall not wear a garment of divers sorts, as of woolen and linen together." This God is concerned about trivia, but doesn't command us not to discriminate or enslave?

The original sin narrative can only be accepted through a process of conditioning – socialisation, not through the process of constructive reasoning. Shockingly, the concept is not part of the Adam and Eve story as you will read. We are at our best when our core personality and character are defined by wisdom, intelligence, and constructive reasoning, otherwise called common sense. You will fail to convince most believers in the Adam and Eve creation story that many Bible stories cannot be taken literally. No matter how gently you break it to them that snakes or serpents cannot speak and have never spoken at any time in history, you will struggle to change their attitude towards the Bible as being the undisputed **literal** word of a Creator. The closest we can get to snakes talking is to logically assume that they can communicate with other snakes.

The contradictions of the first four characters of the Bible are further evidence that this is an invented story

We are told that the Bible was originally written in three languages, the Old Testament in Hebrew and Aramaic, and the New Testament in Greek. We should expect a book inspired by God to be consistent and accurate in conveying the name of the first four humans. We should expect that God would be capable of giving them names we can understand and there would be no need to change them. We should also expect that this short narrative would be written by one person and in one language. So, with this context in mind, here is the etymology of the names of the first four people on earth claimed by the Bible – it should not be necessary to do an etymology to establish the original names:

Adam – "Its meaning comes from the **Hebrew** word "adamah" meaning "earth," from which Adam is said to be formed. The name also refers to the reddish color associated with human skin." **[Why change it to Adam? Why change a God's inspired name? Adamah is easily pronounceable]**

Eve –"It is a **Latin or English** given name for a female, derived from the Latin name Eva, in turn originating with the Hebrew (Chavah/ Havah – chavah, to breathe, and chayah, to live, or to give life)." **[Why keep changing it? If Chavah was the inspired name why not write this?]**

Cane – "It is late Middle English: from Old French, via Latin from Greek *kanna*, *kannē*, of Semitic origin." [**They didn't even bother to use a name that's related to the original Hebrew or Aramaic language. They probably didn't expect anyone to question or doubt anything in the "Holy Book", and they have been mostly right**]

Abel – "It is a biblical first name which **may** derive from the Hebrew Hebel, itself derived from hevel (breath or vapour), or from the Assyrian for son." **[There is no certain knowledge of the linguistic origin of this name]**

Why would holy-inspired men feel the need to, or feel comfortable changing the names given to them by their God considering the awe and fear in which they hold him, and names have meaning? Why would they think they have the authority to change the names when this makes them inaccurate? Answer: they made them up. If this was a real story they would not do this. This would be like a teacher deciding to change your child's name. A teacher would not do this and you are mortal and not a fearsome God! In the case of Cane, they cannot even claim that they changed it because it's not connected to the claimed original languages, Hebrew and Aramaic.

The proof that gods and Holy Books are manmade concepts can be made glaringly obvious with a simple question in the form of an analogy: If you had a son whose address you are aware of but he does not know you as his parent because he has been given contradicting stories about his parent's identity, and you wanted the child to know you are his real parent, what would be the only and simple solution? The obvious answer is you would present yourself to your son in a manner that leaves no doubt in his mind. This would be especially necessary if the consequence of the child continuing to acknowledge the wrong person as his parent would be detrimental to him. Has this happened? No! An all-wise God whose number one priority is for us to know that he exists, and desires worship and praise would ensure that we know exactly who he is. But as you have read, ***if humanity's worship of God was the reason for our existence the Bible would have made this claim, and it would have been said to Adam and Eve.***

Who is the real God to worship?

In **Exodus 20:3** it states, "Thou shalt have no other gods before me", and just in case adherents missed it, it is repeated in **Deuteronomy 5:7**, "Thou shalt have no other gods before me", and in **chapter 28:14**, "And thou shalt not go aside from any of the words which I command thee this day, to the right, or the left, to go after other gods to serve them." In **Exodus 34:14**, "For thou shalt worship no other god: for the Lord, whose name is Jealous, is a jealous God." This acknowledgement of the existence of other gods is repeated in **Psalms 136:2**, "O give thanks unto the God of gods: for his mercy endureth forever." Is this scripture claiming that God created other gods, or is this another example of how contradictory and confusing the Bible is? This is further evidence that the Bible was not inspired by an infinitely intelligent being, God, who inspired it as a guide that is supposed to inform us in the knowledge of him as the only God. Such a message would not laud the God of gods. This is the language of polytheism.

Additional confusion about God's identity and how he created humans

If **Genesis 1:26-27** is added to the question of God's identity, it either adds confusion or clarity. It states in **verse 26**. "And God said, let **us** make man in **our image**, after our likeness. **Verse 27**, "So God created man in **his own image**, in the image of God created he him; male and female created he them." This claims three things, **verse 26** claims two Creators; **verse 27** claims one Creator, and that man and woman were created at the same time. Yet, in **Genesis chapter two** there is a second and different creation story. In **verse 7** it states, "And the Lord God formed man of the dust of the ground and breathed into his nostrils the breath of life, and man became a living soul." Then **verses 8-17** claim God planted a garden with trees for food; the tree of knowledge of good and evil; install rivers; placed the man in the garden and commanded him not to eat from the tree of good and evil. Then in **verse 18**, it occurred to him that, "It is not good that the man should be alone; I will make a helpmate for him."

This sounds like an afterthought, which makes no sense. Then from **verses 19-20** it is claimed God proceeded to create animals and birds and brought them to Adam to name them. **Verse 20** ended with a nonsensical statement: "but for Adam, there was **not found** a helpmate for him." God was **looking for one?** Where? There was no one else on the planet. In **verses 21-22** it's claimed God put Adam to sleep, extract one of his ribs, and made the woman. This is a different creation story. The first story claimed they were created at the same time, but in the above story, there is a wide activity gap between their creation, and the woman is created by a different method, from a rib. Why would an inspired story be told twice with different facts by the same writer? Once again, this is evidence that this is not a story inspired by an infinitely intelligent being; it is a poorly written story by two persons in this case; one person would not write the same story twice in the same book!

Even if the Bible's creation story was true, an infinitely intelligent being would not say, "It's not good that the man should be alone". Did he temporarily forget why he created the earth? He forgot why he made the man? He forgot the role the man has to play, and that's why he gave him a penis, and that he would need to use it on a woman to be fruitful and multiply?

If this is a real story, what would an all-wise and infinitely powerful God do who confesses to being jealous of us worshipping other gods, but doesn't want us to? Is there a better solution than appearing at a time when we have the means to record him? How about appearing to the entire world and ensuring that we all hear and see him speak? Is there any solution more powerful that would ensure that we stop worshipping different gods, and therefore give him no reason to be jealous? This would also solve the problem of religious confusion, and bloody conflicts that are rooted in religious beliefs.

Religious doctrines dictate that disobeying God will result in varying degrees of severe punishment. So, why would such a god leave the question of "his" identity in doubt if the consequence of getting it wrong would be severe, and administered by him? Considering that the God in the Christian Bible is depicted as being very talkative and spoke to humans on numerous occasions over thousands of years, and in many ways[14], why the deafening silence now? After thousands of years of mass killings in the name of God, why would the real "God" not clarify "his" identity in an irrefutable manner, like making an appearance for us to record him? This would save so many lives and leave no room for doubt as to his true identity. In **Exodus 19:9** it states, **"And the Lord said unto Moses, Lo, I come unto thee in a thick cloud that the people may hear when I speak with thee and believe thee forever.** And Moses told the words of the people unto the Lord."

Consider how deeply people believe and fear various Gods they have never seen or heard, but only read about them in their religious texts. Do you think belief in different Gods would remain if there is a God, and he spoke to humanity from the clouds, as mentioned in **Exodus 19:9**, and did it to all peoples of the world? Since it's claimed he has done it before there is no reason why he can't do it again. And since there is no logical or beneficial reason to let "Satan" continue to mislead[15] his children, he would then destroy him, write it off as a mistake, and proceed to have the world and the affairs of humanity back to the way "he" wanted it, as it is claimed he wanted it in the beginning. Yet, the claimed all-powerful, all-wise, and all-knowing God has done no such thing according to religions. So, we are left with a situation where our **geography of**

---

[14] See Addendum for other claims and ways under "God spoke to us"

[15] For this to be a reality, our minds would have to be taken over and directed to do things that we were not aware of doing similar to being hypnotised. In reality, we are consciously aware of the things we do.

birth largely determines our religion, and which God we worship is based on belief, not on direct contact with any being. We know this is true because all the major religions have "Holy Books" that inspire different religions and they only accept their book as being accurate. There is no intervention from the real "God" to establish the truth.

When we combine the fact that we are born almost empty of a guiding software that dictates behaviour, with the fact that geography of birth largely determines religious belief, these facts should be indisputable evidence of our programmable nature. A deadly example of this programmability that should serve as a caution and warning is the story of the Peoples Temple and its leader Jim Jones who led from America over 900 members of his religious group to a settlement in Guyana called Jonestown, where he orchestrated a mass suicide with poisoned Flavor Aid, in November 1978.

The belief in Satan as being evil incarnate is not supported by the Bible

The belief in the existence of Satan or the Devil is part of the foundation of religious belief. Yet, as you will read, the concept of Satan as a being who is evil incarnate is not supported by the Bible, therefore, it is largely manufactured by preachers, theologians, and Hollywood. As already stated, in a real story there is no logical reason for such a being's continued existence since it's claimed he is thwarting God's plans, therefore he would be killed. **1 Chronicles 2:3** confirms the fallacy of this belief because its claim suggests a God who would kill a human being if he thinks they are evil. So, if compared to the Satan story, it suggests a God who is not even-handed and doesn't have firm principles, which is true of many human beings but would not apply to a perfect being. If we can expect consistent principles from other human beings, why wouldn't we expect the same from a perfect being? If there is a God who kills those who are evil, many people in our time who are evil would be killed, but many will live to "a ripe old age". So, **1 Chronicles 2:3** claiming, "And Er, the firstborn of Judah, was evil in the sight of the LORD; and he slew him" is a mythological story.

Since Satan is supposedly evil incarnate, Er, a mere mortal would be, at most, compared to Satan, a negligible threat to God's plans. And yet he supposedly killed him and leaves Satan to reign unrestrained terror on earth for the past thousands of years. This is a poorly written mythological story. Fortunately, our religiosity has not led our courts to accept Satan as a co-defendant in any criminal trial. Evil is an action preceded by thought and we are solely responsible.

If we believe in the narrative of the power of Satan and that evil didn't exist before he instigated it, we shouldn't blame or prosecute anyone for a crime. How can we mere mortals resist such a powerful being? However, this narrative contradicts God introducing the tree of the knowledge of good and evil to Adam and Eve. This can only be interpreted that it was God who introduced the knowledge of evil to the first people. So, where does Satan fits into this, since it's claimed he was responsible for "original sin"?

How are we supposed to be able to tell which God is real? If the religious all-wise God existed, he would know of our limitations and that it's necessary not to leave it to chance, as he would have foreseen what's happening now. Billions of us **sincerely** believe in a different "one and only God". Also, if Satan is real, God would know that such a powerful spirit would find it easy to deceive us into worshipping different gods, or him. This is another good reason why an all-wise God would not leave such a being unchecked, especially not for thousands of years, unless he is not in a hurry to fix the problem. If this is a true story the inescapable conclusion would be that he doesn't mind allowing Satan to supposedly cause all the suffering and destruction over so many years, even though we would not be capable of defeating such a powerful adversary. And yet, despite this, it's believed God will punish us when Satan supposedly succeeds in taking us off course. This makes no sense.

What possible benefit a loving parent would get from allowing this to continue when he would know from day one we are not capable of defeating an immortal being we have never seen nor heard? In the real world, would a loving parent leave their baby in the presence of a wild dog and expect the baby to defend itself and survive? If the Jesus story was his second attempt to get humanity back on the right track after his mass drowning led by Noah failed, and Satan was responsible, why would he allow such a powerful nemesis to exist who has successfully kept humanity on the wrong track? This makes no sense. An average person would get rid of any obstacle that makes it difficult to solve a problem, especially if that obstacle is harmful to their children. So, an all-wise and loving God would know this as well and do the same thing. **Therefore, this is definitive proof that the Bible and its God are manmade dogma**.

Many say they know God is real because they felt him, or he spoke to them and they spoke to him. How would they know it was not Satan they felt? According to the Scriptures, he is an immortal angel who was created by God and used to be in God's inner circle. Such a being would be well capable of deceiving anyone, especially since they can't see whoever they believe is talking to them. Interestingly, there is never any eyewitness who can verify these conversations with God even when they were in proximity. This means the voice was in their heads.

If I, a mere mortal can easily recognise that this would easily happen if Satan was real and his main purpose is his dedication to deceive and destroy us, humans, a Biblical all-wise God should have no problem in coming to this conclusion well in advance, and therefore ensure that it doesn't happen. This raises questions that expose the fallacy of the story. Why not just destroy him? How can a God who is pure love and goodness create a being that is pure evil? Wouldn't this be tantamount to the impossibility of extracting oil from water?

But God is not all good, the Bible claims he introduced the tree of good and evil to Adam and Eve – he introduced evil to the world. This would disqualify us from being responsible for committing evil acts. God would be solely responsible – he would be the root cause. If this is a real story such a God would be considered as being weird and diabolical for introducing the knowledge of evil to us but doesn't want us to have this knowledge and will destroy us for having this knowledge.

Virtually every religion and denomination holds the view that other religions are false. Different Christian denominations will differ on translation or interpretation, and consider the differences of great significance, to the point where they are not regarded as knowing the truth, and therefore, they will not earn God's reward. An example is observing or not observing the Sabbath. If it's a different religion they would regard their religious text as a made-up story that would be attributed to Satan, and they would have no interest in reading their "made-up" texts, hence, generally speaking, for example, Christians will not read the Quran and Muslims will not read the Bible as a source of guidance. Within the Christian faith, it is said there are over 45,000 denominations. It's not necessary to examine every denomination to prove a basic point; they have varying interpretations of "God's words" which leads to different practices, even when they use identical Bibles! **Their Gods have never settled any of these disputes because they only exist in their imaginations.**

The reasons for there being many different denominations with various practices are due to traditions, contradictions in Biblical text, and because it is poorly written. It is so poorly written that adherents will tell you that someone who is "qualified" needs to interpret it for you. An example of religion being based on tradition is that the vast majority of Christians do not give recognition to a Sabbath day – the formation of their denomination informed the tradition and this is usually more powerful than specific scriptures. So, they can ignore **Exodus 20:8,** Remember the Sabbath day to keep it holy because the founder of their denomination did not recognise it based on his or their interpretation. Also, many do not share the same belief in terms of the nature of "Jesus" whom they believe came to earth to "save" humanity from "sin". **There would not be thousands of denominations if a supernatural one and only God was responsible for the Bible and was in contact with Christians** to make sure they are not misled. **We would also not have thousands of religions if such a God was in touch with humanity**.

According to Kersey Graves in *The Bible of Bibles: "There are not less than eleven hundred and fifty pious effusions ... claiming to have originated from the fountain of divine revelation."* How can such diversity come from the same source when in many instances they teach vastly different things? This is all man-made because of the results it produces – insurmountable divisions and conflicts. The foundation upon which religious adherents accept the identity of their God and believe that he exists is the belief in divine revelation. It's based on the assumption that there has to be a Creator or organised personality, and the indoctrination into believing that the world and human behaviour are not the way they are meant to be. At the root of this belief is the belief that good and evil are distinctive and external forces to humanity, and they are the embodiment of two beings, God and Satan. This "rabbit hole" leads to accepting that God has words and instructions that we need to know and follow. This is the basis of believing in God since no one has ever seen or spoken to God, and no such God has spoken to humanity.

The Triangle of Helplessness

Since all of us supposedly have a problem that only God can fix, and God wants to fix it, God would speak to all of us, not just a few. The belief in external forces of good and evil (God and Devil) can be described as the triangle of helplessness. It can take us away from the reality that it is our thoughts and actions that dictate our lives. The belief in an external force of good and evil cause believers to credit bad outcomes to "the Devil", and good outcomes to "God", this belief limits or eliminate the reality of self or group determination, and cause us not to take responsibility for the state of human affairs. So, believers act like their lives are determined by two powerful opposing forces and they are just along for the ride because everything is in God's hands.

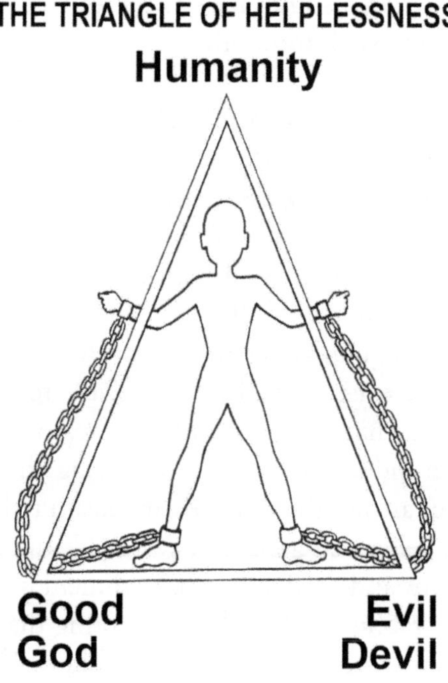

The claim of divine revelation can easily be discredited and dismissed with a simple common sense analysis: let's suppose you knew someone who spoke 3000 languages and dialects fluently and they had twelve relatives who each spoke one of these languages. This person had a message that was of paramount importance to each of these people and wished to communicate it to them. Because the importance of the message was a life and death matter it had to be communicated in a manner that left no room for misunderstanding. The Bible does not fit this description. Would it make sense that this person would communicate in one language that requires translation to the other eleven relatives? Are we all aware that things get lost in translation? There are things in Chinese that have no translation in English. This reasoning should not be necessary to dismiss the idea that religious texts are the result of divine revelation. The existence of innumerable denominations and many religions that have existed for up to thousands of years without correction from "God", is evidence that no communication from a Creator has taken place because all of them cannot be right. Religions are the result of man's desire to organise, politicise, and commercialise mythical concepts as a tool of control and power. The following is a minute listing of the divisions in Christianity.

The four biggest Christian denominations

Christianity – 2.6 billion
Catholicism – 1.345 billion.
Protestantism – 900-1000 million.
Eastern Orthodoxy – 220 million.
Oriental Orthodoxy – 62 million.
Non-trinitarian Restorationism – 35 million.

Catholicism

"Adherence to the forms of Christian doctrine and practice which are generally regarded as Catholic rather than Protestant or Eastern Orthodox."

Protestantism

Here are a few of the Protestant churches

Presbyterian, Episcopal, Lutheran, Baptist, Methodist, and Wesleyan

"55% reported using **the King James Version**, followed by 19% for the New International Version, 7% for the New Revised Standard Version (printed in both Protestant and Catholic editions), 6% for the New American Bible (a Catholic Bible translation) and 5% for the Living Bible."

Eastern orthodox churches

The Orthodox Study Bible uses **the New King James Version of the Bible** "In terms of the number of adherents, nontrinitarian denominations comprise a small minority of modern Christians. The largest nontrinitarian Christian denominations are The Church of Jesus Christ of Latter-day Saints, Oneness Pentecostals, Jehovah's Witnesses, La Luz del Mundo, and the Iglesia ni Cristo."

Oriental Orthodox churches

Their Bible

"As far as the Oriental Orthodox Church is concerned it recommends the use of **the Peshito bible**. The Peshito bible is similar to the RSV edition of the holy bible of the Catholic Church. The Peshito bible is also known as the Syriac bible. The Septuagint, Greek, and King James are most common.

The primary theological difference between the two communions [**Eastern Orthodox and Oriental Orthodox**] is **the differing Christology**. Oriental Orthodoxy rejects the Chalcedonian Definition, and instead adopts the miaphysite formula, believing that the human and divine natures of Christ are united."

Wouldn't we be better off if our main drive was based on our recognition that we are social beings, and the human experience works best when we act on the truth that we are more effective when we work as a team? What if our only value system was rooted in this truth, and we had no religion? The answer is obvious, we would have fewer conflicts and more harmony, and the only basis on which we would regard people as being evil would be their actions, not their beliefs.

No human was born with built-in knowledge of a specific "Creator" in terms of name and description; this has to be passed on from parent or society. This is confirmed through observation. Geography and history play a huge role in which religion people embrace. If we were born in the Middle East there is an overwhelming probability that we would be Muslims, if we were born in the West, we are likely to be Christians. And if we were born in ancient times we would worship whichever god or gods that our society worshipped, and they are not the same as the current set, in either names or descriptions.

The above speaks to the fact that we are born almost empty of any knowledge or ability, and need a philosophy (software) to function – the first religious software that we absorb tends to stick depending on its intensity and duration. We have to learn almost everything. For example, if we never hear words we couldn't speak. If no one mentioned a concept of god we would have none, or perhaps we would make up one. In terms of general and scientific knowledge, we learn through the process of observation and experiments. And it's only through the process of growth and development that we advanced and created societies. Before having organised societies, we were nomads, and it was only because we discovered how to domesticate plants and animals that we were able to, in the main, abandon nomadic lifestyles and stop being hunter-gatherers. None of these things were taught to us by "God".

All of the stuff we have learned to do up to the present happened through a process of evolving and growing in knowledge and understanding. Religious people claim that all our talents and ability are gifted to us by our Creator. This would suggest that all the abilities we have are in line with the direction that our all-wise "father" wants us to follow. This opens them up to questions that they can't supply rational answers to. For example, did our all-wise and loving "father" want us to know how to split the atom, and therefore created weapons of mass destruction? If not, why give us this ability? They would say, God, didn't want us to be like robots so "he" gave us free will. So, we have to know how to cause mass destruction to qualify to be humans? Since the vast majority of humans will not kill or commit murder in their lifetimes, such knowledge is not a requirement to be human.

The current motivation that drives the belief that there has to be a Creator is the desire to understand how we got here, or how we came to exist. This desire is universal. It is the same motivation that drives the theory of evolution, however, in the case of evolution, speaking from a layman's point of view, we have evidence that life evolves as in the case of caterpillars evolving into butterflies. But we have no evidence that the various gods of religions exist. All the evidence point to the opposite.

The concept of original sin is not in the Bible

Christian teachings provide a narrative that "In the beginning" Adam and Eve "sinned" and that necessitates that all future humans are required to be "saved" from being punished by God. How did the plan of a perfect being, with infinite wisdom and power, got knocked off course? What was the powerful force that derailed his plan? It can only be a mythological story that would claim a serpent **he created** derailed it. Of greater significance, you will read shortly that the idea that humanity inherited the "sins" of Adam and Eve is not in the Bible.

The idea of God creating a serpent to thwart and defeat his plans and designs, or permitting him to do it, is absolutely ridiculous. If God knew, when he created the serpent, that his machinations would bring "death and sin and all our woe" unto the world, the act would prove him to be an unprincipled being. And, if he did not know it, he must have been ignorant and short-sighted, and not fit to be a God. To assume that God could be outwitted by a serpent is to place him lower on the scale of intelligence than a snake. Kersey Graves - The Bible of Bibles 1870

If this is a real story, it's illogical that a lowly serpent that an all-powerful being created could derail the plan of its Creator by deceiving his superior creation, humans, and the Creator is blameless, therefore, it's more reasonable and logical to credit all the blame to the Creator.

To believe in the Adam and Eve story we would have looked at the incalculable size of the universe, innumerable stars, planets, and galaxies, our grand earth, and accept the illogical idea that all of this was put in place for us to enjoy everlasting life by a powerful Creator who also created a serpent that messed up his plan.

If you wanted to find out about your most ancient ancestors and you have two options of information, an account by your parents received from their parents, or an account that was written by those who were alive at the time, which one would be more reliable? Without a doubt, the eyewitness account would be more reliable.

The purpose of the above analogy is to make the point that if humans came into the world as claimed in the Adam and Eve story and had first-hand and intimate experiences with their Creator who communicated with them, the most accurate description of "God" would be from the first set of people. However, the earliest humans had widely different practices, names, and beliefs about "God" in comparison to now. And they certainly didn't worship any of the current Gods or those of recent centuries. They did not know deities called Jesus, Yahweh, Jehovah, or Allah. In short, they did not know of any of the characters mentioned in any of the current Bibles or Quran.

This is significant because current religious texts provide a narrative of "In the beginning" claiming that "The Creator" spoke to, guided, and help humans over thousands of years. So, if this long intimacy with a Creator was true, we would not have a reality where there are hundreds of books that were and are regarded as inspired Holy Books, but they were and are the foundation of different religions. However, the compelling evidence is as explained in chapter one, the ancient and longstanding worship of goddesses.

A brief study of history will tell us that at every juncture of human existence, religious people believed that their 'God' was real. It seems that history tends to repeat itself. This track record of inventing myths and gods should have made us at least cautious in accepting religious beliefs at face value, especially because most of us inherited our beliefs, but this has not been the case. Most of us have not been cautious in accepting beliefs. However, in the main, we are not to be blamed because we were indoctrinated before we got to the age of reason. The people who believed in the various gods throughout history never thought of them as myths. New civilisations supplant old civilisations and gradually what the old civilisations believed in is now taught as being myths and called pagan. It is therefore possible that thousands of years from now current Gods will be regarded as myths.

The absurdity and falsity of punishment for original sin

Many scriptures are claimed to reference or validate the claim of original sin in the Bible. Here are three that are worth mentioning. However, none of them can change the narrative of the Adam and Eve story. If this story was about informing us that all future humans would inherit the sins of Adam and Eve and therefore be born guilty of sin it would say so, but it does not mention sin. None of the three scriptures qualify as being related to the Adam and Eve story because it is about being coaxed by **a serpent** to disobey God and the gaining of knowledge, and **sin was not mentioned**. If the knowledge that evil exists makes us evil or bad this should qualify God as being evil or bad since he introduced it into the garden and therefore had the knowledge. Or **they** "know good and evil" as stated in **Genesis 3:22**.

One - Revelation 12:9 "And the great dragon was cast out, that old serpent, called the Devil, and Satan, which deceived the whole world: he was cast out into the earth, and his angels were cast out with him". Stating that Satan deceived the whole world cannot connect to the story because Satan was not part of the Adam and Eve story.

The Bible does not claim Adam and Eve were tempted by the Devil

The foundation of Christianity is based on the belief that 'in the beginning' the mythical Satan thwarted God's perfect plan, by deceiving Adam and Eve in the garden to disobey God. This is not in the Bible, so the foundation of Christianity does not even have the Bible to lean on, which is the basis of the religion. Therefore, it does not even have the basis for the pretence of divine revelation!

Two - Genesis 3:22 "Then the LORD God said, "Behold, the man has become like **one of us** in knowing good and evil. Now, lest he reaches out his hand and take also of the tree of life and eat, and live forever". The man knowing good and evil by eating the fruit cannot relate to the principle of "original sin" because the principle is about the transfer of sin from Adam and Eve to all future generations.

Three - Psalm 51:5 "I was brought forth in iniquity, and in sin did my mother conceive me". At best this is someone reciting an opinion about his birth. It cannot be connected to the creation story. There are two types of sins that are part of the Christian dogman, original or inherited sin, and doing something that is considered to be bad. This scripture doesn't say which one.

"Any God who would sentence you to an eternity of torture by fire for not believing in HIM, yet refuses to provide unambiguous and tangible evidence of HIS existence, is NOT a God. It has to be a myth." Anonymous. It's a certainty that believers would reject the idea that the Bible says God introduced evil to humanity. However, how else can this be interpreted? Isaiah 45:7 I form the light, and create darkness: I make peace, and CREATE EVIL: I the Lord do all these things. (KJV)

The basic premise of Christianity's claim of divine revelation is that God has provided a moral guide, that is, vital and critical instructions in their Bible for humanity to adhere to and gain his approval and avoid his punishment. Logic says, if this is true it would have been given to the earliest human population. However, even if we use Christianity's timeline of six thousand years as the age of humanity, it would mean God neglected to give us a moral guide or provide a saviour for over four thousand years. Billions of us lived and died without these 'benefits'. An infinitely intelligent being would not be this negligent.

Considering that it is claimed the Old Testament took over a thousand years to be written and the New Testament was written four hundred years after, it's easy to assume the claim in **Revelation 12:9** above was written close to two thousand years after Genesis. Unjustifiably connecting this scripture to "original sin" is an attempt to connect the mythical Satan to the claimed deception of the mythical Adam and Eve. **The mythical Satan has to be connected to humanity's fabled "fall from grace" for him to hold centre stage and justify the necessity of Christianity.** He is the invented bogeyman that it needs to save us from.

However, **Revelation 12:9** does not change the fact that the Bible claims the **serpent** tempted Eve. Considering how critical the existence and role of Satan is to the validity of Christianity and other religions, and since the narratives in the Bible are said to have been inspired by an all-wise God and the events are historical, Genesis account of the eating of the fruits would have been written the way people believe to be true, that is, Satan tempted Eve. The fact that this was not written can only mean the writers of Genesis were not involved in the Christianity narrative. If they were, they would have written that Satan tempted Eve. This is necessary for Satan to be the cause of humanity's fabled fall from grace, and provide the link for the need for a saviour. The claims that Satan is evil incarnate are tenuous at best because it hardly has any scriptures to support this. On the other hand, God is credited with many merciless killings and egregious behaviour such as the psychopathic deception in **Exodus 4:21-23** outlined in the Prologue and chapter six. It, therefore, raises the question as to how is it that Satan is regarded as being evil incarnate. Why is he the villain of the story?

If the Biblical account of reality is true, God would be the only eyewitness to the Adam and Eve story. Therefore, because the temptation story is pivotal to the need for Christianity, and Satan is supposed to be the catalyst, if this was the intended message to the writers, the Bible would have stated it as such.

Apart from the story of Job in which it claims God used Satan to test Job's loyalty, what other evil has he been credited with to justify his reputation? You will see in a list of references to Satan in the **addendum** that Bible scriptures don't support the evil incarnate reputation. The conclusion is then obvious, this mythical character is magnified by Hollywood, religious institutions, and preachers who blame him for the evils of mankind to give themselves power and jobs – the writers were not involved in Christianity's doctrine. **The entire Bible narrative was not coordinated by great intelligence of any description to support Christians' core beliefs.** Since Satan's goal is to create chaos and destruction in our lives, and it's claimed he started by introducing sin to the world, we should expect him to 'run riot' after the Adam and Eve story. Yet, he is not credited with the reason for the degeneration of the people who it's claimed God killed through mass drowning. If the evil of the people was the inevitable consequence of Adam and Eve's disobedience, it raises the question of why didn't an all-wise God not destroy Adam and Eve and start over to avoid this mass drowning? He told them if they ate from the forbidden tree they would die. This is a story devoid of the cohesion and precision that would be natural to an all-wise and infinitely intelligent being.

Saint Augustine was responsible for the concept of original sin in Christianity

How many Christians are aware that original sin is a phrase coined outside of Biblical narratives? According to Wikipedia: "The belief began to emerge in the 3rd century, but only became fully formed with the writings of **Augustine of Hippo** (354 AD – 430 AD), who was the first author to use the phrase original sin (Latin: *peccatum originale*). Influenced by Augustine, the councils of Carthage (411–418 CE) and Orange (529 CE) brought **theological speculation** about original sin into the official lexicon of the Church." Augustine also made significant contributions to the development of just war theory.

Since Christianity claims **original sin** is the reason humanity arrived at the juncture where we need a saviour, and the above proves that the concept originated and exists outside of their "Holy Book", that is, it cannot even claim to be from the mythical divine revelation, the entire story falls apart on the above evidence alone. Since the concept is illogical and it's not in their Bible, on what basis can they continue with the Christianity narrative?

As you have read, the concept of original sin is based on the work of Christian theologian St Augustine. Wikipedia further states, "His writings influenced the development of Western philosophy and Western Christianity, and he is viewed as one of the most important Church Fathers of the Latin Church in the Patristic Period." Further commenting on Augustine's work, it states: "The sin of Adam is inherited by all human beings. Already in his **pre-Pelagian** writings, Augustine taught that original sin is transmitted to his descendants by **concupiscence**[16] which he regarded as the passion of both soul and body, making humanity a *massa damnata* (mass of perdition, condemned crowd)....Although earlier Christian authors taught the elements of physical death, moral weakness, and a sin propensity

[16] **Concupiscence** is an ardent, usually sensual, longing. In Christianity, particularly in Roman Catholic and Lutheran theology, concupiscence is the tendency of humans to sin.

within original sin, Augustine was the first to add the concept of inherited guilt (*reatus*) from Adam whereby an infant was eternally damned at birth." **This philosophy was not universally accepted.**

"Augustine's understanding of the consequences of original sin and the necessity of redeeming grace was developed in the struggle against **Pelagius** and his Pelagian disciples."

Pre-Pelagian writings refer to **Pelagianism**. "**Pelagianism** is a heretical Christian theological position that holds that the original sin did not taint human nature and that humans by divine grace have free will to achieve human perfection." The narrative of St Augustine and Pelagianism is a story about a conflict of ideas between non-supernatural humans about Christianity theology, and St Augustine won. His idea was brought into the official lexicon of the Church in 529 CE, and now it's considered the undisputed word of God even though it's not in the Bible. This is simply amazing.

And now, the belief in original sin is used as the basis for the need to be "saved" or be "born again", and the only way to avoid punishment after death. This theology is believed to be related to the story of Adam and Eve. However, the only narrative that can be drawn from the eating of the fruit story is the tenuous claim that it resulted in Adam and Eve not living forever. This is based on an interpretation of **Genesis 2:17**, "But of the tree of the knowledge of good and evil, thou shalt not eat of it: for **the day that thou eat thereof thou shalt surely die**." The conclusion is tenuous because **they didn't die after they ate the fruit.** Some believe it means spiritual death while others don't, as they believe they will live forever on earth in the next life. Some even believe that this is how the knowledge of death came into the world. When asked how this fits into animals killing each other for food, they claim that in the beginning all animals were herbivores, and the sin of Adam and Eve caused this to change. They say this to be consistent with the belief that we were not supposed to know death. Belief often destroys the logical mind. The physiology of a herbivore and a carnivore is vastly different. So, they are inadvertently claiming that the eating of the fruit by humans caused the bodies of plant-eating animals to drastically change physically and biologically. Snakes gain venom, and no more sharks, etc. It's amazing how destructive belief can be to human minds.

> ***Moral evils must be treated as the fruit of the imperfections of our nature and not as the product of sin punishing devils, who first originate and stimulate crimes, and then join with God in punishing the criminal with fiendish cruelty; then applying a remedy which is a thousand times worse than the disease.* (*The Bible of Bibles* by Kersey Graves, 1870).**

There is nothing in the creation narrative that suggests that the descendants of Adam and Eve and future humans will be punished for their disobedience. And as you have read, St Augustine more or less invented the concept, and yet it is the very basis on which Christianity rests even though it was not considered to be divinely inspired. If it was, they would have amended the Bible and included it in the story. The problem is, they would have to include it in the punishments mentioned in Genesis unless they are happy with the conclusion that God is absent-minded and forgot to mention it when he was dishing out punishments, as you will read about in **Genesis 3:14** below. We could conclude that the following scriptures were inspired by St Augustine as they are worded to support the concept of the transfer of "sin" and are used to claim original sin is real:

Psalm 51:5 Behold, I was shaped in iniquity; and in sin did my mother conceive me. **Romans 5:12-14** Wherefore, as by one man sin entered into the world, and death by sin; and so death passed upon all men, for that all have sinned: **13** (For until the law sin was in the world: but sin is not imputed when there is no law. **14** Nevertheless death reigned from Adam to Moses, even over them that had not sinned after the similitude of Adam's transgression, who is the figure of him that was to come."

The use of these scriptures to validate original sin should always fail because if the transfer of sin was the major consequence of the disobedience of adam and Eve, it would have been written in Genesis. Since God would be the one that dictated this consequence, if the writer intended to make this claim he would have written this when he related the Adam and eve story instead of it being written in the New Testament, **Romans 5:12-14**, over a thousand years later. The other reason should be obvious. If all descendants of Adam and Eve inherited their sins, a real story would not include God engaging in the mass slaughter of humans in the Noah story, and provided no means for them to be "saved" and redeem their inherited sins. **This will be expanded on in chapter four.**

The punishments for Adam and Eve, and the Serpent

The main perpetrator, the mythological serpent/snake received the least punishment which was not much of a punishment. **Genesis 3:14,** "And the LORD God said unto the serpent, Because thou hast done this, thou art cursed above **all cattle**, and above every **beast of the field**; upon thy belly shalt thou go, and dust shalt thou eat all the days of thy life."

If the serpent was an evil spirit, Satan, in disguise, being cursed and crawling on its belly would not qualify as punishment. Therefore, the writer had no such idea in mind.

Snakes are perhaps the most agile of creatures, far better than we are. They can run on the ground, swim, and climb virtually anything. For Adam and Eve their punishments were:

Genesis 316-19 Unto the woman he said, I will greatly multiply thy sorrow and thy conception; in sorrow thou shalt bring forth children; and thy desire *shall be* to thy husband, and he shall rule over thee. **17** And unto Adam he said, Because thou hast hearkened unto the voice of thy wife, and has eaten of the tree, of which I commanded thee, saying, Thou shalt not eat of it: cursed is the ground for thy sake; in sorrow shalt thou eat of it all the days of thy life; **18** Thorns also and thistles shall it bring forth to thee, and thou shalt eat the herb of the field; **19** In the sweat of thy face shalt thou eat bread, till thou return unto the ground; for out of it was thou taken: for dust thou *art*, and unto dust shalt thou return.

The Bible does not claim Satan disguised himself as a serpent

Religious adherents believe it was Satan who took on the form of the serpent even though the Bible doesn't say so. This is a mythological story. **This is further evidence that man invented holy books**, and without holy books, there is no Biblical God, as it claims no one can see God and live, and we have not heard from him either. So, why would rational beings believe in someone they have neither seen nor heard?

The belief in Christianity that we were meant to live forever on earth is an impractical idea because the earth has finite space, so death is necessary to avoid overcrowding and for the earth to be able to provide enough food. They can only be blamed for believing in an idea that defies logic. However, the belief that humanity was meant to live forever is based on the assumption that God telling Adam he will die as punishment meant he would have lived forever if he had not disobeyed. Some are questioning if the Bible meant spiritual death. Either conclusion is problematic. Those who conclude that it means spiritual death are inadvertently admitting that the Bible lacks clarity, and therefore causes believers to question its meaning. However, whether this mythology meant spiritual death or physical death, this text should cancel the belief in "hell" as punishment for "sin". This is because **death was declared as one of the punishments for eating the mythical fruit of the knowledge of good and evil, sin and hell were not mentioned as the consequences.** Also, there was no mention of forgiveness and their punishment was lifelong. This paint a picture of an extremely callous and merciless parent, and this is a contradiction of the claimed loving father whose mercy endureth forever.

We should not be surprised when adherents follow what they believe their God wants them to do. It's similar but much more powerful than we humans imitating our role models. One of the closest to this lifelong punishment based on religiosity is practiced by Jehovah's Witnesses. It is called shunning or dis-fellowship. It is a punishment implemented by a panel of elders and calls on all other members of the congregation to reject the person both socially and emotionally, even if they are a family member. So, those with the misfortune that all their family and friends are members would suffer a punishment almost as torturous as solitary confinement in prison. What is the horrific "crime" that merits this potentially destructive punishment? Randy Wall was expelled for admitting to being drunk on two occasions and verbally attacking his wife.

The fact that millions of people believe that their loving father in "heaven" sanctioned the inhumane practice of shunning is simply amazing and speaks to how awful religious beliefs can be. They will not see the contradiction of their God sanctioning such punishment yet tolerate the Devil for thousands of years according to their belief.

History teaches that there are no limits to horrific punishments that people will accept as being sanctioned by their God. The acceptance of the mind-bending idea that God will punish a person for something their ancestors did is an example of this. Religious belief inhibits the ability to see contradictions in their Bible or beliefs. So, believers will not see the contradiction that such an act would paint about their God. It paints him as a maniac and psychopath and the opposite of the description of their "Creator" as being loving, merciful, and most important, intelligent. Those who believe in everlasting hellfire will not conclude that not even the most despotic human would engage in such behaviour, and very few humans can engage in torturing someone for days or weeks. No crime justifies everlasting torture. So, based on this fact, those who believe their God will punish us without mercy, paint the inescapable conclusion that we are better beings than their God – most of us are more merciful.

Regarding original sin, St Augustine must have had psychopathic tendencies to come up with this idea.

Why would a rational person believe someone exists that they have never seen nor heard, especially if it's claimed this person wants them to know that he exists?

As you have read above about the punishment for Adam and Eve, there is no mention of hellfire as punishment. Perhaps God forgot to mention it? A perfect being would not forget. This would be like a parent listing your punishment but forgetting to mention that they were going to torture you. The Bible mentions hell but it's used in various contradictory ways, so a definitive meaning cannot be ascribed to it, therefore, this is an example of pastors interpreting scriptures to use as a weapon against their flocks. The claim of hellfire as punishment is evidence that man invented God and holy books unless they are claiming God forgot to mention this critical bit of information when he was admonishing the mythical Adam and Eve and laying out the consequence of their **"horrendous crime"** of eating fruit from a tree that **he chose** to make.

Based on the story, the fruit tree was placed in the garden for no other reason than to tempt them – what's the point of a fruit tree if the fruits are not meant to be eaten? He didn't give them the capacity to resist temptation, and since he supposedly knows all things, he would know they were going to give in to temptation, and yet he punished them for that which was not their fault. Since we humans are born with all our inclinations, capacities, and characteristics, and religions teach that God created us, God punishing us would be tantamount to a watchmaker blaming and punishing the watch for being inaccurate.

Several Scriptures teach that death is a consequence of sin, including Genesis 2:16-17, Genesis 3:3, Genesis 3:19, Romans 5:12-21, and 1 Corinthians 15. However, **Genesis 3:19** cannot be misconstrued as meaning anything besides physical death.

Example of contradictions of the meaning of hell in the Bible

Psalms 9:17 "The wicked shall be turned into hell, and all the nations that forget God."[17] **Revelation 20:14** "And **death** and **hell** were cast into the lake of fire. This is the second death."

There is no definitive meaning that can be ascribed to "hell", as you can see above. There are forty-three scriptures found that referenced hell. There are forty-three that have no definitive meaning, are unclear, contradictory, and confusing. Of the forty-three, four seem to suggest that Jesus went to hell before resurrection! Out of the six that allude to hell as a place for punishment, only one gives a description that matches the common understanding of the concept, but without the fire: "**Psalms 9:17** The wicked shall be turned into hell and all the nations that forget God." See other scriptures in the addendum. **This much confusion disqualifies the use of hell as a definitive concept in the Bible that can be used to frighten people into submitting to religious dogma.** Why is hellfire such a common belief? This points to a common practice in the teaching and preaching of Christianity, the misrepresentation and cherry-picking of scriptures to suit the agenda. And in this case, the agenda is fear or "**spiritual terrorism**". This has to be the greatest of egregious deceptions.

Without the principle of punishment and reward, current religions have no value. So, after the fallacy of punishment such as hellfire is exposed, next is the reward of heaven. What does the Bible say about heaven? Is it definitive? There is no definitive description of it and how to get there. If this was not true we would not have many denominations with different practices they regard as "God's will". Therefore, they have no clarity on what "The will of my father" means.

---

[17] We would be thrown into hell for forgetting a God we have neither seen nor heard? Amazing. What an awful mythological story.

This standard of writing should never be accepted as coming from an intelligent person much less an infinitely intelligent being.

Matthew 7:21 "Not every one that said unto me, Lord, Lord, shall enter into the kingdom of heaven; but he that doeth **the will of my Father** which is in heaven." There are over five hundred references to heaven but none of them add any clarity to the above scripture. Many of them make no sense, and some add confusion and contradiction. Here is a major contradiction:

Matthew 3:1-2 "In those days came John the Baptist, preaching in the wilderness of Judaea, **2**. And saying, Repent ye: for the kingdom of heaven is at hand." Since it claims getting to heaven can be achieved because Jesus died for our sins and was accepted as our saviour. He never told anyone about the principle on which Christianity is based, his dying for the sins of humanity. And since he was still alive when John was preaching, and only his blood can save us, how would repentance of their sins save them and there was no saviour? Here are a few more references to heaven:

Nehemiah 9:6 Thou, even thou, art LORD alone; thou hast made **heaven**, the heaven of heavens, with all their host, the earth, and all things that are therein the seas, and all that is therein, and thou preserves them all; and the host of heaven worshiped thee. **[What?]**

Mark 13:25 And the stars of **heaven** shall fall, and the powers that are in heaven shall be shaken. [This is suggesting that heaven is what we see in the sky, space, and stars]

Job 26:11 The pillars of **heaven** tremble and **are astonished** at his reproof. [This is suggesting it's a physical structure with **pillars** holding it up and that the **pillars** are persons! To add to the confusion, **1 Samuel 2:8** states in part, **"...**for the **pillars** of the earth are the LORD'S, and he hath set the world upon them." We know the earth doesn't sit on pillars, but **Job 26:7** states, "...he hanged the earth upon nothing." **A perfect source of information would not dictate such contradictions**]

Why and how would a non-physical being live in a physical or non-physical place? Isn't this like believing that a ghost lives in a house?

Ezra 7:23 Whatsoever is commanded by the God of **heaven**, let it be diligently done for the house of the God of **heaven:** for why should there be wrath against the realm of the king and his sons? **[What?]**

2 Chronicles 2:6 But who is able to build him a house, seeing the **heaven** and heaven of heavens cannot contain him? Who am I then, that I should build him a house, save only to burn sacrifice before him? **[What?] John 6:32** Then Jesus said unto them, Verily, verily, I say unto you, Moses gave you not that bread from **heaven**; but my Father giveth you the true bread from heaven. **[What?] Revelation 21:1** And I saw a new **heaven** and a new earth: for the first heaven and the first earth were passed away; and there was no more sea. **[What?] 2 Kings 1:10** And Elijah answered and said to the captain of fifty, If I be a man of God, then let fire come down from **heaven**, and consume thee and thy fifty. And there came down fire from heaven, and consumed him and his fifty. **[What?] Matthew 24:30** And then shall appear the sign of the Son of man in **heaven**: and then shall all the tribes of the earth mourn, and they shall see the Son of man coming in the clouds of heaven with power and great glory. **[What?] Daniel 4:23** And whereas the king saw a watcher and a holy one coming down from **heaven**, and saying, Hew the tree down, and destroy it; yet leave the stump of the roots thereof in the earth, even with a band of iron and brass, in the tender grass of the field; and let it be wet with the dew of heaven, and let his portion be with the beasts of the field, till seven times pass over him; **[What?] Psalms 76:8** Thou didst cause judgment to be heard from **heaven**; the earth feared, and was still, **[What? The earth feared?] Matthew 18:18** Verily I say unto you, Whatsoever ye shall bind on earth shall be bound in **heaven**: and whatsoever ye shall loose on earth shall be loosed in heaven. **[What?]**

No matter what the language style was, every style of writing has to be coherent, otherwise, it was written by semi-illiterates and not by intelligent persons or directed by an infinitely intelligent being. The world's Christians hold divine revelation to a low standard.

More examples of confused and contradictory explanations of Hell

Acts 2:31 He seeing this before, spoke of the resurrection of Christ, that his soul was not left in **hell,** nor his flesh did see corruption. **[This is suggesting that Jesus went to hell before his resurrection] Acts 2:27** Because thou wilt not leave my soul in hell, neither wilt thou suffer thine Holy One to see corruption. **[Too identical for it not to be the same as Acts 2:31] Psalms 16:10** For thou will not leave my soul in hell; neither wilt thou suffer thine Holy One to see corruption. **[Too identical for it not to be the same as Acts 2:31] Revelation 1:18 I am he that lives and was dead**; and, behold, I am alive forevermore, Amen; and have the keys of hell and of death. **[Seems to be referencing the same story as Acts 2:31] Psalms 86:13** For great is thy mercy toward me: and thou hast delivered my soul from the lowest hell. **[What? Soul delivered from hell?] Proverbs 23:14** Thou shalt beat him with the rod, and shalt deliver his soul from hell. **[A living person's soul went to hell?] Job 26:6** Hell is naked before him, and destruction hath no covering. **[What?]**

"The great flood is a story from ancient Egypt. Every year the Nile Delta became flooded and washed away the Egyptians' world. This caused great tragedies because it was very destructive. The people called it "The waters of chaos". The people eventually learn to celebrate the coming of the waters because without it the deserts would remain dry and nothing would grow, and there would be famine. The celebration was called "The Argha Noa". It was the coming of the great flood that washed away the old world and brought new life." The Naked Truth documentary

The above story became the mythical Ark of Noah, the subject of chapter four

CHAPTER FOUR

The story of Noah and the flood – the second failed attempt to have perfect humans?

This story is one of the strongest pieces of evidence that man invented Holy Books and God

Since it is believed that Satan started humanity on a path of destruction in the garden of Eden, and is regarded as evil incarnate, one would expect the Bible to have a narrative outlining his evil activities that led God to perform the mass drowning in Genesis, but it doesn't. There is no mention of Satan in Genesis. Fifteen verses mention Satan in the Old Testament. Eleven of them are in the book of Job. Satan commits no evil act in the other four verses as you will read in the Addendum. So, of the 39 books of the Old Testament only in the book of Job Satan committed evil acts, and God permitted him to do it in some sort of wager. All the other killings and bad things in the Old Testament are claimed to be performed by God! A presumed Christian or someone being sarcastic wrote on news24.com:

"I am constantly amazed at the mysterious way in which our Lord works. Take God's kill rate in the Bible: 2.5 million people. What can the Devil boast? A measly 10 souls. I mention this because we need to watch Satan as he is notoriously sneaky. While God is in-your-face and honest, one never knows what the Devil has been up to, and better the Devil you know!

Of course, the 2.5 mill excludes the deaths resulting from the Great Flood, the obliteration of Sodom and Gomorrah, general plagues, famines, and other miseries. Then God's kill rate rises to an impressive 24 million. And even those ten who Beezlebub killed were not entirely his own work. They were the seven sons and three daughters of Job, and God only allowed it as part of a bet. Technically speaking, those deaths should be shared five-a-piece, as some of that blood was earned via God's hands."

The writings of the Old Testament do not support the central claim of Christianity. Without the claim that humans were made perfect and this was destroyed by Satan, and this caused the need for redemption through a saviour, there is no basis for Christianity. The belief in the mythical Satan is inseparable from the belief in a mythical saviour. The claimed role of a Devil seems to be an afterthought that was inserted in this poorly written mythological story, and it has no cohesion with the Satan or Devil narrative. The worship of the mythical Triad of Jupiter, Juno, and Minerva that preceded Christianity in the Roman Empire did not have a Devil or Satan character as part of it. The Devil is a late invention. There are 57 verses that mention Devil and they are all in The New Testament and 15 says, "a devil", not "the devil".

If the story of Noah is a real story it would be the biggest mass killing in the history of the world. It is indicative of the power of socialisation that religious people all over the world accept the idea that a loving God would kill almost everyone on earth to solve the presumed problem of evil but failed, and his killing included millions of innocent babies, unborn babies, children, and animals. And this gruesome act was done without warning. The reasons given for his gruesome actions were:

Genesis 6:5-7 And GOD saw that the wickedness of man was great in the earth and that every imagination of the thoughts of his heart was only evil continually. **6** And it repented the LORD that he had made man on the earth, and it grieved him at his heart. 7 And the LORD said, **I will destroy man whom I have created from the face of the earth; both man, and beast, and the creeping thing,**

and the fowls of the air; for **it repented me that I have made them**. This story makes even less sense when we put it in the context that the narrative states in **Genesis 3:22,** "And the Lord God said, Behold the man has become as **one of us**, to know good and evil…" How did Adam and Eve come to know good and evil? The story claims God introduced the tree of the knowledge of good and evil to them!

The reason given in **Genesis 6:5-6** for the mass killings of humans makes no sense when viewed in conjunction with God commanding people to engage in mass slaughter as claimed in **I Samuel 15:2-6,** "Now go and smite Amalek, and utterly destroy all that they have, and spare them not; but slay both man and woman, **infant and suckling**, ox and **sheep, camel and ass**." You will read other stories like this in chapter six, and there are many such stories in the Bible. Since murder is regarded as our worse evil, what could these people have done that would be more offensive to God than what he commanded in the above scripture? All the people he drowned could not have engaged in murder because this would be impractical. The vast majority of them would not have engaged in either murder or killings, so mass drowning would be unjust. So, this mythological story makes no sense and is the product of a demented mind.

Based on God's violent tendencies there is no purpose or morality in this story. Therefore, the reasons given are not compelling to justify such mass slaughter. This story cannot serve as a moral guide, so, all we have left is the immoral implication that it's okay for parents to slaughter their children if they are displeased with their behaviour, even if they, the parent, engaged in worse behaviour.

It makes no sense that God grieved and regretted his decision to make humans and animals, and then chose to kill most but continued with the rest. We do not continue doing what we regret doing. Why would he regret putting animals on earth? In effect, this would be regretting at least creating the earth, because without other life on earth many plants cannot survive, and there is no life. Just claiming that God regrets making animals should mark this as a silly mythological story.

Introducing Noah – this story is disconnected from the principle of original sin

Genesis 6:9 "These are the generations of Noah: Noah was a **just man and perfect** in his generations, and Noah walked with God."

Genesis 9:20-27

20 And Noah began to be a husbandman, and he planted a vineyard. **21** And **he drank of the wine and was drunken, and he was uncovered within his tent.** **22** And Ham, the father of Canaan, saw the nakedness of his father and told his two brethren without. **23** And Shem and Japheth took a garment, and laid it upon both their shoulders, and went backward, and covered the nakedness of their father, and their faces were backward, and they saw not their father's nakedness. **24** And Noah awoke from his wine and knew what his younger son had done unto him. **25** And he said, Cursed be Canaan; a servant of servants shall he be unto his brethren. **26** And he said, Blessed be the LORD God of Shem, and Canaan shall be his servant. **27** God shall enlarge Japheth, and he shall dwell in the tents of Shem, and Canaan shall be his servant.

Dissecting Noah's story at face value

How could Noah be perfect when we are told we all inherited original sin, and Jesus is the only solution?" However, it makes sense because the concept of original sin is not in Genesis. So, whoever wrote it didn't have original sin or Christianity in mind, therefore, there is no contradiction. This is proof that the Bible creation story was not written with "original sin" in mind. If it did, it would not describe Noah as being perfect. Since right now the theology is that we cannot either go to heaven or start over on paradise earth without erasing "original sin", the same principle would have applied then to Noah and all the people.

The Noah story is disconnected from the Christian narrative of the need for a saviour. If original sin was part of the Bible story, and it claims that it is the result of Adam and Eve's disobedience, the Noah story would have to be in harmony with the need to rid humanity of original sin which is claimed to be the prerogative of Jesus. Drowning most of humanity and starting over with a few "sinners" is a massive contradiction that should destroy the credibility of Christianity adopting original sin as its main principle that justifies needing a saviour.

It's unthinkable that the earth only had one good family, and the one most favoured, Noah, was a drunkard. Interestingly, God did not reprimand the "just and perfect" man for being drunk, yet Christians regard this as a sin, and in some cases, they punish such action severely. Since mass slaughter cannot be a substitute for being "saved" what was the point of this action? There is no point because it's not connected to anything. It's like a violent movie that stands on its own. This story is so poorly written, that it neglects to explain the purpose of such a monumental action and we can only assume its objective.

The story of Noah and the flood cannot be a true story that represents the action of an all-wise, just, and all-knowing being or any intelligent being. To accept this story, one has to accept that this infinitely intelligent and loving being carried out this mass slaughter without a positive intent. If we assume it was intended for perfect humans to be the consequence it failed. Repeated failures of this magnitude are reserved for imperfect humans like a tin-pot despot, not a perfect being for whom it is claimed all things are possible. This would represent his second major failure to have humanity behave the way he wants. Since this event is claimed to have happened, humanity has engaged in far worst numbers of varying evil acts such as mass murder, torture, genocide, and slavery to name a few.

Even if we accept the illogical narrative that a perfect, infinitely intelligent, and all-powerful God would fail at creating two perfect beings, it would be reasonable to assume that this claimed mass slaughter of almost every living being to correct his mistake would be the final solution, right? The fact that currently, the world is far more violent and evil is living proof that this story is unrelated to our reality. However, the story wasn't written with the claim of starting with perfect beings – it's an assumption we have made based on the claimed preserving of two of each animal and one family. If this is a real story, an all-powerful God would not fail, therefore, if such a God took such action, it would not be a story of him failing. So, this story came from the despotic imagination of men. If this mass killing was real it depicts a God who killed untold numbers of innocent animals, babies, unborn children, and lots of good human beings without achieving anything.

The invented irrational God

Because the writers of the Bible did not have original sin in mind, the stories will contradict Christianity's doctrines. If original sin was the intended doctrine, there would not be a story about Noah being perfect since everyone is supposed to inherit the sins of Adam and Eve, and therefore imperfect. Secondly, there would not be a story of starting over with imperfect beings, Noah and his family. Thirdly, there would not be a story of mass drowning that did not solve the problem. An infinitely intelligent being would not be incompetent and irrational. Augustine invented original sin thousands of years after Genesis was written.

Ultimately, this story is a description of a God who does not fit Christians' assumption of him creating perfect humans. Genesis did not claim Adam and Eve were created perfectly. And their "crime" was gaining God's knowledge of good and evil, and this made them become like God. How can this be a bad thing unless God didn't want them to kill the way he did? This would be a case of doing what I say but not what I do. If this was the case, why create them in his likeness? In **Genesis 1:26** it says, "Let **us** make man in our image and likeness". And to reiterate, if we were made in God's likeness then we are like God. And if God is always perfect, so are we. A strange, contradictory, and confusing mythological story.

The mythology of an irresponsible God, and the impossible Ark

Genesis 6:5-7 can be interpreted as God regretting that he created mankind in his likeness because it is this "likeness" that would have led us to do everything we did and do. How could it be otherwise when we played no part in our design? Believers should question the legitimacy of a story that claims a perfect being's plans went wrong and he intends to punish us for this if we don't follow his new instructions. Rational minds should see the contradiction of a perfect and infinitely powerful being making mistakes, having regrets, and yet not taking responsibility, but deciding to punish us instead.

Just like in the Adam and Eve story, Satan was not blamed for the evil of humanity in the Noah story

Genesis 6:11 & 13 The earth also was corrupt before God, and the earth was filled with violence. **13**. And God said unto Noah, The end of all flesh has come before me; for the earth is filled with violence through them; and, behold, I will destroy them with the earth.

Size of Noah's Ark – impossible to hold two of every species on earth

Genesis 6:15 And this is the fashion which thou shalt make it of: The length of the ark shall be **three hundred cubits**, the breadth of it **fifty cubits**, and the height of it **thirty cubits**. How could a real story about an infinitely intelligent being giving instructions on the size of a vessel that is to house millions of animals and the measurements given were ridiculous to the point of being laughable? The measurements said to have been given by God converted into metres are:

Length 160 metres, Width 26.7 metres, and Height 16 metres

The length is merely 40 metres (25%) longer than the longest football/soccer (90-120m) field in England. The width is only a small fraction, that is, twenty-nine percent of the width of the said field (45-90m). The height is merely sixteen (16m) metres (16m).

The size of the Ark is consistent with the story being a poorly written fable that would insult the intelligence of children. Such an Ark can't hold two of every species of animals unless creation didn't happen in one act as the Bible claims, and the earth didn't have millions of species of animals at the time, just a handful. Therefore, after the flood, God created the vast majority of animals, and he forgot to explain this to us.

Further evidence that the Bible doesn't support Christianity's doctrine of worship and praise

Genesis 9:1-2

"And God blessed Noah and his sons, and said unto them, Be fruitful, and multiply, and replenish the earth. **2.** And **the fear of you and the dread of you shall be upon every beast of the earth**, and upon every fowl of the air, upon all that moves *upon* the earth, and upon all the fishes of the sea; into your hand are they delivered."

As highlighted in chapter three God told Adam and Eve to be fruitful and multiply and gave them dominance over the animals but **did not require worship and praise.** And once again, despite many covenants with Noah, none of them was about worship and praising him. And one of his requirements doesn't make sense: **Genesis 9:5,** And surely your blood of your lives will I require; at the hand of every beast will I require it, and at the hand of man; at the hand of every man's brother will I require the life of man. **[What sort of people made up this story?]**

As already stated, the Noah story does not fit the narrative of getting rid of original sin, and perfect humans enjoying the great life that is supposed to follow. So, it does not support Christianity's doctrine that God wishes to alleviate our "sins". **Genesis 9:2** magnifies this point. Why would God tell Noah that the "**fear of you and the dread of you shall be upon every beast of the earth**?" This is suggesting that Noah killed for fun and sport as we do now. Animals do not fear anyone or anything that is not a threat to them. And since all living things on earth are not edible to humans, the only other reason they would fear him is if he engaged in wanton killing. Also, since many creatures do not fear humans, how would Noah instill fear and dread in them? Why would this be desired by an all-wise and infinitely caring God who intended tranquillity on earth?

The mass killing of animals would have been unnecessary for an all-wise God

If this is a real story it would have been easy for an all-powerful God to minimise his wanton mass slaughter. Even though there is no rationale for a sane parent much less a loving God to virtually kill all his children (including unborn babies) and start over, if we assume that they were somehow all evil, this could not extend to the animals. God had the option to leave the innocent creatures on earth in a safe place since it's claimed all things are possible for him. There is no reason given, and there is no logical reason why he should kill almost all the creatures on earth. This would have been a wanton act.

This unnecessary act would have caused a major problem for Noah and his family if this is a real story. How would they cope with living with the toxicity of millions of decaying bodies with all their harmful toxic wastes getting into the water supply?

A major contradictions of God's claimed plan for humanity

In Genesis 11:6-8 the story degenerated into a major contradiction of what Christians believe is the plan that God has for humanity. The following narrative makes no sense and would achieve the opposite of what he is believed to want to achieve. "And the LORD said, Behold, the people is one, and they have all **one language**; and this they begin to do: and now nothing will be restrained from them, which they have imagined doing. 7 Go to, **let us** go down, and there **confound their language, that they may not understand one another's speech**. **8** So the LORD scattered them abroad from thence upon the face of all the earth: and they left to build the city."

Verse 6 states that the people speaking one language would empower and benefit them, and yet **verse 8** claims he destroyed this without giving a reason. Humans do not benefit from not understanding each other, and lack of understanding is a common factor that causes divisions and strife. What sort of person would enable problems that he would also kill to solve? This would be like an episode of a film about psychos.

The question is, now that these people have been punished with summary drowning without a judgement day, was death the finality of their punishment, or are they going to be punished on the fabled judgement day? As you read in chapter three there is no definitive meaning of hell or burning in hellfire. So, if this story was real, the people in the Noah story would be the only ones to suffer definitive punishment, the terror of drowning. And according to **Genesis 9:9-11** God promised not to do this again. **9** "And I, behold, I establish my covenant with you, and with your seed after you. **10** And with every living creature that *is* with you, of the fowl, of the cattle, and of every beast of the earth with you; from all that go out of the ark, to every beast of the earth. **11** And I will establish my covenant with you; **neither shall all flesh be cut off anymore by the waters of a flood; neither shall there anymore be a flood to destroy the earth**."

So, since we are not going to be drowned, and there is no definitive claim of hell as a place for our punishment, religions should not preach hellfire anymore – we will just live and die, as is natural. This is a certainty.

Based on the story, the people killed in the flood were not given an option to redeem themselves, that is, they didn't get a saviour to die for them, and they were not given a Holy Bible to guide them. An oversight, incompetence, or a poorly written fable? This mass killing would include, presumably, the majority of the great and mighty nations of Abraham God initiated in **Genesis 18:10** by enabling his wife to have a child beyond childbearing age. This means his claim or prediction that they would have a great and mighty nation failed. If not, why would he kill his great and mighty nation?

Genesis 18:17 And the LORD said, Shall I hide from Abraham that thing which I do; **18** Seeing that Abraham shall surely become a great and mighty nation, and all the nations of the earth shall be blessed in him?

We now get to the character that Christianity is supposedly based on, and he is supposedly the son of God. So, using Christians' dating of the earth, after over four thousand years without a means to redeem ourselves and gain forgiveness, God finally came up with a solution for humanity to erase original sin and other sins. The great plan was to send his son to earth for us to kill him so that he doesn't have to punish us, and we can live forever.

CHAPTER FIVE

The story of Jesus – the third failed attempt to have perfect humans?

Father, Son, and Holy Ghost, three essences but one God – Since belief in the Trinity is the dominant interpretation of the Christian God, most Christians at least inadvertently believe God send himself to impregnate a woman with himself so he could be born as a human being, pray to himself – and then get us to kill him as a sacrifice to himself so he can forgive sins he created himself to save us from hell created by himself. This sounds like something even he wouldn't believe. Paraphrasing unknown author

No story demonstrates the power of socialisation more than the story of Jesus coming to earth to die for the "sin" of humanity. It is a story that follows a pattern of the God in the Bible requiring blood sacrifices which are usually animals. It doesn't make any sense that the Creator of all things would desire and entertain the killing of his creations to please himself. What possible benefit could a God gain from this? Billions of people have accepted this to be a real story, a testament to the power of socialisation. Here are a few of the many stories of sacrifices:

Leviticus 3:1 And if his oblation is a sacrifice of peace offering, if he offers it of the herd; whether it be a male or female, he shall offer it without blemish before the LORD. **Numbers 29:36** But ye shall offer a burnt offering, a sacrifice made by fire, of a sweet savour unto the LORD: one bullock, one ram, seven lambs of the first year without blemish. **Leviticus 9:4** Also, a bullock and a ram for peace offerings, to sacrifice before the LORD; and a meat offering mingled with oil: for today the LORD will appear unto you. **Leviticus 23:19** Then ye shall sacrifice one kid of the goats for a **sin offering**, and two lambs of the first year for a sacrifice of **peace offerings**[18]. **Exodus 23:18** Thou shalt not offer the blood of my sacrifice with leavened bread; neither shall the fat of my sacrifice remain until the morning. **Leviticus 1:2** Speak unto the children of Israel, and say unto them, If any man of you bring an offering unto the LORD, ye shall bring your offering of the cattle, even of the herd, and of the flock.

Numbers 29:36 suggest he likes the smell of burnt flesh, and Leviticus 23:19 claims baby goats were acceptable for the remission of sin. Why differentiate between cattle and herd since cattle make up a herd? Perhaps he wanted a lot?

After perhaps thousands of years of animal sacrifice, this time the blood sacrifice required is human, but it will be his immortal son in human form. Or will it be himself in human form? The concept of the Trinity says three essences, but one God – Father, Son, and Holy Ghost. It is the dominant principle in Christianity. In ancient Rome offering sacrifices to the gods was a common practice and this included the **king of the Roman gods**, Jupiter. Sheep were often sacrificed to Jupiter. The sacrifice of a human being to a god would be a major shift. However, the story of Jesus as the sacrifice was not based on humans offering a sacrifice to an imaginary god such as Jupiter, it is based on an imaginary God getting humans to unknowingly **sac-**

[18] In the real world, it means reducing hostility. In ancient times it was common to appease an angry god with sacrifices. However, they claim it means "a thanksgiving to God" in the Bible. This doesn't make sense to this author, however, you decide.

rifice his son to himself, or himself to himself. Such an idea would have probably shocked and confused the ancient Romans.

So, why wasn't this solution offered to the descendants of Adam and Eve instead of drowning them? The simple answer is that much of the Bible is a compilation of stories that are not related to each other, and as you have read, key principles of Christianity are not in the Bible such as the principle of original sin. The mass drowning of humanity does not fit with the principle of original sin since Jesus is supposed to be the only solution to avoid punishment after death.

Christians use **Isiah 64:6 quoted below** to claim Jesus is the only solution for "sin". This strengthens the conclusion that the Noah story is incohesive with the central principle of Christianity, **the born-again theology**. This is another example of this being a poorly written manmade dogma.

Isiah 64:6 is interpreted as meaning that God doesn't place any value on us doing good deeds and living a good life. We could live an exemplary life that is devoted to others and do no wrong, but if we never accept his son as our saviour we will be punished. As you will see **Isiah 64:6** doesn't say this. However, this is quite common in Christianity. A lot of beliefs in Christianity are manufactured by theologians and pastors either through the interpretation of scriptures or invented ideas that become part of the belief even though they are not in the Bible. The manufactured interpretation of **Isiah 64:6** is an excellent recruitment tool. It's diabolical and clever to convince potential victims that living an ethical and moral life and doing good doesn't count in their God's value system. We can only blame them for believing that this nonsensical dogma makes sense. **However, Job 15:16** confirms that their God regards us as being unsavoury. It's this guilt trip that drives many to embrace religion. A famous song, "Amazing Grace" stokes this indoctrination of guilt with the lyrics, "…save a **wretch** like me." We even put this guilt trip on innocent children by telling them they were born in "sin". This should qualify as child abuse with the use of ignorance as a weapon!

Isaiah 64:6 But we are all as an unclean thing, and all our righteousness are as filthy rags, and we all do fade as a leaf; and our iniquities, like the wind, have taken us away. Job 15:16 How much more abominable and filthy is man, which drinks iniquity like water? [Living a righteous life means nothing to God? Amazing.]

If doing good and serving our fellow man was ***the only possibility of not being punished*** and rewarded with going to heaven, would those who believe and are God-fearing engage in centuries of disunity, cruelty, oppression, and bloodshed? No. it would be at least less likely. If this was a true story wouldn't this be what an all-wise God would offer as the way to earn his favour? Would an all-wise, infinitely intelligent, and loving parent reject his children's choice of being righteous when this would result in a better outcome? No. We are told that his better solution was for us to kill his son, and accept him as our saviour. This outrageous idea should be definitive proof that man invented scripture and God. However, it is also a clever way to recruit more of the vunerable into Christianity, a social and commercial institution.

The acceptance of this story as being real can be damaging to that which defines us as humans, our capacity to reason. The acceptance of such a story at least limits our growth and development. Let's break it down and also have a closer look at the Adam and Eve story, and interrogate it as if it was real:

- Even if we allow for the non-Biblical concept of us needing forgiveness for "original sin" co-opted into Christian doctrine by St Augustine, the solution could easily be more sensible by requiring us to ask for forgiveness for bad deeds, and the sole requirement is for us to do good deeds. This would, at minimum, eliminate going to wars in the name of God, and claiming his protection unless it was genuinely in self defence. We are yet to hear of any war declared in the name of Satan. St Augustine must have had a convoluted and sick mind if he considered the option of us asking for forgiveness but rejected this as being too simple and without sacrificial violence. The fact that so many have accepted the idea of original sin without question is the most amazing part of this story.

- Even if we allow the macabre idea of a blood sacrifice, the story claims Jesus is immortal, as he had risen from the dead. Therefore, he can't be killed, so there was no sacrifice. Giving up his human life cannot rescue this narrative since he is immortal and his human experience was just temporary.
- Since Jesus is immortal and therefore can't be killed, people should recognise the weakness of the doctrine and be repulsed by the idea of an innocent person being sacrificed for the actions of guilty persons, so that they suffer no consequence for their evil acts. Also, an all-wise and infinitely intelligent God would not require humans to perform a symbolic killing of a god when we are admonished by him not to kill. This would be a major contradiction and nonsensical. If we include the non-Biblical original sin dogma, it paints him as being so unforgiving about Adam and Eve disobeying him by eating an apple from the "tree of knowledge of good and evil" that he decided that all future generations will be guilty by default of the transgression of Adam and Eve, and could be punished for it (if we are not 'saved'). And yet he wanted us to kill his son so that he can forgive us for things we do and didn't do. This would be like a parent desiring his children to live a perfect life, but forcing them to commit a crime. What a monumental, nonsensical, and ignorant idea St Augustine championed and so many of us bought, and so did I before I got to the age of reason. What sort of parent would require the symbolic killing of his son by some of his children so that he can forgive and not kill his other children? We have to

perform mental gymnastics that is injurious to our minds for this to make sense, or don't think at all.

- **Genesis 2:25** states "And they were both naked, the man and his wife, and were **not ashamed**." Why would they be ashamed of being naked? In **Genesis 3:6-7** the answer was given and it makes no sense. "And when the woman saw that the tree was good for food, and that it was pleasant to the eyes, and a tree to be desired to make one wise, she ate the fruit and gave some to her husband and he also ate. **7.** And **the eyes of both of them were opened, and they knew that they were naked**, and they sewed fig leaves together and made themselves aprons." Why did eating the fruit from the tree cause awareness of being naked and the cause for **being ashamed?** God made the tree to represent the knowledge of good and evil **(Genesis 2:17)**. Since the knowledge of something good is not a cause for being ashamed, then God linked being aware of being naked to knowing evil. This makes no sense.
- This is the third scripture found where the Bible states there is more than one Creator. **Genesis 3:22** "And the Lord God said, Behold the man has become as **one of us**, to know good and evil, lest he put his forth his hand, and take also of the tree of life and eat and live forever. The others are **Genesis 1:26 and Genesis 11:7**
- **Genesis 3:22** is claiming God and his co-creator knew good and evil, therefore they are responsible for this consciousness. They placed it in the reach of Adam and Eve, created the serpent that caused them to eat from its tree, punished them for doing so, and then Saint Augustine added that all future generations would also be held responsible. How can the people of the world grow if they are indoctrinated into believing such an illogical, unjust, and twisted fable? **Genesis 3:22** also suggests that knowing good and evil is necessary to be a Creator, so how can it be a bad thing?
- Since Christians accept that Jesus came to die for our sins, why would they be unhappy with those who facilitate his

death? No Christian will name their son Judas. Since Jesus didn't come to die of old age or climb up onto the cross and crucify himself, someone had to cause his crucifixion, and Judas was nominated for this job. So, if logic counts, Christians should hold him in high esteem, but this is not the case, and it's safe to conclude that God has not explained this to them – some people speak of his betrayal and death as if it was not supposed to have happened. However, the story gets stranger. Since crucifixion is supposed to be God's master plan to save humanity, why would the Devil help to make this happen? According to **John 13:2,** "And supper being ended, **the devil having now put into the heart of Judas Iscariot, Simon's son, to betray him**." The story still gets stranger. **Matthew 26:24** suggests that the person who betrayed Jesus will suffer. "**The Son of man goes as it is written of him: but woe unto that man by whom the Son of man is betrayed! It had been good for that man if he had not been born.**" It gets even stranger. **Matthew 26:25** suggests that Jesus confirmed to Judas that he will betray him. "Then Judas, which betrayed him, answered and said, Master, is it I? He said unto him, Thou hast said." Why would the Bible which is supposed to be God's wisdom describe him as a traitor when he should be regarded as a facilitator?

- Since his role in the crucifixion was necessary, why "Woe unto him"? How can such a contradictory story be regarded as divine revelation? Another piece of evidence that this is a manmade story and cannot be attributed to any infinitely intelligent being is that this supposedly divine plan was not explained as being divine to Judas, **a disciple**. As a result, his story ended as we are accustomed to seeing in a typical tragic Hollywood movie. According to **Matthew 27:1-5**, "When the morning had come, all the chief priests and elders of the people took counsel against Jesus to put him to death: **2.** And when they had bound him, they led him away, and delivered him to Pontius Pilate the governor. **3.**

> Then Judas, which had betrayed him, when he saw that he was condemned, repented himself, and brought again the thirty pieces of silver to the chief priests and elders, **4.** Saying, I have sinned in that I have betrayed the innocent blood. And they said, what is that to us? See thou to that. **5. And he cast down the pieces of silver in the temple, and departed, and went and hanged himself."** Did he hang himself? It depends on which scripture you read. According to **Acts1:18-19** he didn't return the money or hang himself: **18.** Now this man purchased a field with the reward of iniquity, and falling headlong, he burst asunder in the midst, and all his bowels gushed out. **19** And it was known unto all the dwellers at Jerusalem; insomuch as that field is called in their proper tongue, Aceldama, that is to say, **the field of blood**." In **Matthew 27:6-8** the priests took the money and bought the land called the field of blood. **6** And the chief priests took the silver pieces, and said, it is not lawful for to put them into the treasury, because it is the price of blood. **7** And they took counsel, and bought with them the potter's field, to bury strangers in. **8** Wherefore that field was called, **The field of blood**, unto this day. **[contradictions rule supreme]**

If the Jesus story is a real story, and his coming to earth was to provide evidence to humanity regarding the identity of the real God, and his crucifixion was to save us from his father's punishment, the result is another unmitigated failure. How can a story about an all-wise, all-powerful, and infinitely intelligent God who is repeatedly incompetent be anything but mythology? Based on the current state of affairs, he will have to destroy or punish billions of us because of the divisions and beliefs in different gods, and numerous different interpretations of poorly written "Holy" texts. Out of an estimated seven billion people on earth, there are only over two billion of us who identify as Christians. An infinitely intelligent being would be capable of communicating his message in such a way that there would be no room for misunderstandings. Is there a better way that this could have been accomplished? Yes, there are three: In **Exodus 19:9** it stated, **"And the Lord said unto Moses, Lo, I come unto thee in a thick cloud that the people may hear when I speak with thee, and believe thee forever.** And Moses told the words of the people unto the Lord." This is the most powerful option, speak to the world directly, as is claimed he did with Moses and his people. Apart from talking in the clouds, he could communicate the information in all our brains or through a universal dream. The next option will be covered shortly when the concept of divine revelation is examined closely.

The story of Jesus fails the history test – time, place, people, custom, and events

Every story that is claimed to be historical should be able to pass the test of accuracy on any of six principles, people, customs/practices and beliefs, place, time, events, and credibility.

1. The relevance of time to the Jesus story

The minimum expected from documents claimed to be inspired by a perfect infinitely intelligent being is accuracy. The Bible, having many contradictions, untruths, illogic, and gibberish would disqualify it from being written by an intelligent person, much less an infinitely intelligent being. There are two important time principles about the telling of the story on which it fails. Firstly, an infinitely intelligent, all-wise, and all-powerful being who wish to record his monumental plan for "human salvation" for future generations to read would ensure that the events were recorded in real-time by eyewitnesses. However, not only was it not written in real-time, there is no definitive answer as to when they were written, and the answers are problematic. The writers are also unknown. Celebrities in our time who wish to preserve an accurate account of their lives are far more accomplished, they hire biographers to document it. **A Google search of "When was the New Testament written" produced various estimates**:

"They were written **between approximately 70 and 100 AD**, and were the end-products of a long process of development; all are anonymous, and almost certainly none are the work of eyewitnesses."

John Drane, a Christian theologian wrote:

"The New Testament has 27 books, written **between about 50 and 100 AD**, and falling naturally into two sections: the Gospels, which tell the story of Jesus (Matthew, Mark, Luke, and John); and the Letters (or **epistles**) - **written by various Christian leaders** to provide guidance **for the earliest church communities."**

Interestingly, John Drane writes about **The Epistles** as if it was not aimed at the entire world for then and in perpetuity as a guide. Such a view should eliminate it being a divine revelation to humanity. However, even though theologians tend to view the Bible differently, the power of socialisation doesn't stop them from embracing ideas that should render Christianity to be invalid.

The consensus found through this research is that the writers of the Bible are not known.

History.com – Even after nearly 2,000 years of its existence, and centuries of investigation by biblical scholars, we still don't know with certainty who wrote its various texts, when they were written, or under what circumstances.

When were the Gospels written and by whom? "The four canonical Gospels were probably written **between AD 66 and 110**. All four were anonymous (with the modern names added in the 2nd century), almost certainly none were by eyewitnesses, and all are the end-products of long oral and written transmission. Mark was the first to be written, using a variety of sources." Wikipedia

"The most probable date of composition is around **80–100 AD**, although some scholars date it significantly later, and **there is evi-**

dence that it was still being substantially revised well into the 2nd century." Wikipedia

The consensus that the writers are unknown, and uncertainty as to when the scriptures were written strengthen the observation that if something this important was organised by an infinitely intelligent, and all-powerful being, it would not have this many unknown factors. Unknown factors weaken credibility.

Christianity tradition credits the four Gospels to Matthew, Mark, Luke, and John. Both common sense (logical thinking) and Bible scriptures discredit this. Authors never title their books "according to" as it is with all the four Gospels. This is like saying "This book, according to me." None of the authors put their names on the books. If Matthew wrote Matthew, this scripture would not be written in this way: **Matthew 9:9** "And as Jesus passed forth from thence, **he saw a man, named Matthew**, sitting at the receipt of custom: and he said unto him, Follow me. And he arose, and followed him." At the beginning and end of the book of John, it states, **John 1:6** "There was a man sent from God, whose name *was* John." And **John 21:24-25** "This is the disciple who testified of these things, and wrote these things: and **we know** that **his testimony** is true. **25** And there are also many other things which Jesus did, the which, if they should be written every one, I suppose that even the world itself could not contain the books that should be written. Amen."

Saying "we know" is stating that there was more than one writer, and starting with **John 1:6,** they are writing about John. And since he is only referenced in the Bible and not by any historian, this is a made-up story. This point will be expanded on shortly.

So the evidence suggests the disciples didn't write the New Testament, and the authors are unknown. However, whoever wrote them were not eyewitnesses and they didn't have any supernatural help. This is evident because of the contradictions. Here are a few of many:

Matthew 2:1 Now when Jesus was born in Bethlehem of Judaea in the days of Herod the king, behold, there came **wise men from the east to Jerusalem**.

Luke 2:8-10-11-16 - 8 And there were in the same country **shepherds** abiding in the field, keeping watch over their flock by night. **10** And the angel said unto them, Fear not: for, behold, I bring you good tidings of great joy, which shall be to all people. **11** For unto you is born this day in the city of David a Saviour, which is Christ the Lord. **16** And they came with haste and found Mary, and Joseph, and the babe lying in a manger.

Matthew 17:20 And Jesus said unto them, Because of your unbelief: for verily I say unto you, If ye have faith as a grain of mustard seed, ye shall **say unto this mountain,** Remove hence to yonder place, and it shall remove; and nothing shall be impossible unto you. **Luke 17:6** And the Lord said, If ye had faith as a grain of mustard seed, ye might **say unto this sycamine tree**, Be thou plucked up by the root, and be thou planted in the sea; and it should obey you.

An extraordinary story of omitted verses from the book of St. Mark

Apart from the King James Versions, if you search new translations of the Bible for **St. Mark 16:15-18** you will find it but you will also see this message:

"The earliest manuscripts and some other ancient witnesses do not have verses 9–20."

This is declaring that these verses are late additions. This is very significant for two major reasons. Firstly, it strengthens the fact that Divine Revelation is a fallacy. Secondly, the scriptures are the basis for the most lucrative part of Christianity, Pentecostal healing ministries, and televangelism.

St. Mark 16:15-18 And he said unto them, Go ye into all the world, and preach the gospel to every creature. **16** He that believeth and is baptized shall be saved; but he that believeth not shall be damned. **17** And these signs shall follow them that believe; In my name shall they **cast out devils**; they shall **speak with new tongues**; **18** They shall take up serpents; and if they drink any deadly thing, it shall not hurt them; they shall **lay hands on the sick, and they shall recover**.

2. Other issues with time and the Bible – how were the sixty-six books chosen?

The other problem regarding time is that it took a long time for the compilation of the Bible. The question is, why? No one with any awareness of the history of Christianity disagrees that the Bible has been edited several times. Yet, despite this, and **the process of compilation was done through centuries of voting books in and out before settling with the current sixty-six books**, and there are other versions, adherents regard whichever version they have as the undisputed word of God. In response to this, one adherent claimed that God would never allow us to change the essential message. This is an example of religiosity stepping in and common sense taking flight. We should all know that just changing a word or two in a sentence can drastically change its meaning.

How could a book go through all these political changes and be regarded as the end product of Divine Revelation? The process of writing then and now would be the same. A writer gets inspired mentally to write something and they act on it until it's finished. It's reasonable to conclude that if a supernatural force was involved it would be a lot quicker and more precise. As you will see further in this book **the Old Testament was claimed to have been written over a thousand years.** This length of time should destroy its credibility of being divine.

The next credibility issue is that it took a long time to decide which sixty-six books to comprise the Bible, and this was because of how the decisions were made. The question of how it was decided throws up interesting answers and all of them point to a central theme, they were all decided by human beliefs and actions, not by a supernatural force. Here are the quotes:

International Bible Society – Biblica

"The 39 books of the Old Testament form the Bible of Judaism, while the Christian Bible includes those books and also the 27 books of the New Testament. This list of books included in the Bible is known as the canon. That is, the canon refers to the books regarded as inspired by God and authoritative for faith and life. No church created the canon, but *the churches and councils gradually accepted the list of books recognized by believers everywhere as inspired.*" **[They accepted the ones in circulation that believers liked and this would be subjective – they chose the popular ones. No claim of communication from God. Could you identify any hint of supernatural force involvement in the above narrative?]**

There is no logical reason for there being an Old and New Testament when the objective is supposed to be the narration of one story, the story of the origin of humanity, how we came into existence, and the rules we are supposed to follow. The explanation for the differences between old and new is that the New Testament represents a new dispensation. And this is characterised as God changing his mind about things such as stoning someone to death as punishment. So, God is like us, he changes his mind now and again. However, we know that Natural Science governs our existence. So, Natural Science which is embedded in Nature must be in harmony with whatever is responsible for our existence.

"It was not until 367 AD that the church father Athanasius first provided the complete listing of the 66 books belonging to the canon. **[Over 350 years after the crucifixion?]**

- He distinguished those from other books that were widely circulated and he noted that those 66 books were the ones, and the only ones, universally accepted. **[The church father Athanasius didn't decide based on input from his God]**
- The point is that the formation of the canon did not come all at once like a thunderbolt, but was the product of **centuries of reflection**." **[No communication from God?]**

A Google Searched question and answer

"When did they decide what books would be in the Bible?"

"While there was a good measure of debate in the Early Church over the New Testament canon, the major writings were accepted by almost all Christians **by the middle of the 3rd century**."

Someone must have noticed the lack of answers that included claims of Godly input so they wrote this on **biblword.net:**

"It must be noted that although the canon of Scripture was discussed and debated by men, **we believe** that ultimately it was God who led the Church to decide on which books he wanted to be included in His divine Word." **[It's just a belief, "God" didn't speak to them either]**

The Bible's major credibility issues

Voting books in and out and the editing of books should destroy claims of a supernatural force involvement. Also, the most commonly used Bible is the King James Version. It would not be called a "version" if it was a copy of the original and merely translated into a different language, and there is now a **New King James Version**, and changes have been made – only two have been identified. The **NKJV** uses the word "slave" sixty-five times while the original **KJV** uses it once. The new version says **grain** instead of **meat**. This is significant because, instead of claims of many meat sacrifices to God, it's now grain sacrifices. Why would it take this long to make such a major change? A book that claimed to be inspired by God had this major error, and for more than a thousand years God didn't inspire anyone to change it?

What standard of writing and communication to humanity would have more credibility than the Bible, and supersede human capabilities? Kersey Graves has said it so well it's best to quote him:

"We will inquire, in the first place, what a divine revelation would be. Coming from a perfect being, it would of course be perfect, and perfectly adapted to the moral and spiritual wants of the whole human race. Such a revelation would be so clear, explicit, and unequivocal in its language with respect to every doctrine, principle, and precept, and every statement of fact, that no person of ordinary mind could possibly misunderstand it; and no two persons could differ for a moment with respect to the meaning of any text embraced in it. It would need no priest and no commentator to explain it; and, if any attempt should be made to explain it, it would only "darken counsel", render the matter more obscure, and would amount to the blasphemous assumption that Omniscience can be enlightened, and his works improved. And a divine revelation should be communicated to the whole human race; for, if restricted to one nation, it would render God obnoxious to the charge of partiality. And, in order to make it practicable to communicate to all nations, it would be necessary to comprehend it in a universal language constructed for the purpose, or else impart it to the world through all the three thousand languages in use by different nations and tribes. But, as such a revelation has never been known on the earth, it is at once evident that no such revelation has ever been communicated to man by Infinite Wisdom." – The Bible of Bibles by Kersey Graves, (1870).

Kersey Graves's suggestion that the purpose and strategy of a divine revelation would be to inspire people in every language cannot be faulted. In this scenario, every nation would claim and accept the message as their own, and this would demonstrate an action that no human could accomplish. Currently, the majority of people on earth do not regard the major religions or their holy texts such as the Bible, the Quran, and the Torah, as being relevant to their lives. How can they be blamed when we consider the following: *"There are not less than eleven hundred and fifty pious effusions ... claiming to have originated from the fountain of divine revelation."*

On what basis can one be sure that the book they believe in is a divine revelation when all of them cannot be right, therefore they could all be wrong? Based on the logical standard quoted from Kersey Graves and the absence of irrefutable communication from an all-powerful Deity, all we have is belief, no facts. The acceptance of religion and its texts have resulted in centuries of wars and oppression, and this demonstrates the strongest proof that religions are false – they divide us and have been responsible for our worse behaviour, and the "God" they claim to represent has not intervened to point us to the right message, but often, it is the belief in the dogma – the words of God within their "Holy texts" that are directing the carnage.

3. The relevance of verification of people in the Bible

The people mentioned in the Bible have to be verifiable, especially because it was written in a well-documented era. Many years before and during the time the Jesus story is claimed to have happened are well-documented by known historians. King David is linked in two genealogies of Jesus and yet David is a mythological figure. He is only referenced in the Bible, and Goliath whom it claims David slew with a sling and a stone is also a mythological figure with a claimed height of 9.75 feet.

Wikipedia – "David Hebrew: Modern: *Davīd*, Tiberian: *Dāwīḏ*) is described in the **Hebrew Bible** as the third king of the United

Monarchy of Israel and Judah. In the Books of Samuel, David is a young shepherd and harpist who gains fame by slaying the giant Goliath."

Peter is an English or Scottish name and both languages are about 1,400 years old, and the Jesus story is claimed to be up to 33 AD which is 1,989 years ago. The name **Mary** was derived from the ancient Hebrew name **Miriam**, so why would the inspired writers not record her as such? The obvious answer is the writer wrote a name in modern times without any mystical influence. It has to be significant that the majority of the disciples, Mary, and others who it was claimed to be close to Jesus had no last names, and for those with other names, it's not clear if they are last names. This diminishes credibility. See in **Addendum, "Bible characters, tradition, historical or spurious claims?"** for additional information on Bible characters.

4. The relevance of time, place/location, and custom to the Jesus story

The central claim of Christianity is that Jesus represents the only true God, his father, or they are one, as parts of a Trinity. The people of the region where the Bible claims the Jesus story started were worshiping many gods and goddesses during the time of the story. Religious people today regard them as Godless people because the "people" they were worshipping were not real, and this is confirmed by the fact that all the gods and goddesses they worshipped are now categorised as mythology. Therefore, as far as Christians are concerned they would have no experience, knowledge, or communication with supernatural "real" beings such as the God of the Bible, angels, the Lord Jesus, and the Holy Ghost. With this context in mind, the Bible's account of how the Jesus story began is patently false and definitive evidence that man invented Bible texts and the God they claim inspired the story. According to **Luke 1:26-35 KJV:**

26. "And in the sixth month the angel Gabriel was sent from God unto a city of Galilee, named Nazareth, **27** To a virgin espoused to a man whose name was Joseph, of the house of David; and the virgin's name *was* Mary.**28** And the angel came in unto her, and said, Hail, *thou that art* highly favoured, the Lord *is* with thee: blessed *art* thou among women. **29** And when she saw *him*, she was troubled at his saying, and cast in her mind what manner of salutation this should be. **30** And the angel said unto her, Fear not, Mary: for thou hast found favour with God. **31** And, behold, thou shalt conceive in thy womb, and bring forth a son, and shalt call his name JESUS. **32** He shall be great, and shall be called the Son of the Highest: and the Lord God shall give unto him the throne of his father David: **33** And he shall reign over the house of Jacob forever, and of his kingdom, there shall be no end. **34** Then said Mary unto the angel, how shall this be, seeing I know not a man? **35** And the angel answered and said unto her, the Holy Ghost shall come upon thee, and the power of the Highest shall overshadow thee: therefore also that holy thing which shall be born of thee shall be called the Son of God."

If this is a real story Mary would be unfamiliar with everything the angel said to her. Apart from the fact that, like us, she would have no experience of having conversations with supernatural beings[19], and therefore she would either faint, burst into hysteria, or run away screaming. The story is told as if she was familiar with the characters mentioned by the angel. Since this supposedly took place before the Bible was written, and King David only exists in the Bible, she would have no idea who he was talking about. What's the chance that a giant existed and was killed with a sling and a stone being a real story and it's only mentioned in the Bible? A legendary king in the Roman Empire would be well documented. However, every aspect of King David's life is strictly Bible narratives, not historical – his lineage, his father, and his mother. This is a mythological story.

[19] Any claim by individuals of God talking to them is either delusional or a deceiver. If God can talk to one person, he can talk to all of us. With all the religious divisions and confusion in the world, it would be pointless to talk to a few of us when he has a plan for all of us.

Mary would be unfamiliar with the single God concept of the "Most High", and "Holy Spirit", and yet the story claims she spoke as if she fully understood everything that was said, except for being puzzled as to how she can be pregnant when she never had sex. This is the only natural part of the story. In today's world Christians are fully aware of Muslims, and vice versa. If a Christian woman was told that she was going to have a baby for Allah would she entertain this conversation? No. Would the situation improve if she had no reference regarding the deity mentioned? No, she would probably think the person was crazy. And if the communication was in the form of a supernatural spirit, she would think it was an evil spirit. If it is a real story, Mary's reaction would not be an intellectual one.

There were twelve main gods and goddesses that were worshipped in the ancient Roman Empire, chief among them were **Jupiter - God of the sky; Juno - Queen of the gods; and Minerva Goddesses of wisdom**. They practiced polytheism, as did most of the world. Some of the other gods and goddesses were **Saturn** - god of Time; **Neptune** - god of the Seas; **Pluto** - god of the Underworld; **Venus** - goddess of Love and Beauty; **Mars** - god of War; **Mercury** - Messenger of the gods; **Apollo** - god of the Sun; **Diana** - goddess of the Hunt; and **Ceres** - goddess of Agriculture and Familial Love.

5. The relevance of location/place of Jesus's story

Outside of the Bible's account there are no credible records of the existence of Jesus, his disciples, Mary, and other persons the Bible claims had close connections to Jesus in the location this drama is supposed to have happened. The history of this area is well documented, yet there are no burial sites for any of the characters, and none of the many historians from that locality have written about these people. As you can confirm, many of the characters in the Bible who are claimed to be closely connected to the Jesus story only exist in the Bible.

If we contrast this with ancient Egyptians who existed thousands of years before, some of their remains are in museums. Josephus is said to be the most notable Jewish historian, and yet scholars have found just one short reference for Jesus in his works which scholars have dismissed as a forgery. This makes sense. What is the chance of a person who had the following experiences was not well documented during a time that is well documented? It's claimed he was followed by twelve disciples and at times great multitudes; he performed many miracles such as raising the dead, healing the sick, making the blind see, turning water into wine, walking on water, and powerful people were aware of him and his powers. He was installed by the Roman Empire as the son of God in the Roman Catholic Church. A brief outline of his fame according to the Bible:

"**Matthew 4:25** And there followed him great multitudes of people from Galilee, and from Decapolis, and from Jerusalem, and from Judaea, **and from beyond Jordan**.

Matthew 14:1&5 At that time Herod the tetrarch[20] heard of the fame of Jesus, **5** And when he would have put him to death, he feared the multitude, because **they counted him as a prophet.**

Matthew 12:15 But when Jesus knew it, he withdrew himself from thence: and great multitudes followed him, and he healed them all.

Mark 3:7 But Jesus withdrew himself with his disciples to the sea: and a great multitude from Galilee followed him, and from Judaea.

Matthew 14:13 When Jesus heard of it, he departed thence by ship into a desert place apart: and when the people had heard thereof, they followed him on foot out of the cities.

Matthew 20:34 So Jesus had compassion on them, and touched their eyes: and immediately their eyes received sight, and they followed him.

[20] Son of King Herod

Luke 12:1 In the meantime, when there were gathered together an innumerable multitude of people, insomuch that they trode (trampled) one upon another,

Luke 5:15 But so much the more went there a **fame abroad of him**: and great multitudes came together to hear, and to be healed by him of their infirmities.

Matthew 21:14-15 And the blind and the lame came to him in the temple; and he healed them. **15** And when the **chief priests** and **scribes** saw the wonderful things that he did, and the children crying in the temple, and saying, Hosanna to the Son of David; they were sore displeased"

If put in the context of a time when medical knowledge was limited compared to now, how would they react to such miracles? A person who did any or all of the above would be a legend throughout that region and everywhere that those people travelled, and **Luke 5:15** suggests this. The people of the time these events supposedly happened had less scientific knowledge and were more superstitious than we are currently. What is the chance of someone raising a person from his grave and this didn't cause mass hysteria? That would be the outcome now, and people would likely think it's "Satanic or demonic". And yet the Bible claimed the crowd that was with him was calm and "bears record or witness." This is suggesting that they acted like this was a normal regular occurrence. **John 12:17**, "The people, therefore, that was with him when he called Lazarus out of his grave and raised him from the dead, bare record."

It's implausible for a person who had these powers and fame not to have been well documented.

A major event of the following magnitude would have been recorded by many people around the world.

Luke 23:44-45 claims the following happened during Jesus' crucifixion: "And it was about the sixth hour, and there was a darkness **over all the earth** until the ninth hour. **45** And the sun was darkened, and the veil of the temple was rent in the midst."

6. The relevance of the slaughter of the innocent by King Herod and the Jesus story

The story of the mass killing of children by Herod **(Matthew 2:16)** in an attempt to kill Jesus is only written in the Bible, and only in the book of Matthew. What's the chance of such a horrific crime being committed during a time that had many writers, was well documented, and yet no one else recorded it? Herod was regarded as a wicked man.

Yet, here are writers who wrote about him but did not mention that which would be, at minimum, one of the worse crimes in history:

- Rabbinical writers - wrote about his wicked acts in minute detail
- Josephus - wrote, "The Life of Herod". The book claimed Herod died 4BC!
- Roman historians

Matthew 2:16

"Then Herod, when he saw that he was mocked of the wise men, was exceeding wroth, and sent forth, and slew all the children that were in Bethlehem, and in all the coasts thereof, from two years old and under, according to the time which he had diligently inquired of the wise men."

Roman historians and others would record such an unmissable story of the mass slaughtering of babies and children. For example, "**Marcus Velleius Paterculus (c. 19 BC – c. AD 31)** was a Roman historian, soldier, and senator. His Roman history, written in a highly rhetorical style, covered the period from the end of the Trojan War to AD 30, but is most useful for the period from the death of Caesar in 44 BC to the death of Augustus in AD 14." **Marcus Velleius Paterculus** was alive during the time the Bible claimed Jesus lived in the Roman Empire. There was also, among others, Seneca the Elder, Born in 54 BC in Córdoba Spain, and Died in 39 AD, in Rome, Italy, and he didn't write about him either. Christianity was not a religion during this time, so there would be no basis such as a religious bias for these historians not to record these personalities. There would be no reason not to record the mass slaughter of babies and children.

7. The relevance of Mary's descendants to the Jesus story

The Roman Empire approved the church in **AD 380** and installed Christianity which claimed that a woman named Mary gave birth to the Son of God under their jurisdiction. And even though Mary is venerated as the "Holy mother of God", there is no trace of her ever existing or her descendants who would have been at least Jesus's brothers and sisters. Since they were related to the Son of God, they would have been involved in the church. If this is a real story, this family lineage would have been preserved by the Roman Empire and they would be around today as the greatest power in the Catholic Church and Christianity generally. They would be like "Holy Royals". Since Christians believe the Bible is the inspired words of God, they shouldn't object to us interpreting scriptures as being literal when there is no reason not to. So, it's a given that the following scripture is claiming Jesus had brothers and sisters. Therefore, Mary would have descendants.

Mark 6:3 "Is not this the carpenter, the son of Mary, the brother of James, and Joses, and of Juda, and Simon? And are not his sisters here with us? And they were offended at him." **Matthew 12:46-50**
46 While he yet talked to the people, behold, his mother and his brethren stood without, desiring to speak with him. **47** Then one said unto him, Behold, thy mother and thy brethren stand without, desiring to speak with thee. **48** But he answered and said unto him that told him, Who is my mother? and who are my brethren? **49** And

he stretched forth his hand toward his disciples, and said, Behold my mother and my brethren! **50** For whosoever shall do the will of my Father which is in heaven, the same is my brother, and sister, and mother. **John 2:12** After this, he went down to Capernaum, he, and his mother, and his brethren, and his disciples: and they continued there not many days."

Apart from the unlikely lack of descendants, there is a more powerful case to be made that if this is a real story Mary would be the first leader of the Catholic Church. You may agree with this conclusion after examining the narrative attributed to the beginning of the Catholic Church. But first, consider this narrative about Mary:

The figure Mary is highly venerated in the Catholic Church. She is so highly venerated that many prayers are offered up to her similar to those aimed at Jesus. One such prayer is called Hail Mary. It says, "Hail Mary, blessed are thou amongst women and blessed is the fruit of thy womb Jesus. Holy Mary mother of God, pray for us sinners now and at the hour of our death, Amen." Another prayer says: "Holy Mary, help those in need, give strength to the weak, comfort the sorrowful, pray for God's people, assist the clergy, intercede for the religious. Mary all who seek your help, experience your unfailing **protection**. Amen."

Considering the degree of veneration bestowed on Mary, if this is a real story, there is no logical, spiritual, or emotional reason why she would not be head of the Catholic Church as the first Bishop or Pope. How could anyone be more qualified than a woman, who was believed to have done something unprecedented, that is, gave birth to the Son of God? The Biblical apostle St. Peter is listed as the first Bishop or pope. This is how it is explained:

Wikipedia: "According to Catholic **tradition**[21], the Catholic Church was founded by Jesus Christ. The New Testament records Jesus' activ-

---

[21] Synonyms: belief, legend, folklore, lore, myth, superstition, culture, symbolism etc.

ities and teaching, his appointment of the twelve Apostles, and his instructions to them to continue his work." There are two important points to note from this quote, it says catholic **tradition**, not Catholic history, the New Testament records, and not the church's records. This is the definition of tradition:

"The root word means to pass along **beliefs and customs**. Tradition can be **created and developed** during the present and continue into the future."

Wikipedia – "The Catholic Church teaches that the coming of the Holy Spirit upon the apostles, in an event known as Pentecost, signalled the beginning of the public ministry of the Church. Catholics hold that Saint Peter was Rome's first bishop and the consecrator of **Linus** as its next bishop, thus starting the unbroken line which includes the current pontiff, Pope Francis."

So, the founding church of Western Christianity claims that the church started shortly after the "crucifixion", and the first Bishop or pope was Saint Peter, an apostle of Jesus. However, Saint Peter is a Bible story and character only, and the Bible was written many years after the start of the church. **It is not a recorded Roman Catholic Church history story, nor a story credited to historians.** Its authors are unknown, and it's based on belief, tradition, legend, folklore, lore, or myth. The justification of Peter being the foundation of the church is based on Bible scripture, **Matthew 16:18-19**, and it states, "And I tell you that you are Peter and on this rock, I will build my church, and the gates of Hades will not overcome it. I will give you the keys of the kingdom of heaven…"

Let's used simple common sense deduction to break this down and reveal major flaws in this narrative:

- The Old Testament is claimed to have been written at different times between about 1200 and 165 BC. An all-powerful God would not take this long to inspire the writing of supposedly vital instructions and moral guides for humanity. One can only guess how many people would be involved in writing it over such a long time.

- If this is a real story, the story of Jesus and the beginning of his church with Peter would not be based on tradition or legend. An all-powerful God orchestrating the saving of humanity would arrange for this to be well documented for that time. Therefore, the Jesus story and the formation of the church would be well documented, but they aren't. The Bible does not qualify as a well-documented narrative – it provides no information about the formation of the church. Yet, this would have been easy since there were historians around at that time, and place. **But even more compelling, Jesus, having not broadcasted and proved his identity to the entire world, had another powerful option. With his infinite powers and wisdom, would have recorded his life in its entirety and ensured that it was available for then, and future generations.** If this was done and included extraordinary knowledge that was undisputedly above our scope at the time, the only proof of his divinity that would supersede this is God speaking from the clouds. It is implausible that he nominated Saint Peter to start his church, and he did, but the church has no record of him – he didn't leave any record of his activities or a chronicle of his and Jesus' time together. You have read that Peter is an English name, but another credibility issue that applies to all named disciples is the lack of last names for almost all of them. Peter is particularly implausible because the full name of the founder of the church would be known. **According to the Encyclopedia Britannica, "Accounts of Peter's life and ministry rely on the four Gospels, the Acts of the Apostles, the epistles of Peter, and the epistles of St. Paul."** It was not from the church's historical records or historians. Also, according to **Luke 6:14**, "Simon, whom he [Jesus] also named Peter…" So, his name was Simon, and in **Mark 3:16** it says, "And Simon he surnamed Peter." So, he was given a surname, and most of the disciples had no surname either. This is not plausible for such important persons in the story. In further reference to St Peter, the Encyclopedia also cited tradition which also means legend, mythology, etc. It states, "According to **tradition**, he eventually went to Rome, where he suffered martyrdom by being crucified upside down." All authors of the Bible are unknown – no historical evidence, just legends.

- If this is a real story, Peter and all the Disciples would know Mary as Jesus's mother, the Mother of God, and therefore, they would have revered[22] her. Yet, there is no mention of this in the Bible. So, irrespective of whether Jesus had told Peter to start the church, Mary would be part of that church. How could the unprecedented Mother of God not be a part of the first church to carry out her son's work, especially in the context of how she is venerated currently?

Biblical sexism is definitive proof it is manmade dogma

As **I Timothy 2:12** indicates in chapter one, the Bible is the foundation of sexism. The concept of the Trinity is a central principle in Christianity. It is supposed to be a real story about the Creator(s) of **life** and the universe, yet God is characterised as a father who has a son but no mother. There is evidence that suggests that this was deliberate and part of a religious strategy to remove women from the representation of Deity. This would be a major shift from the long-standing religious **Polytheism** at the time to the current religious **monotheism**. In monotheistic religions, it's easy to get rid of the principle of the goddess since there is just one God. This had to be the intention because it is the only explanation that would explain why Mary is an obscure figure in the Bible story, and there is no mention of her as Holy Mother of God. If this is a real story it is a given

[22] Put this in the context of goddess worship was common at the time the story supposedly took place.

that Mary would have been revered as a goddess on earth by the disciples and all who believe in the divinity of Jesus, **because goddesses were worshipped then**. So, why not tell the story believably and logically? The obvious answer is, that it was part of a deliberate plan to remove the female representation of a deity as was customary in all religions and spiritual concepts. The fact that there is no goddess in Christianity and the other dominant religions is evidence that this was the intention, and it worked.

After centuries of violence, oppression, and indoctrination most religions don't recognise the concept of a goddess. It is now primarily regarded as mythology.

Pick a religion, Christianity, Islam, or Judaism. How long would it take to change the minds of believers from any of these religions? Do you think it would be a few years, decades, or hundreds of years? We know for sure it wouldn't be quick, especially if the change is drastic. So, within the context of the mythological polytheistic worship that was the norm at the time, there would be mass confusion and upheaval if someone among them was regarded by many as the only true God incarnate, and was demonstrating his credentials with miracles. If this was true it would not take the Roman Empire hundreds of years to recognise it and to decide what was its true doctrine. And since the Christian religious leaders were divided and confused hundreds of years later, it means there was no infinitely intelligent being (God) involved in the stories they believed in. The same principle applies today, religious leaders and the masses are divided on doctrine, and no God has intervened to give them clarity even though many believers claim they have a personal relationship with God.

A look at the people's beliefs at the time should show how big the shift was. The gods at the time tend to have wives and children, and some children will have wives and children as well. Christianity is God and son, no mother, and the unknown gender of the Holy Ghost. Perhaps this was the birth of the single-parent concept.

The three most important Roman gods were **Jupiter** (protector of the state), Juno (protector of women), and **Minerva** (goddess of craft and wisdom). Other major gods included **Mars** (god of war), **Mercury** (god of trade and messenger of the gods), and **Bacchus** (god of grapes and wine production). **Jupiter** was the god of the sky and thunder, and king of the gods in ancient Roman religion. **Jupiter (god)** - **Parents:** Saturn and Ops - **Consort (wife)**: **Juno** - **Children: Mars**, **Minerva**, Vulcan, Bellona, Juventas, and Hercules.

Juno (was an ancient Roman goddess, the protector and special counsellor of the state. She was equated to **Hera**, queen of the gods in Greek mythology. A daughter of Saturn, she was the **wife of Jupiter** and the mother of Mars, Vulcan, Bellona, and Juventas.

"Minerva is the Roman goddess of wisdom and strategic warfare, justice, law, victory, and the sponsor of arts, trade, and strategy. Minerva is not a patron of violence such as Mars, but defensive war only. **Minerva** is one of the three Roman deities in the **Capitoline Triad**, along with **Jupiter** and **Juno." If the triad is the principle on which the Holy Trinity is based, it is a major change. As you can see, it's Father, Wife, and Daughter.** Significantly, there are two women in the triad. The scarcity or non-existence of women deities in the current major religions, compared to ancient times is indicative of the high esteem women were held before the installation of Christianity. In Christianity, even the angels are men! This cannot be a coincidence. This was part of the process of removing the female representations of deities.

Mars: was the god of war and also an agricultural guardian, **consort(s)**: Nerio and others including Rhea Silvia (he raped her), Venus, Bellona **Children:** Romulus and Remus, Cupid

The Capitoline Triad – Jupiter, Juno, and Minerva

Christianity is polytheism disguising as monotheism

It's widely accepted that Christianity is a monotheistic religion, but is it? The Capitoline Triad is supposed to represent father, wife, and daughter, and they were referred to as god and goddesses. Christianity has three personages that are regarded as immortal, and immortality is a central characteristic of the god concept. There being three immortal personages in Christianity is no different than the **Capitoline Triad**. The "difference" is imaginary, that is, adherents chose to interpret it as three in one, **even though it's not in their Bible.** The convoluted concept of the **Trinity** formulated during the Council of Nicaea was perhaps intended to disguise the polytheistic nature of Christianity. It got ratified by the ecumenical councils, and now it is the dominant accepted doctrine. Those who made up the Christian story were no different than those who made up the Capitoline Triad – they were thinking from a polytheism point of view. However, the major difference was the removal of female representation.

Was the removal of the female representation of Deity a major reason for the conception and implementation of Christianity? Lots of evidence in this research points to this conclusion, and this includes the powerful evidence from two **ecumenical councils** – see below. For some reason, many adherents had issues with the concept of a female Deity. Since they were not disputing that Mary gave birth to Jesus, this suggests they didn't hold women in high esteem. Considering that they and the world worshipped goddesses for thousands of years, it must have taken many years of intense social engineering for any populace to abandon this concept and have low regard for women. Even if this is a real story, their objection to her was not personal because she would have been before their time and the Bible has no derogatory account of her. Here is a possible reason as to how the disparaging attitude towards women came about. As you have read in chapter one, the woman came to be regarded as the temptress.

The Biblical Adam and Eve creation story was one of a few such stories in human history. And they would have been born out of the desire to explain the origin of our existence. This was probably the first one that is unkind to the woman. Since there was a high regard for females before this, perhaps another factor came into play which was the desire to understand human behaviour, and the differences between the sexes. So, if men began to regard women to have a "nature" that is antithetical to men, it could foment a desire to restrict and control them.

The following iconography is an indication of the degree of negativity that the belief that Eve is to blamed for humanity's "fall from grace" fomented in early Christians. We know that not only did early Christians interpret Bible stories as being literal, but they were also very responsive to its dictates, and the result was mass slaughter over disagreements about Bible doctrines. Therefore, portraying the image of a serpent as a mirror image of Eve undoubtedly had the effect of suggesting women's nature is that of a dangerous serpent, and not to be trusted, and this is very likely related to women's persecution and execution as witches by early Christians as you have read in chapter one. How can we make this connection?

Even though the Bible doesn't say so, it is believed up to this day by many that the serpent was Satan the devil, and early Christians who killed women as witches defined witches as the devil's consort. So, if Eve was portrayed by early Christians as a mirror image of the serpent and it was believed to be the devil, and subsequently women were more likely to be regarded as witches, and witches were regarded as companions of the devil, there is the connection. So, it is very likely that the iconography was inspired by **Genesis 3** where the serpent is portrayed as sly and deceiving. Another mythical story with the same message of women being deceivers is Samson and Delilah in **Judges 16** where Delilah is said to have betrayed Samson and it resulted in many deaths. You have read in chapter one about the large disparity of disparaging names for women versus men. So, consider that the Bible has forty references to harlots, thirty-six references to whore or whoredom, and only one reference to sodomite. And this reference is in the context of a disclaimer: **Deuteronomy 23:17** There shall be no whore of the daughters of Israel, nor a sodomite of the sons of Israel.

Considering the veneration men had for women for thousands of years, these stories must have been around a long time before they took roots in the consciousness of men.

The Fall of Man
Mythology

By Rebecca Kennison
Part woman, part serpent

"Adam, Eve, and a female serpent at the entrance to Notre Dame Cathedral in Paris, France. ***The portrayal of the image of the serpent as a mirror of Eve*** was common in earlier Christian iconography as a result of **the identification of women as the ones responsible for the fall of man and source of the original sin.**" Wikipedia

A major contradiction to the story of Constantine and his role in Christianity

There is a widely accepted belief that Constantine converted to Christianity.

This is another example of using a real person to validate Biblical mythology. The Bible has no credibility as a history book. Given the time Constantine lived the following narrative is more likely to be true: "About four years prior to chairing the Council, Constantine had been initiated into the religious *order of Sol Invictus*, one of the two thriving cults that regarded *the Sun as the one and only Supreme God* (the other was *Mithraism*). Because of his Sun worship, he instructed Eusebius to convene the first of three sittings on the summer solstice, 21 June 325 (*Catholic Encyclopedia*, New Edition, vol. I, p. 792), and it was "held in a hall in Osius's palace" (*Ecclesiastical History*, Bishop Louis Dupin, Paris, 1686, vol. I, p. 598)."

You have read in **Matthew 2:16** the myth of King Herod's mass killing of children and babies, and it is confirmed to be a myth because Herod died in 4 BC. Since BC stands for before Christ, this would mean he died before it's claimed Jesus was born.

Another example of inserting real people into this mythological story of Jesus' birth is repeated in **Luke 2:1-6** but with a major contradiction. It states: "And it came to pass in those days, that there went out a decree from Caesar Augustus, that all the world should be taxed. **2** (*And* this taxing was first made when Cyrenius was governor of Syria.) **3** And all went to be taxed, everyone into his own city. **4** And **Joseph also went** up from Galilee, out of the city of Nazareth, into Judaea, unto the city of David, which is called Bethlehem; (because he was of the house and lineage of David:) **5 To be taxed with Mary his espoused wife, being great with child**."

This account placed Jesus' birth at around 6 CE because this was when the tax mentioned was put in place. Wikipedia states, in part, "Luke appears to have conflated Quirinius' census with the death of Herod, and most critical scholars acknowledge a confusion and misdating by Luke." This comment disregard the high standard a Divine Revelation should be held. Instinctively they concluded the author was confused, perhaps because they don't accept the Bible was divinely inspired.

Other evidence against the claim of Constantine's conversion

The Catholic Church is the foundation of Christianity as we know it today. So, logic suggests that the following article in the **Catholic Encyclopedia** written in 1907 talking about stories accredited to the church would merit some attention:

According to Johann Peter Kirsch an ecclesiastical historian and biblical archaeologist, writing in the **Catholic Encyclopedia 1907 Vol. 14 page 370-71:**

"This was the era of Constantine the Great, when the public position of the Church so greatly improved, a change which must certainly have been very noticeable at Rome; it is consequently to be regretted that **there is so little authoritative information concerning Sylvester's pontificate**[23]. At an early date **legend** brings him into a close relationship with the first Christian emperor, but in a way that is contrary to historical fact. These **legends** were introduced especially into the "Vita beati Sylvestri" which appeared in the East and has been preserved in Greek, Syriac, and Latin in the "Constitutum Sylvestri"—an apocryphal account of an alleged Roman council that belongs to the **Symmachian forgeries** and appeared between 501 and 508, and also in the **"Donation of Constantine"**. The accounts given in all these writings concerning the persecution of Sylvester,

[23] Johann claimed there is no evidence of a Pope named Sylvester. So, everything is legendary including the baptism of Constantine.

the healing[24] and baptism of Constantine, the emperor's gift to the pope, the rights granted to the latter, and the council of 275 bishops at Rome, are entirely legendary[25]."

Wikipedia
"The ***Donation of Constantine*** is a **forged Roman imperial decree** by which the 4th-century emperor Constantine the Great supposedly transferred authority over Rome and the western part of the Roman Empire to the Pope. Composed probably in the 8th century, it was used, especially in the 13th century, in support of claims of political authority by the papacy." "The *Donation of Constantine* is a document fabricated in the second half of the eighth century, purporting to be a record by the Emperor himself of his conversion, the profession of his new faith, and the privileges he conferred on Pope Sylvester I, his clergy, and their successors. According to it, Pope Sylvester was offered the imperial crown, which, however, he refused. This fictitious tale describes the sainted Pope Sylvester's rescue of the Romans from the depredations of a **local dragon** and the pontiff's miraculous cure of the emperor's leprosy by the sacrament of baptism."

Catholic Encyclopedia Vol III Page 712 1907

Our documentary sources of knowledge about **the origin of Christianity and its earliest developments** are chiefly the New Testament Scriptures and various sub-Apostolic writings, the authenticity of which we must to a large extent take for granted here.

A breakdown of the above evidence against Constantine's conversion to Christianity and the lack of historical records of Christianity.

---

[24] **The spurious claim that Constantine was cured of leprosy by Pope Sylvester I** and, in gratitude, surrendered his power and lands to the pope and the pope then generously gave that power back, allowing the emperor his reign.

[25] Synonyms of legendary: Fabled, fabricated, imagined, fictional, invented, unreal etc.

Three strong points against it:

- The Catholic Encyclopedia volume XIV 1907 account of ecclesiastical historian Johann Peter Kirsch claiming Pope Sylvester didn't exist, if combined with:
- The **Donation of Constantine** which makes the implausible claim that Constantine offered his crown to Pope Sylvester[26] is regarded as a **forgery**. And it is the same forged document that claims Constantine's conversion.
- The same forged document was used by the church to try to gain political authority for their religion.
- The story of Pope Sylvester includes a **mythical dragon**. This confirms his mythical status.
- Volume III of the **Catholic Encyclopedia 1907** also states the church had no direct records of the origin of Christianity and its earliest development, and yet the conversion of Constantine is claimed to be part of its earliest development. They got their information from the same source we get it, the New Testament and other religious texts – **not historical documents or their church records**. It's implausible that history of this magnitude would not have been recorded by the church. If Saint Peter who the Bible claimed Jesus nominated to start HIS church was a real person, he would have recorded the history. Since God didn't speak to humanity from the clouds, the other option is documentation, and if this was not done, both Saint Peter and God can be charged with incompetence and carelessness of extraordinary magnitude. Since this does not fit the description of an infinitely intelligent being, it's all fiction of the greatest magnitude.

What seems certain in terms of Constantine's role in what became Christianity is that he commanded the first ecumenical council that led to others. The aim was to stop religious conflicts and killings

[26] His existence, at minimum, is questionable

which were threatening to destabilise his empire and create a unified state recognised church. This was not accomplished. Up until now since the formulation of the Nicene Creed, the belief in the Trinity is not universally accepted in Christianity.

The title of this book is a definitive statement that Christianity is a fictional story, and its content is proof. However, this research throws up a question, why is the Bible so poorly written and has so many contradictions? The inevitable conclusion is that there was no coordination between writers. However, here is a narrative of how, at least, the New Testament was written. The sources of the scriptures mentioned are a plausible basis for why the Scriptures are so poorly written. It provides a more detailed possibility that fits the inconsistent, many times incomprehensible, and confusing style of the Bible. The highlighted texts are the most relevant to this point:

The Cenacle – Constantine's Fake Bible

"Constantine "never acquired a solid theological knowledge" and "depended heavily on his advisers in religious questions" (***Catholic Encyclopedia***, New Edition, vol. xii, p. 576, passim). According to Eusebius (260-339), Constantine noted that among the Presbyterian factions "strife had grown so serious, vigorous action was necessary to establish a more religious state", but he could not bring about a settlement between rival god factions (*Life of Constantine*, op. cit., pp. 26-8). His advisers warned him that the bishops' various religions were "destitute of foundation" and needed official stabilization (ibid.).

Constantine saw in this confused system of **fragmented dogmas** the opportunity to create a new and combined State religion, neutral in concept, and to protect it by law. When he conquered the East in 324 he sent his Spanish religious adviser, Osius of Córdoba, to Alexandria with letters to several bishops exhorting them to make peace among themselves. The mission failed and Constantine, probably at the suggestion of Osius, then issued a decree commanding all bishops and their subordinates "be mounted on asses, mules, and horses belonging to the public, and travel to the city of Nicaea" in the Roman province of Bithynia in Asia Minor.

They were instructed to bring with them the **testimonies they orated to the rabble**, "bound in leather" for protection during the long journey, and surrender them to Constantine upon arrival in Nicaea (*The Catholic Dictionary*, Addis and Arnold, 1917, "Council of Nicaea" entry).

Their writings totaled, "in all, two thousand two hundred and thirty-one scrolls and legendary tales of gods and saviors, together with a record of the doctrines orated by them" (Life of Constantine, op. cit., vol. ii, p. 73; N&PNF, op. cit., vol. I, p. 518)."

The suggestion is that it was from these writings that the New Testament was put together, and this means it would have come into existence after 325 AD

The ecumenical councils that shaped Christianity

Wikipedia - In the history of Christianity, the **first seven ecumenical councils** included the following: the **First Council of Nicaea in 325**, the **First Council of Constantinople in 381**, the **Council of Ephesus in 431**, the **Council of Chalcedon in 451**, the **Second Council of Constantinople in 553**, the **Third Council of Constantinople from 680–681** and finally, **the Second Council of Nicaea in 787**. These seven events represented an attempt by Church leaders to reach an orthodox **consensus**[27], restore peace and develop a unified religion.

[27] Reach an agreement on religious doctrine which means they would vote on it. God didn't speak to them and gave them a single message.

Two Councils that had to deal with the rejection of Mary as Mother of God

The Council of Ephesus in 431. The council was called after Patriarch Cyril of Alexandria appealed to Pope Celestine 1 to condemn Patriarch Nestorius of Constantinople for heresy due to Nestorius' refusal to use the term *theotokos* (Mother of God) in relation to the Virgin Mary. **The Second Council of Constantinople 553,** "The council also condemned the teaching that Mary could not be rightly called the Mother of God (Greek: Theotokos) but only the mother of the man (*anthropotokos*) or the mother of Christ."

The belief that eventually became Christianity was one of many diverse beliefs within the Roman Empire and the world. Similar concepts were common in Greece and Egypt, except for the exclusion of female representation – they had Father, Wife, and Offspring. They were all called gods or goddesses, and never thought of as anything but polytheism.

According to Wikipedia "Constantine called the Council at Nicaea to resolve **the dispute in the church** which resulted from the widespread adoption of **Arius' teachings**, **which threatened to destabilize the entire empire**." So, why did Arius' teachings caused so much strife that Constantine thought it posed a threat to the empire?

It caused great strife because if Arius, a theologian, teachings were adopted, it would drastically change the theology and shift power from those who taught the doctrine that became the Trinity. It is claimed that he taught that there was just one God, and Jesus was not equal to God, and therefore was created by God. While the other factions taught that there is one God but three essences and that Jesus is part of that essence – a three-in-one being – all three always existed. This mind-bending idea is probably an attempt to explain **Genesis 1:26** which claims God said, "Let **us** create man in our own image…" This is suggesting there is more than one God or Creator which was not acceptable to the new religion. So, the process of the

Nicaea Council formulated the Nicene Creed. Its doctrine is now known as the Trinity and it is used to justify **Genesis 1:26.** Currently, one explanation of "**Us**" is that God was speaking as a Trinity, and another is that he was speaking to Jesus which would be the same thing from a Trinitarian point of view since they are believed to be one. In effect, the claim is that Arius was teaching that there is more than one god, a little **god**, and a big **God**. However, the Trinitarian view was the mind-bending concept that Jesus, his father, and the Holy Ghost are equal in status, but they are not separate, they are one. A father and son is one person combined with another entity? What injury does this inflict on the development of our minds to accept this as a real story?

Worldhistory.org "The First Council of Nicaea produced what became known as the concept of the **Trinity**[28]. This concept expressed the belief that Christ was of the identical essence of God, who had manifested himself in the earthly **Jesus of Nazareth**. It produced the innovation of a creed that dictated what all Christians should believe. The Nicene Creed was now enforced by the legions of the **Roman** emperor, and **Arianism** was condemned as heresy. However, those who sided with Arius continued to incorporate his teachings in their communities. One of Constantine's sons, **Constantius II** (r. 337-361 CE), was an Arian Christian." So, the Council of Nicaea in **325** had not ended the Arian controversy – the disagreement with the concept of the Trinity.

"The **First Council of Constantinople** in **381** was called by the Roman Emperor Theodosius 1. When Theodosius ascended to the imperial throne in 380, he began a campaign to **bring the Eastern Church back to Nicene Christianity**." This Council didn't achieve full acceptance of the doctrine. So, the **Council of Chalcedon** was called in **451 CE** by the **Roman Emperor** Marcian. Part of the debate

---

[28] The council of Nicaea didn't produce the concept of the Trinity, it gain consensus on its principle and produced a dissertation on it called The Nicene Creed. The idea was already widely accepted and that is why there was strife after Arius opposed the concept.

was to settle the question of whether Christ was human or divine, a man who became God (through the resurrection and ascension) or **God who became a man**[29].

Encyclopedia Britannica

Trinity, in Christian doctrine, is the unity of Father, Son, and Holy Spirit as three persons in one Godhead.

So, even though the theology of the Trinity was ratified by the Council at Nicaea in 325 AD, the matter was not settled even up to 451 CE. **This was 126 years after establishing the Nicene Creed and it was ratified and became known as the Trinity.** If added to the date of the claimed crucifixion, this is over four hundred years after. Therefore, after over 400 years after the crucifixion supposedly took place, **the central plank of Christianity's doctrine, the belief in the Holy Trinity** was uncertain – not firmly established. Based on this, all this time had passed and there was no communication from God to settle this critical point, even though it is claimed he inspired the Bible and frequently spoke to humans? **The inability to decide on Christian doctrine after so many years should eliminate the idea of supernatural force involvement in the central doctrine of Christianity.** How does the Nicene Creed prove this point?

- It proves this point because the concept was decided by acrimonious debates and then a vote – there was no supernatural intervention and this pattern continued to the **451 CE <u>Council of Chalcedon</u>**, and it is still not universally accepted today. Therefore, we can safely conclude there has been no Divine Intervention to settle this matter.
- The Trinity concept makes the numerous Biblical accounts of Jesus praying laughable because he would be praying to himself.

[29] God became man or God became Jesus is a central principle of the Trinity.

- There is no definitive scripture that fits the description of the Trinity. In the following one of many scriptures where Jesus described himself as the "Son of Man", two parts of the Trinity are regarded as being different – that is, they are not the same person:
- Luke 12:10 And whosoever shall speak a word against the **Son of Man [Jesus]**, it shall be forgiven him: but unto him that blasphemed against the **Holy Ghost** it shall not be forgiven. [We can speak ill of him but not the Holy Ghost? If they are one personage, there wouldn't be a difference in punishment – **this is suggesting that they have different statuses!**]
- This next scripture also references them as separate entities: **Matthew 28:19** Go ye therefore and teach all nations, baptizing them in the name of the Father, and of the Son, and of the Holy Ghost.
- If this is a real story, this next scripture would justify us concluding that God suffers from having a split personality because he would be talking to himself: **Luke 3:22** And the Holy Ghost descended in a bodily shape like a dove upon him, and a voice came from heaven, which said, Thou art my beloved Son; in thee, I am well pleased. [This is another claim that God has spoken from the clouds to humans, why not now?]

The elephant in the room

Why would they need to settle the Trinity question if they had spiritual guidance? If such a God existed and this was his major push to establish himself as the only true God, such guidance would be easy and necessary for him as it is now. However, even this logical assertion falls short to explain why after hundreds of years he didn't communicate this to them, and now after thousands of years, he has not communicated it to current Christian adherents, or the world.

Encyclopedia Britannica

Neither the word "Trinity" nor the explicit doctrine appears in the New Testament

The fact that the central belief in Christian doctrine is not supported by the book that is the basis of the religion should be undisputable proof that the religion is based on manmade dogma – not supernatural inspiration. Nearly two billion people believe in the concept. If the acrimonious process of how the Nicene Creed was formulated is accepted as true, this should further consolidate it as manmade dogma.

Also of great significance, the belief in original sin, a central tenet in Christianity, is not from what Christians regard as divine revelation – the Bible. It came from the mind of Augustine. So, Augustine's theology and the Trinitarian theology are now bounded as one – and now is the foundation of Christianity, and both of them are not in the Bible. This is the power of socialisation, and it flourishes because societies have never interrogated it intellectually. They allow it to be transmitted intergenerationally without questions.

Between 325 and 787 is 462 years. This long process of establishing the Bible as doctrine is in line with having controversial and unclear traditions that require sorting out by human beings. It does not fit a Divine Revelation. Wikipedia: "**The Nicene Creed of 325** explicitly affirms the Father as the "*one God*" and as the "*Almighty,*" and Jesus Christ as "*the Son of God*", as "*begotten of ... the essence of the Father,*" and therefore as "*consubstantial with the Father,*" meaning, "*of the same substance.*" "The purpose of a creed is to provide a doctrinal statement of correct belief." **A highly disputed** Creed decided what the correct belief was, and it was later amended in 381 AD. The Nicene Creed formulated the current dominant Christian doctrine, the Holy Trinity, and gave it official recognition. Here is the actual creed:

The Nicene Creed – Encyclopedia Britannica

"A modern English version of the text is as follows, with the *Filioque* clause in brackets:

I believe in one God, the Father almighty, maker of heaven and earth, of all things visible and invisible. I believe in one Lord Jesus Christ, the Only Begotten Son of God, born of the Father before all ages. God from God, Light from Light, true God from true God, begotten, not made, consubstantial with the Father; through him, all things were made. For us men and our salvation he came down from heaven, and by the Holy Spirit was incarnate of the Virgin Mary, and became man. For our sake he was crucified under Pontius Pilate, he suffered death and was buried, and rose again on the third day in accordance with the Scriptures. He ascended into heaven and is seated at the right hand of the Father. He will come again in glory to judge the living and the dead and his kingdom will have no end. I believe in the Holy Spirit, the Lord, the giver of life, who proceeds from the Father [and the Son], who with the Father and the Son is adored and glorified, who has spoken through the prophets. I believe in one, holy, catholic, and apostolic Church. I confess one Baptism for the forgiveness of sins and I look forward to the resurrection of the dead and the life of the world to come. Amen."

Why do we have a poorly written Bible filled with contradictions and stories that should only be regarded as mythologies? Apart from the plausible explanation that Constantine summoned many documents from adherents to the Council of Nicaea, the following is also relevant:

We currently have many different religious beliefs in the world. During the time of the Roman Empire, there were a lot more gods and goddesses being worshipped, and like now they are all based on myths and legends that were thousands of years old. These concepts spread from Egypt and Greece to Rome and were adopted in various versions with different characters in different countries. This is the basis of there being so many crucified Saviours as documented by Kersey Graves in his book, **the world's sixteen crucified saviours**. Emperor Constantine decided to establish one of the many doctrines as the only officially recognised religion.

This official recognition began the process to consolidate the new doctrine into a unified church. The Bible eventually became a compilation of oral traditions (myths) transcribed into texts, variations of ancient spiritual concepts transcribed into texts, and other texts written by church leaders. And this is one of the reasons why the Bible is so filled with contradictions, and often nonsensical stories. This point can be strengthened with a question. How many of the books in the Bible can be regarded as moral guides, elevated knowledge, or relevant to our lives today? If not all or any, what's their purpose? It's a struggle to find any such books. Apart from the inadequate Ten Commandments, what divine lessons are in it that are transformative that humanity didn't practice before the advent of the Bible?

Another reason many Bible stories are often nonsensical and unintelligible is that some of the original stories are based on astronomy. It is difficult to convert this into an anthropomorphic story about the "Son of God" without it being nonsensical. Perhaps by mistake, they included in the Bible **Psalms 84:11** "For the LORD God is a **sun** and shield: the LORD will give grace and glory: no good thing will he withhold from them that walk uprightly." There are many other astronomy references in the Bible and stories that were corrupted from ancient stories. It is claimed that "amen" said at the end of a prayer is in reference to the Egyptian **sun god** Amen-Ra. Is there evidence to support this? A **single eye** was the symbol of Amen-Ra. In **Matthew 6:22,** "The light of the body is the eye: if therefore thine **eye be single**, thy whole body shall be **full of light.**" This seemingly nonsensical verse makes at least some sense if applied to Amen-Ra, **the sun god.**

Critical things the Bible omitted saying that would help humanity

Apart from the Bible's inadequacy as a moral guide, its lack of value is compounded by its **omissions** and **complicities**. If an all-wise and loving God was involved in the Bible he would not omit to state that women should have equal standing as men, instead **1 Timothy 2:12** states, "I do not permit a woman to teach or **to have authority** over a man; she must be silent." And it doubled down in **1 Corinthians 14:34-35,** "Let your women keep silence in the churches: for it is not permitted unto them to speak; but *they are commanded* to be under obedience, as also said the law. **35** And if they will learn anything, let them ask their husbands at home: for it is a shame for women to speak in the church." Why would God not want women to speak in a supposedly spiritual organisation? The Bible omits to say, do not enslave human beings, instead it's complicit in giving the practice "divine" legitimacy by stating:

New International Version of the Bible

Ephesians 6:5 the following scriptures should also disqualify the Bible as coming from a divine source

"Slaves, obey your earthly masters with respect and fear, and with sincerity of heart, just as you would obey Christ. **Leviticus 25:42-46,** Because the Israelites are my servants, whom I brought out of Egypt, they must not be sold as slaves. **43** Do not rule over them ruthlessly, but fear your God. **44** Your male and female slaves are to come from the nations around you; from them you may buy slaves. **45** You may also buy some of the temporary residents living among you and members of their clans born in your country, and they will become your property. **46** You can bequeath them to your children as inherited property and can make them slaves for life, but you must not rule over your fellow Israelites ruthlessly."

Instead of providing a scientific understanding of the correct human diet, it states in **Genesis 9:3,** in part, "Every moving thing that lives shall be food." This is not correct, and it's devoid of knowledge and wisdom, because not every living thing is compatible with our body's physiology. Doctors have stated that 70% of diseases are diet and lifestyle related. The Bible also states the seemingly opposite of this scripture and also nonsensical, in **Romans 14:21**, "It is good neither to eat flesh, nor to drink wine, nor *anything* whereby thy brother stumbles, or is offended, or is made weak." Then in **Deuteronomy 14:21, it** gives the most immoral and outrageous instruction regarding eating, "Ye shall not eat of anything that dies of itself: thou shalt give it unto the stranger that is in thy gates, that he may eat it; or thou mayest sell it unto an alien: for thou art a holy people unto the LORD thy God. Thou shalt not seethe a kid in his mother's milk." In the NIV its evil intent is even more glaring, "Do not eat anything you find already dead. You may give it to the foreigner residing in any of your towns, and they may eat it, or you may sell it to any other foreigner. But you are a people holy to the LORD your God. Do not cook a young goat in its mother's milk."

The celebration of Easter is the celebration of an astronomical story

Easter is the most important festival of the Christian calendar. It is claimed to mark the Resurrection of Jesus three days after his death by crucifixion. However the date is not fixed, it has to be calculated. Death has a fixed date. If a well-known person dies the date would be known, and even if it is not known and a date was chosen, it would not change every year. The date of Easter has to be calculated, and how it is calculated is evidence that the story is an astronomical story. The calculation begins with determining when is the Spring Equinox, or the Vernal Equinox which marks the astronomical start of spring. The March or spring equinox is the moment the Sun crosses the celestial equator – an imaginary line in the sky above Earth's equator – from south to north. This happens on March 19, 20, or 21 every year, but most of the time March 20th.

There is also an equinox in September. Here is an example of how it's calculated:

Easter 2022 – spring equinox Sun March 20th – first full moon after, Sat 16th April – first Sunday after, 17th April

Easter 2035 – spring equinox Tues 20 March – first full moon after, Fri 23rd March – first Sunday after, 25th March – Easter will be on the 25th March 2035

Since Easter or its celebration is not mentioned in the Bible, who determined the date? Wikipedia, **"The Council of Nicaea decreed that Easter should be observed on the first Sunday following the first full moon after the spring equinox March 21".** So, the body of people in the Roman Empire who decided the central Christian doctrine, the Trinity, also decided how to calculate the date for Easter. This is another example of manmade dogma, not divine revelation. How can it be anything but an astronomical story when the people who decided the central tenets of Christianity used observable astronomical phenomena as part of the story? These are the same people from a civilisation that anthropomorphised planets such as Jupiter and Mars and worshipped them for centuries.

What is the significance of the **spring** equinox, **full moon**, and **Sunday** to this story?

Let's start with a central tenet in Christianity. Jesus represents the ending of the old and the beginning of the new – to be born again through him **(rebirth).**

Spring equinox (Jesus **the Sun** brought new life)

"For many ancient religions and cultures, spring is symbolic of rebirth, and in the case of **Eostre**, rabbits and hares were typical imagery of rebirth. Ancient Saxon tribes of northern Europe practiced a holiday they referred to as **Eostre**. This was in honor of the Germanic goddess of spring **Eastra**." "Good fortune, wealth, and **procreation** are frequently associated with rabbits. Rabbits have become a symbol of **rebirth** in many modern societies."

Full moon

"The Sun symbolizes **the supreme cosmic power** – the life force that enables all things to thrive and grow. In some cultures, the Sun is the Universal Father. **Correspondingly, the Moon symbolizes death, birth, and cycles**." So, the full moon represents the momentary death of **the Sun**. The **Sun of God** dies momentarily then rises.

Sunday

The etymology of Sunday: "**Sunday comes from Old English Sunnandæg, which is derived from a Germanic (*Sonntag*) interpretation of the Latin, dies Solis, "sun's day.**" "Germanic and Norse mythology personifies the sun as a **goddess** named Sunna or Sol. **In Roman culture, Sunday was the day of the Sun god**. In pagan theology, **the Sun was the source of life, giving warmth and illumination to mankind.** It was the center of a popular cult among Romans, who would stand at dawn to catch the first rays of sunshine as they prayed." So, **Jesus represents the Sun's conquest of death (darkness)** and ascending into heaven – the universe. This is an astronomy story.

The etymology of Saturday adds to the astronomical meanings of Christian religions as you will see when applied to how Seven-day Adventists regard the celebration of Easter.

The Romans named Saturday *Sāturni diēs* (**"Saturn's Day"**) no later than the 2nd century for the planet Saturn, which controlled the first hour of that day, according to Vettius Valens. In Roman mythology, Saturn was the father of Jupiter. Saturday is also named after the **Roman god Saturn.**

"Adventists do celebrate Easter in the same way most Protestant churches would but it looks different from other Protestants in how it is celebrated. Friday is still Good Friday, but the Resurrection of Christ is recognized at church service on Sabbath (Saturday), instead of Sunday."

You have seen how the dates of Easter are calculated, it is related to the "Sun's day" or "**Sol Invictus** (Classical Latin, "Unconquered Sun") sometimes known as Helios, and was long considered to be the official sun god of the later Roman Empire."

So, the fact that Seventh-day Adventists recognise Good Friday as the crucifixion of Jesus but reject Sunday worship in favour of Saturday worship is indicative of the ignorance and confusion in religion. The masses of Seventh Day Adventists are unaware of the process by which the date of Easter is determined. If they did and applied simple common sense to it they would know that it is the same calculation that established Sunday as Easter that established Good Friday. Therefore, the two dates cannot be separated. However, since their "Holy day", Saturday, is named after Saturn the Roman God, their branch of Christianity likely came about because of a split in doctrine, and somehow they maintained one of the other gods of Rome as part of their theology. So, they venerate **Sol Invictus** and **Saturn** – but they have no idea that they are involved in astronomy. So they will argue over whether to recognise the **Sun's day** or **Saturn's day**.

Baptism and genealogy of Jesus

Luke 3:21 – 23 Now when all the people were baptized, it came to pass, that Jesus also being baptized, and praying, the heaven was opened, **22** And the Holy Ghost descended in a bodily shape like a dove upon him, and a voice came from heaven, which said, Thou art my beloved Son; in thee, I am well pleased. **23** And Jesus himself began to be about thirty years of age, being (as was supposed) the son of Joseph, which was *the son* of Heli.

Even a casual analysis of **Luke 3:21 – 23** leads to only one conclusion, it was not a true story, was not written by a person who had their thoughts in order, and needless to say, it was not inspired by an infinitely intelligent being. It is also reasonable to conclude it was written by two persons who did not coordinate their work. Since the Bible is supposed to be the inspired words of an infinitely intelligent being, God, and Jesus is supposed to be God's son, such a being would not inspire a disjointed narrative with a pointless genealogy about Jesus. And since he is supposed to be God's son and the writer was supposedly inspired to record this from God, if this was a divine revelation, the same writer who wrote that God said this is my son I am well pleased would not write, "being (as was supposed) the son of Joseph." Also, such a being would not inspire a disjointed narrative starting with, "beginning at about thirty" and an opinion of him being the son of Joseph, and then a genealogy that concluded with Adam as the son of God in verse 38.

According to the Christian narrative, the purpose of God sending his son to die is to establish his identity as the son of God and to make it known that his father was the only true God. Therefore, it makes no sense to inspire two genealogies of Jesus as is written in the Bible. It makes even less sense because Matthew's genealogy hardly matches Luke's genealogy. The difference is vast, including **Matthew listing Jacob as Joseph's father**, and **Luke listing his father as Heli**. There cannot be a genealogy of someone who was not sired by a sperm and egg, however, in mythologies, everything is allowed. Perhaps in this mythology, they are claiming God injected Joseph's sperm into Mary. If this was the case, he was Joseph's son, and if he was the genealogy makes sense, and Jesus was not the son of God. Furthermore, the story of Jesus brings into focus the mythological nature of the God story. If we are all God's children, Mary would be God's daughter, and if she had a son, he would be God's grandson. Therefore, if Jesus was God's son, he was also his grandson. If this narrative with all its contradictions is not enough to prove the story is a myth, consider these facts about the genealogy.

The genealogy according to Matthew starts with "Jesus Christ, son of David, son of Abraham". This makes no sense since Joseph is the only man the Bible claims has a connection with him. Secondly, the David listed as Solomon's father refers to King David who is listed as the father of Solomon. Now here is the clincher, as already explained, young King David who is claimed to have slain a giant named Goliath is a Biblical mythological story only, and his mother and father are also only accredited to religious texts. How can a famous king's mother and father not be well documented? Solomon is described in Wikipedia as "Solomon, was, **according to the Hebrew Bible** and **Christian Old Testament,** a fabulously wealthy and wise monarch of the United Kingdom of Israel who succeeded his father, David." **"The conventional dates of Solomon's reign are derived from biblical chronology."** So, he and his legendary father, King David, were not documented by historians? This is mythology.

Titles of Jesus

Jesus never said to anyone "I am the son of God". You will read shortly that at least one of his devoted disciples was unaware of this. Forty-six references to the Son of God were found in the Bible. Of the forty-six, there are six examples where one can conclude he claimed ownership of the title, here they are: **John 9:35-37** Jesus heard that they had cast him out; and when he had found him, he said unto him, Does thou believe in the Son of God? **36.** He answered and said, who is he, Lord, that I might believe in him? **37** And Jesus said unto him, Thou hast both seen him, and it is he that talked with thee. **Matthew 26:63-64,** But Jesus held his peace. And the high priest answered and said unto him, I adjure thee by the living God, that thou tell us whether thou be the Christ, the Son of God. **64** Jesus said unto him, **Thou hast said**: nevertheless I say unto you, hereafter shall ye see the **Son of man** sitting on the right hand of power, and coming in the clouds of heaven [**a coy admission**]. **John 5:25** Verily, verily, I say unto you, The hour is coming, and now is, when the dead shall hear the voice of the **Son of God**: and they that hear shall live. **Luke 22:70** Then said they all, Art thou then the Son of God?

And he said unto them, Ye say that I am. **John 10:36** Say ye of him, whom the Father hath sanctified, and sent into the world, Thou blasphemes; because I said, I am the Son of God? **John 11:4** When Jesus heard that, he said, This sickness is not unto death, but for the glory of God, that the Son of God might be glorified thereby. **Mark 3:11-12 makes the story even more strange, it claims that his identity as the son of God was supposed to be a secret or at least not well known.** "And unclean spirits, when they saw him, fell down before him, and cried, saying, Thou art the Son of God. **12** And he straitly charged them that they should not make him known."

Since there are forty-six references to the Son of God and only six claimed to be said by him, one could conclude that he was very reticent in declaring his identity as **Matthew 26:63-64** indicated, and it is strange that a coy admission would be given followed by describing himself as the **Son of man**, and they wrote it with a capital **'S'** as done when saying Son of God. And as is common with Bible scriptures, there is also a contradiction, a fatal flaw that invalidates the scripture. The fatal flaw is that he would not have been referred to as "The Christ" because it meant "anointed one" and many fit that description. See the definition below. The other forty references to the Son of God were said by others. However, this is where the story gets interesting. There were **181 references** to him as **"The Son of man",** and he referred to himself **seventy-seven** times as the **son of man!** There are thirteen references by others to him as such. In the book of Ezekiel (Old Testament), there are eighty-seven references to the **Son of man**, but it's unclear who it is referencing. However, most of the time they used capital 'S' in Son, as used in the obvious references to Jesus, or when the narrative is attributed to him as in **John 12:23** "And Jesus answered them, saying, the hour has come, that the **Son of man** should be glorified."

What is the meaning of "anointed one"?

"Christ comes from the Greek word (chrīstós), meaning "**anointed one**". The word is derived from the Greek verb, meaning "to anoint."

In the Greek Septuagint, Christos was used to translate the Hebrew (Mašíaḥ, messiah), meaning "[one who is] anointed". Therefore, Christ was not a sir name. So, it would have been, "Jesus the anointed one." Since it was common practice to be anointed, there were many anointed ones. Therefore, if this is a real story, God would not use it to identify Jesus - he would give a description that was unique to him. During that time if a person was asked, have you seen Christ, they could respond with a question, "Which one?" So, the above scripture is not the result of divine revelation but manmade dogma. **This is further evidence that man invented God and religious text. The custom of anointing is still practiced.**

Anoint

"To smear or rub with oil or perfume for **either *private* or religious purposes**. The Hebrew term for "anoint", masah, **has secular connotations,** such as rubbing a shield with oil."

In response to there being other meanings that are secular, Kyle Blevins wrote, **"Regardless of the original definition or usage**, the intent of anointing is to set apart a person, place, or thing for divine use. It is meant to empower people to accomplish God's work, for protection, or to describe the Messiah's deliverance." He also stated, "While **many could be anointed**, Jesus is the *mashiyach*, or the Messiah, the ultimate anointed one."

Kyle Blevins' words are a demonstration of how desperate adherents can be to give Bible text convenient meaning, and he confirmed his desperation by admitting that many could be anointed – in religion there is no shame in trying to invent facts.

The Bible claims Jesus called himself the Son of man seventy-seven times. Christianity's adherents acknowledge that the **Son of man** means the son of God. They couldn't say anything else because the Bible uses it at least eighty-seven times. However, they should not ignore the oddity of the numerous uses of the **Son of man**. They should be asking why he described himself as the Son of man most of the time, even though he supposedly came to promote himself as the Son of God. This is indicative of the low standard adherents tend to hold a book they believed to be inspired by the infinite power behind the universe. **If the Bible was regarded as a historical narrative written by a mere mortal, it would have been ridiculed and rightfully laughed at.** Why would there be so many references to 'the Son of man'? Can it be a mere coincidence that the main character, Jesus, used it the vast majority of time to describe himself when it doesn't correspond with him being the Son of God? However, the Sun can be regarded as the "Sun of Mankind" because "**Nothing is more important to us on Earth than the Sun**. Without the Sun's heat and light, the Earth would be a lifeless ball of ice-coated rock." Without the Sun nothing grows. It was for this reason that Sun veneration has a long history. Many scriptures that reference Jesus have Sun imageries. Here are some examples:

Revelation 2:18. And unto the angel of the church in Thyatira write; These things said the Son of God, who hath his eyes like unto a **flame of fire**, and his feet are like fine brass. **Matthew 24:30.** And then shall appear the sign of the **Son of man** in heaven: and then shall all the tribes of the earth mourn, and they shall see the **Son of man coming in the clouds of heaven with power and great glory**. **Revelation 14:14** And I looked, and behold a white cloud, and upon the cloud one sat like unto the **Son of man**, having on **his head a golden crown**, and in his hand a sharp sickle. **Luke 21:27.** And then shall they see the **Son of man** coming in a cloud with power and great glory. **Matthew 24:27.** For as the lightning cometh out of the east, and **shines even unto the west**; so shall also the coming of the **Son of man** be. [The **Sun of man will shine** unto the west]

Let's put the Jesus story in the context of the big picture regarding the Christian explanation we are given as to why the affairs of humanity are the way it is. It started with Adam and Eve's disobedience, and Jesus coming to die for our "sins" is supposed to be the solution. We have to disregard the mass killing by drowning in the Noah story as being an attempt to rescue us from our "sinful ways" because this would not qualify since Jesus is supposed to be the only solution, and the mass drowning was not claimed to be a solution. Therefore, it was a stand-alone and pointless mass killing. So, the Jesus story would be the first attempt to get rid of our "sins", or the second attempt to have perfect humans in the context that Adam and Eve were meant to be perfect **even though the Bible didn't say so**. If we pretend for a moment that this is a real story, it is reasonable to expect that Jesus as the solution would be well thought out and well executed, especially coming from an infinitely intelligent being. So, considering that at the time he is claimed to have come to earth we worshipped many gods and goddesses it is reasonable to expect that it would be imperative for him to establish his credibility as the Son of God by declaring who he was and demonstrating his credentials as God's emissary, or from a Trinitarian point of view, he would reveal himself as God. The Bible claims he did it with Moses, Abraham, and others, so why not on this unprecedented momentous occasion? Why the secrecy?

Logic suggests that we can easily dismiss as a solution the claim that his son came for us to kill him so that his father won't punish us for our sins. This plan is made to be even more ridiculous because it was claimed to have been accomplished in mystery, that is, the world didn't know about it. The fact that most people don't accept the Christian story is evidence that even if it was true it was a poorly executed plan. If this is a real story it would be fair to conclude that the planner was incompetent.

If he was announcing himself as the Son of God the authorities would not have written, **Matt 27:37** "And set up over his head his accusation written, THIS IS JESUS THE KING OF THE JEWS." Saying he was the son of God would have been regarded as blasphemy and the punishment was death. This would achieve the objective of dying for our sins and achieve publicity for his mission. This is a trivial point because an all-powerful God who wishes to prevent his children from being punished would have more powerful methods to achieve his objective, and would not require his children to enact a nonsensical and immoral symbolic[30] killing of his son as **a sacrifice to himself! The story claims that because he sacrificed his life, or died for our sins, it provided the route for our punishment from his father to be cancelled.**"

Combining this with the contradictory accounts of his life and no written account by him, and there was no first-hand historical account of his life, the story has no credibility and cannot be the work of any great intelligence. A God could not be this incompetent.

If we put aside the macabre idea that the plan required us to kill his son, logic suggests that it would be necessary for him to reveal himself to the world and in a manner that would leave no doubt – it would be necessary because as stated, people believed in many gods and goddesses at the time, as we do now. Yet, no such action was taken and based on the Bible's narrative, even disciples were not aware of who he was supposed to be and the purpose of his life. For example, the story of his disciple Saint Thomas demonstrates this. As is the case with Jesus, the source of the existence of his disciples and others mentioned in the story is limited to the Bible – there is no credible historical source(s). So, typically, every narrative about Jesus, Mary, or any of his disciples begins with, "According to the New Testament."

According to the Encyclopaedia Britannica, "Thomas's character is outlined in The Gospel According to John. His devotion to Jesus is clearly expressed in **John 11:5–16:** when Jesus planned to return to Judaea, the disciples warned him of the Jews' animosity ("now seeking to stone you"), to which Thomas soon replied, "Let us also go, that we may die with him…" It also states, "Perhaps the best-known event in his life is the one from which the phrase "doubting Thomas" developed. In **John 20:19–29** he was not among those disciples to whom the risen Christ first appeared, and, when they

[30] An immortal being cannot be killed.

told the incredulous Thomas, he requested physical proof of the Resurrection, fulfilled when Christ reappeared and specifically asked Thomas to touch his wounds."

If this was a true story, what else would Jesus discuss with his inner circle except the knowledge to preach and spread the gospel? What would be the point of his identity and mission being a secret?

This is a major contradiction to the claim that his disciples started the spreading of Christianity. For this to be true, he would have to have shared the gospel with them before his death. This has to include his identity and mission to die and resurrect for the sins of humanity. Therefore, they would have known he was God or God's son. Therefore, Thomas who the Bible claim was devoted to him would not doubt his resurrection. Furthermore, Thomas would be aware of the miracles he is claimed to have performed, including raising Lazarus from the dead. This would be confirmation of his identity and powers. This is another example of the story lacking credibility.

How belief in the Capitoline Triad got into the Roman Empire

If the writers of **the Old Testament** were monotheists they would not write "Let us create man in our own image" but it never stated who was "us". The New Testament concept of deities was almost identical to the Capitoline Triad, except for no female representation of Deity, and this Triad was part of a polytheistic belief. However, they eventually described it as one God by adopting the Nicene Creed, even though it comprised three entities. And even those who reject the concept of the Trinity interpret it as being one God who has a son but no mother. So, the mission was accomplished, the demise of the concept of a goddess. The Triad is a copy of the **Etruscan** polytheistic Trio of **Tinia**, the supreme deity, **Uni** his wife, and **Minerva** his daughter. According to **Encyclopedia.com**, the Etruscan civilization was at its height *c.*500 BC and was an important influence on the Romans, who subdued the Etruscans by the end of the 3rd-century BC.

The **Encyclopedia Britannica** states, "They (Etruscans) created the first great civilization on the peninsula, whose influence on the Romans as well as on present-day culture is increasingly recognised. **Etruscan religion** comprises a set of stories, beliefs, and religious practices of the Etruscan civilisation, **heavily influenced by the mythology of ancient Greece**, and sharing similarities with concurrent Roman mythology and religion. As the Etruscan civilization was gradually assimilated into the Roman Republic from the 4th century BC, the Etruscan religion and mythology were partially incorporated into ancient Roman culture, following the **Roman tendency to absorb some of the local gods** and customs of conquered lands." As was common in ancient times, gods were copied and worshipped. So, the Etruscans copied from the Greeks, and the Romans copied from the Etruscans. However, the significance of this is greatly enhanced when put in the context of the fact that "The Roman goddess Diana was venerated from the late sixth century BC as a "three-form" goddess" (Wikipedia), and "In ancient Egypt, there were many triads: the **Osirian** (or Abydos) triad of **Osiris** (husband), **Isis** (wife), and **Horus** (son), the Theban triad of **Amun**, **Mut** and **Khonsu**, the Memphite triad of **Ptah**, **Sekhme**t and **Nefertem**." – **Encyclopedia Britannica.** And yet, despite the similarity with the Trinity, they were all part of a polytheistic culture. Christianity came out of this lineage – just another Triad. Despite innumerable claims of polytheism that go back thousands of years, far more than monotheistic claims, and now we have varying claims of different monotheistic Gods, no supernatural being has intervened to set the record straight, past or present.

In the context of humanity worshipping many gods and goddesses at the time, it makes no sense for God to send his son to earth and his main strategy wasn't to convince **all of humanity** that he represented the one and only true God, as he is currently regarded by Christians. It is implausible that an infinitely intelligent being whose objective was to be known by his entire creation would restrict his presence to a tiny group of people who weren't fully informed as to who he was. This would be like a company in today's world wishing to sell a product globally but only sharing it with a small group of people, hoping that they will spread the message.

In the context of the claim that Thomas was willing to die with him as stated in **John 11:16,** and the claims in the following scriptures, this is another example of proof that this is a disjointed made-up story. How did John know this but not Thomas? **John 1:34** "And I saw, and bare record that this is the Son of God." **John 6:69** "And we believe and are sure that thou art that Christ, the Son of the living God." Significantly, of the gospels, the book of John is the only one that directly referees Jesus as being divine. **John 1:10** highlights this point. However, it also exposes the implausibility of the story – an infinitely intelligent being came to save humanity but it was not only unknown to the world but hardly known by the people close to him or the general public. This makes it a poorly written disjointed fable. **And according to John 1:10, "He was in the world, and the world was made by him, and the world knew him not."**

It should be of great significance that of the four gospels, **John is the only one that repeatedly ascribes divinity and the title Son of God directly to Jesus**. This cannot be said of the others. According to the Encyclopedia Britannica, the "**Gospel According to John** is the fourth of the four New Testament narratives recounting the life and death of Jesus Christ. **John's is the only one of the four not considered among the Synoptic Gospels** (i.e., those presenting a common view). Because of its special theological character, the Gospel According to John was considered in ancient times to be the "spiritual gospel," and it wielded a profound and lasting influence on the development of early Christian doctrine." It makes no sense that the other gospels are so different, and hardly ooze veneration of Jesus as the Book of John. This suggests that the Book of John was added to strengthen the dogma to be in line with current Christian beliefs. Apart from the first line in **Mark 1:1**, it is only in the book of John that the author directly references Jesus's divinity, and as you have read, the authorship of these books is unknown. Here are the gospel's references to Jesus's divinity:

Matthew 4:3 And when the tempter [the Devil] came to him, he said, If thou be the Son of God, command that these stones be made bread.

Matthew 4:6 And said unto him [the Devil], If thou be the Son of God, cast thyself down: for it is written, He shall give his angels charge concerning thee: and in their hands they shall bear thee up, lest at any time thou dash thy foot against a stone.

Matthew 14:33 Then they that were in the ship came and worshipped him, saying, Of a truth thou art the Son of God.

Matthew 22:42 Saying, What think ye of Christ? Whose son is he? They say unto him, The Son of David.

Matthew 26:63 But Jesus held his peace. And the high priest answered and said unto him, I adjure thee by the living God, that thou tell us whether thou be the Christ, the Son of God.

Matthew 27:40 And saying, Thou that destroys the temple, and builds it in three days, save thyself. If thou be the Son of God, come down from the cross.

Matthew 27:43 He trusted in God; let him deliver him now, if he will have him: for he said, I am the Son of God.

Matthew 27:54 Now when the centurion, and they that were with him, watching Jesus, saw the earthquake, and those things that were done, they feared greatly, saying, Truly this was the Son of God.

Mark 1:1 The beginning of the gospel of Jesus Christ, the Son of God;

Mark 3:11 And unclean spirits, when they saw him, fell down before him, and cried, saying, Thou art the Son of God.

Mark 5:7 And cried with a loud voice, and said, What have I to do with thee, Jesus, thou Son of the most high God? I adjure thee by God, that thou torments me not.

Mark 15:39 And when the centurion, which stood over against him, saw that he so cried out, and gave up the ghost, he said, Truly this man was the Son of God.

Luke 1:35 And the angel answered and said unto her, The Holy Ghost shall come upon thee, and the power of the Highest shall overshadow thee: therefore also that holy thing which shall be born of thee shall be called the Son of God.

Luke 4:3 And the devil said unto him, If thou be the Son of God, command this stone that it be made bread. [Repeat Matthew]

Luke 4:9 And he brought him to Jerusalem, and set him on a pinnacle of the temple, and said unto him, If thou be the Son of God, cast thyself down from hence:

Luke 4:41 And devils also came out of many, crying out, and saying, Thou art Christ the Son of God. And he rebuking them suffered them not to speak: for they knew that he was Christ.

Luke 8:28 When he saw Jesus, he cried out, and fell down before him, and with a loud voice said, What have I to do with thee, Jesus, thou Son of God most high? I beseech thee, torment me not. [Repeats Mark]

Luke 22:69 Hereafter shall the Son of man sit on the right hand of the power of God

Luke 22:70 Then said they all, Art thou then the Son of God? And he said unto them, Ye say that I am.

John 1:34 And I saw, and bare record that this is the Son of God.

John 1:49 Nathanael answered and said unto him, Rabbi, thou art the Son of God; thou art the King of Israel.

John 3:16 For God so loved the world, that he gave his only begotten Son, that whosoever believeth in him should not perish, but have everlasting life.

John 3:17 For God sent not his Son into the world to condemn the world; but that the world through him might be saved.

John 3:18 He that believeth on him is not condemned: but he that believeth not is condemned already, because he hath not believed in the name of the only begotten Son of God.

John 3:36 He that believeth on the Son hath everlasting life: and he that believeth not the Son shall not see life; but the wrath of God abides on him.

John 5:25 Verily, verily, I say unto you, The hour is coming, and now is, when the dead shall hear the voice of the Son of God: and they that hear shall live.

John 6:69 And we believe and are sure that thou art that Christ, the Son of the living God.

John 9:35 Jesus heard that they had cast him out; and when he had found him, he said unto him, Does thou believe on the Son of God?

John 10:36 Say ye of him, whom the Father hath sanctified, and sent into the world, Thou blasphemes; because I said, I am the Son of God?

John 11:4 When Jesus heard that, he said, This sickness is not unto death, but for the glory of God, that the Son of God might be glorified thereby.

John 11:27 She said unto him, Yea, Lord: I believe that thou art the Christ, the Son of God, which should come into the world.

John 13:31 Therefore, when he was gone out, Jesus said, Now is the Son of man glorified, and God is glorified in him.

John 19:7 The Jews answered him, We have a law, and by our law he ought to die, because he made himself the Son of God.

John 20:31 But these are written, that ye might believe that Jesus is the Christ, the Son of God; and that believing ye might have life through his name.

1 John 3:8 He that committed sin is of the devil; for the devil sinned from the beginning. For this purpose the Son of God was manifested, that he might destroy the works of the devil.

1 John 4:10 Herein is love, not that we loved God, but that he loved us, and sent his Son to be the propitiation for our sins.

1 John 4:15 Whosoever shall confess that Jesus is the Son of God, God dwelled in him, and he in God.

1 John 5:5 Who is he that overcomes the world, but he that believeth that Jesus is the Son of God?

1 John 5:9 If we receive the witness of men, the witness of God is greater: for this is the witness of God which he hath testified of his Son.

1 John 5:10 He that believeth on the Son of God hath the witness in himself: he that believeth not God hath made him a liar; because he believeth not the record that God gave of his Son.

1 John 5:11 And this is the record, that God hath given to us eternal life, and this life is in his Son.

1 John 5:12 He that hath the Son hath life; and he that hath not the Son of God hath not life.

1 John 5:13 These things have I written unto you that believe on the name of the Son of God; that ye may know that ye have eternal life, and that ye may believe on the name of the Son of God.

1 John 5:20 And we know that the Son of God is come, and hath given us an understanding, that we may know him that is true, and we are in him that is true, even in his Son Jesus Christ. This is the true God, and eternal life.

1 John 4:9 In this was manifested the love of God toward us, because that God sent his only begotten Son into the world, that we might live through him.

2 John 1:3 Grace be with you, mercy, and peace, from God the Father, and from the Lord Jesus Christ, the Son of the Father, in truth and love.

2 John 1:9 Whosoever transgresses, and abides not in the doctrine of Christ, hath not God. He that abides in the doctrine of Christ, he hath both the Father and the Son.

The art of global deception

There are a few world leaders and institutions past and present that can be credited with the kind of big lie in the following quote, perhaps fittingly it was said by a man credited with one of the worse crimes in history. "The broad mass of a nation…will more easily fall victim to a big lie than to a small one." Adolph Hitler, *Mein Kampf* (1925)

The 2021 world population was 7.9 billion. The two major religions, Christianity and Islam population are listed on Wikipedia as 2.3 billion (31.11%), and 1.9 billion (24.9%) respectively. In its notes, it states, "These figures may incorporate populations of **secular/nominal adherents...**" A nominal Christian is described as "a person who has not responded in repentance and faith to Jesus Christ as his personal Saviour and Lord" The vast majority of Christian nations fit this description. This fact, the size of the Islamic population, the many other religions, and non-believers is evidence that there was never an all-wise and all-powerful God who wanted the entire world to know that he exists, and wanted us to acknowledge and worship him. If such a God exists he would have accomplished this task. If we mere mortals had children who are unaware of our existence, we know where they are, and want them to know us, we would accomplish this with ease.

Since killing is a "sin" why would an all-wise God use a symbolic brutal killing of his son as the basis for forgiveness to be possible when he could simply require us to ask for it, and he grants it to those who ask?

Currently, people cry in remembrance of him "sacrificing his life" to save us. Yet, the story said he rose from the dead, and this should be expected since he is supposed to be immortal. How could it have been a sacrifice if he was immortal? Therefore, his human experience would be of no consequence, he, therefore, sacrificed nothing. If we mere mortals gave our lives for a cause that would be an extreme sacrifice since it's the only existence we have and know. Is there a more ridiculous story ever imposed on human consciousness? People crying over this story is illogical and speaks to the power of socialisation, and a lack of understanding of the story.

This story is based on an immoral principle, the killing of an innocent person in the place of the guilty. How many of us would not find it abhorrent and appalling if an innocent person was killed as revenge for an act committed by their relative?

What degree of unconsciousness is necessary for anyone to accept the crucifixion as a true story? Does the pointless symbolic killing of a god to please **his father** so that **his father doesn't punish those who inherited original sin makes sense?** Wouldn't the belief in this be tantamount to believing in a vindictive and irrational God who is committed to killing billions of his "children" for an act that they played no part in, that took place thousands of years ago? Such a God would be far worse than mafia bosses who carry out retributions over several generations. What effect does religion have on the human mind and emotions for billions of us to accept as truth that innocent babies are born in "sin"? And since the Bible claims that "the wages of sin is death", this suggests that billions of innocent babies would be punished on" judgement day", because being "saved" is said to be a requirement to avoid God's punishment.

Having said the above, one can understand why someone would suppress their human instinct and accept the horrendous thought of innocent babies being subjected to horrific punishment from God. We can understand it because we have seen and experienced how powerful belief can be. We even have a description for it. We have observed that we can become fanatical. Bible scriptures provide the basis for a programmed and unquestioning mind and emotion to accept this as a true story. If such persons read the following scriptures it explains the widespread acceptance of such extreme immoralities:

Psalm 51:5 says that we all come into the world as sinners: "Behold, I was brought forth in iniquity, and in sin my mother conceived me." **Ephesians 2:2** declares that all people who are not in Christ are "sons of disobedience." **Proverbs 22:15** says "Foolishness is bound up in the heart of a child." **Genesis 8:21** declares, "The intent of man's heart is evil from his youth."

The concept of original sin and its consequences is so greatly accepted that on Christianity.com it's written, "Jonathan Edwards, in his classic work The Great Christian Doctrine of Original Sin Defended." They called the doctrine "great", and they called his work defending the doctrine, "classic".

If there was a God who wanted to come to earth and cancel all our false beliefs of worshipping many gods and goddesses, would the following actions be more effective in convincing humanity than the story of a crucifixion?

Instead of walking on water in front of a few people or turning water into wine, what if Jesus eliminated earthquakes, tornadoes, droughts, hurricanes, tsunamis, and deserts? What if we were only given a perfect balance of sunshine and rain that would guarantee worldwide successful food crops, and thus eliminate hunger and starvation, would the entire world be convinced of his divinity?

What was the point of Jesus living for 33 years? He didn't need to live that long to die for our sins. This would suggest that he had other important things to accomplish before his crucifixion. The only other deeds that would make sense in line with his mission to save humanity from punishment would be to promote his identity and purpose for coming so that the world would not doubt the identity of the only true God, and this would necessitate him doing things to convince the world that he is God's son, or God incarnate. And another way to accomplish this would be to reveal knowledge that was unknown on earth. He did no such thing. What did we get instead? Apart from stories of him healing people in a small part of the world – and we would be better off if we got health care and medical knowledge. We got useless tricks of walking on water which we have seen British magician Dynamo do, and turning water into wine. Now, alcohol consumption is one of our worse problems because of his celebrity endorsement. An all-wise God would not endorse something bad for his children.

The most outrageous contradictions in the Jesus story

If this is a real story would Jesus say these things if he came to symbolically die for our sins? He supposedly said these things during his crucifixion:

Matthew 27:46 And about the ninth hour Jesus cried with a loud voice, saying, Eli, Eli, lama sabachthani? that is to say, My God, my God, why hast thou forsaken me? **Luke 23:34** Then said Jesus, Father, forgive them; for they know not what they do. And they parted his raiment, and cast lots.

The world's sixteen crucified Saviours

This book was written by Kersey Graves in 1870 and it outlines the fact that the Jesus story came after sixteen previous almost identical stories. One such story is that of Krishna whose worship by Hindus dates back to 1200 BC. According to history.com many scholars regards Hinduism as the world's oldest religion. Having asked a Hindu if Krishna was crucified and born of a virgin and was told yes, this is proof that the Jesus story is a copy of older stories, especially if combined with knowledge of the other sixteen mythological crucified saviours. If you can, put this to the test by asking a Hindu the same questions. Kersey Graves lists sixteen previous crucified sav-iours as **Krishna** (India) 1200 BC; **Sakai** 600 BC; **Thammuz** (Syria) 1160; **Wittoba or Vithoba** (India) 552 BC; **Iao** (Nepal) 622 BC; **Hesus** (Ireland) 834 BC; **Quetzalcoatl** (Mexico) 587 BC; **Quirinus** (Rome) 506 BC; **Prometheus** (Rome) 547 BC; **Thulis** (Egypt) 1700 BC; **Indra** (Tibet) 725 BC; **Alcestis** (Greece) 600 BC, **Atys** (Turkey) 1170 BC; **Crite** (Iraq) 1170 BC; **Bali** (India) 725 BC; and **Mithra** (Persia) 600 BC.

In referencing the fact that ancient writers knew about the legends of previous saviours, and the claim that they were crucified, Kersey Graves wrote about their crucifixion, "This important chapter in their history has been omitted by **Christian writers** for fear the relation of it would damage the credibility of the crucifixion of Christ, or lessen its spiritual force. For, like Paul, they were "determined to know nothing but Jesus Christ and him crucified…They thus exalted the tradition of crucifixion into the most important dogma of the Christian faith. Hence, their efforts to conceal from the public knowledge of the fact that it is of pagan origin." He quoted **1**

Corinthians 2:1-2, "And I, brethren, when I came to you, came not with excellency of speech or of wisdom, declaring unto you the testimony of God. **2 For I determined not to know anything among you, save Jesus Christ, and him crucified."**

Here is a good question to ask a religious person, "Which god would you worship if you were born 4000 years ago?" The current gods were not known then.

A few goddesses, gods, and religions from 6000 BC

Gods and goddesses appear in virtually every aspect of ancient Egyptian civilization, and **more than 1,500** of them are known by name [Wikipedia]. Here are a few:

Goddess Wadjet 6000 to 3150 BC one of the earliest Egyptian deities
Goddess Inanna 4000 – 3100 BC Sumer [Egyptian colony]
God Horus 3273 – 305 BC
God Anubis 3100 – 2890 BC
Goddess Heqet 3100 – 2686 BC
Goddess Bastet 2890 – 2686 BC
God Atum 2700 – 2200 BC
God Amun 2700 – 2200 BC
Goddess Isis 2686 – 2181 BC
Goddess Hathor 2686 – 2181 BC
Goddess Maat 2680 – 2190 BC
Goddess Anuket 1803 – 1649 BC
God Aker 2040 – 1782 BC
Roman gods and goddesses – there are twelve major ones as mentioned earlier in this chapter

List of Primordial Greek Gods

These deities represented the fundamental forces and physical foundations of the world and **were generally not actively worshipped, as they, for the most part, were not given human characteristics**; they were instead personifications of places or abstract concepts.

Goddess Achlys – goddess of misery and sadness
God Aether; **Aion**; **Ananke**; **Chaos**; **Chronus; Erebus; Eros; Gaia; Hemera; Hynos**; **Nemesis; Nesoi**; **Nyx; Ourea**; **Pontus; Tartarus; Thalassa**; **Thanatos**; **Uranus**

The Greek Titan Gods – their parents were **Gaia** (Mother Earth) and **Uranus** (god of heavens)
Children of Uranus and Gaia
God Cronos – married older sister Rhea
Goddess Rhea – Cronus' older sister
God Oceanus – eldest son of Uranus and Gaia – married his sister **Tethys**
Goddess Tethys – mother of 300 river gods
God Hyperion – fell in love with his sister, the Titan goddess Theia
Goddess Theia – bore Hyperion three shining children: Helios (the Sun), Eos (the Dawn), and Selene (the Moon).
God Iapetus – father of Atlas, Prometheus, Epimetheus
God Crius – the Titan god of constellations.
God Coeus – married his sister Phoebe
Goddess Phoebe – bore him two children Leto and Asteria. Leto later copulated with the Olympian god Zeus and bore the Olympians Artemis and Apollo.
Goddess Themis
Goddess Mnemosyne – Later, Zeus slept with Mnemosyne for nine consecutive days, eventually leading to the birth of the nine Muses

The Olympian Greek gods were the main Greek gods who lived on the top of Mount Olympus, children of Cronus and Rhea. They rose to power by defeating the Titans in the War of the Titans.

God Zeus – father of gods and humans – respected and feared – wife was Goddess Hera
Goddess Demeter
God Poseidon – brother of Zeus – god of the sea
God Hades – brother of Zeus and Poseidon – god of the underworld
Goddess Hera – sister of Zeus and also his wife
God Apollo – twin with Artemis
Goddess Artemis – the virgin goddess
Goddess Aphrodite – worshipped as the goddess of beauty and passion.
God Ares – the god of war was the son of the Greek gods Zeus and Hera.
God Hephaestus – god of fire and blacksmiths
Hermes – god of wealth, trade, thieves, and travellers
Goddess Hestia – goddess of domestic life
Goddess Athena – goddess of wisdom and strategic warfare
Demigod Dionysus - a god of wine, viticulture ritual madness, and religious ecstasy, he was very beloved among the people and was considered a very important god. He was the son of the **god** Zeus and the **mortal** Semele. [**The birth of Jesus was not the first time a mortal had a baby for a god, in mythology anything goes**]

Indian gods and goddesses

It's difficult to ascertain how many Indian gods and goddesses are there. A google search with this question brings the extraordinary claim that "In fact, there are **over 33 million** Hindu gods in total!" It is safe to say there are hundreds of them. The main deities are:

The *Trimurti* (the Hindu Trinity), also known as the Tridev, consists of Brahma the Creator, Vishnu the Preserver, and Shiva the Destroyer and Reincarnator. Their feminine counterparts are Saraswati, the wife of Brahma, Lakshmi, the wife of Vishnu, and Parvati the wife of Shiva. Wikipedia

The major tenets of Christianity are not supported by the Bible

Apart from the contradictions and immoralities in the Bible etc., the defense of Christianity should be untenable because its biggest tenets and practices are not supported by the Bible. Since the Bible is their guide to the specific God they worship, and this God doesn't intervene and correct their false perceptions, their claim of supernatural guidance is invalid. Concepts that are not supported are the Trinity as you have read, Easter celebration, as you have read, and some others are:

- The veneration of the crucifix as a sacred symbol
- The belief in original sin and that it was caused by the Devil.

The fact that all churches have symbols of the Cross or crucifix and millions of people wear a crucifix in the form of jewelry, and the use of it in movies as having the power to ward off evil is proof that it is firmly embedded in Christian cultures. Apart from the fact that their Bible does not claim it is sacred, the crucifixion story demonstrates that it should not be regarded as such. The evidence is simple, the story included two thieves being crucified as well! So, the crucifix also symbolizes the crucifixion of thieves.

It's logical for Christians to assume that the serpent represented the mythical Satan because we are taught that he was the architect of humanity's downfall. However, there was no ambiguity regarding the identity of the serpent. **Genesis 3:14** leaves no doubt when it stated: "And the LORD God said unto the serpent, Because thou hast done this, thou art cursed above **all cattle**, and above every **beast of the field**; upon thy belly shalt thou go, and dust shalt thou eat all the days of thy life."

If the story intended to claim the serpent was Satan it would have stated it as such. Logic suggests that if this is a real story and the Bible is claiming that Satan was the architect of humanity's downfall, he would be heavily involved in the Old Testament narrative leading up to the story of Noah and God's mass drowning. There is no such claim. There are only ten references to Satan in the Old Testament and only one of them in which it is claimed he interfered with humans, and this is the story you have read, the story of Job in which God authorises him to do evil. See the Old and New Testament references of Satan in the Addendum. In the New Testaments, there were found thirty-three references to Satan, and the strongest claim of Satan's interference with humanity is in **Revelation 12:9** "And the great dragon was cast out, that old serpent, called the **Devil**, and Satan, which deceived the whole world: he was cast out into the earth, and his angels were cast out with him." How he deceived the **whole world** is not stated.

A few religions and their beliefs in brief

Atenism 1991 – 1802 BC Egypt [monotheist belief - Aten is the Source of all life]

Hinduism 1500 – 500 BC India [polytheist belief - embraces many religious ideas]

Zoroastrianism 1000 – 500 BC Indo-Iranian [Zoroastrians believe in one God, called Ahura Mazda]

Judaism 900 – 500 BC Abrahamic religion [**a belief in one transcendent God, Jehovah or Yahweh]**

Jainism 800 – 200 BC India [**Jains believe in reincarnation**. This cycle of birth, death, and rebirth is determined by one's karma]

Confucianism 600 – 500 BC China [believes in **ancestor worship and human-centered virtues for living a peaceful life]**

Buddhism 600 – 500 BC India [believe that the human life is one of suffering and that meditation, spiritual and physical labour, and good behaviour are the ways to achieve enlightenment or nirvana.]

Taoism 600 – 400 BC China [Taoists believe in spiritual immortality, where the spirit of the body joins the universe after death.]

Shintoism 300 – 800 BC Japan [the worship of kami, which are spirits that inhabit the natural world]
Christianity 1 AD to 325 AD (formalised by the first Council of Nicaea – New Testament central doctrine – the Trinity established) [the worship of Jesus, his father, and belief in the Trinity]
Islam 610 to 632 AD [the worship of Allah]

How could a religious person in our time interpret the fact that ancient people worshipped so many gods and goddesses, who are now considered to be myths? They could think that these people were so desperate to worship God for thousands of years they made up their gods. They may also think that these people ignored the real God and invented others. **If people are desperate to worship they would not ignore an obvious all-powerful God who has made contact.** The sensible conclusion should be they had no contact with an all-powerful being. We have no evidence of this either. So, our beliefs are just figments of our imagination. **Nothing is stopping such a God from presenting himself to humanity if he is jealous of us worshipping other gods and wants us to know he exists.**

The Jesus mythology in plain sight

According to the Bible, Jesus was a carpenter

Since **Jesus was** only said to be a carpenter and **never a shepherd** why the iconography of him as "The good shepherd?" As is the norm, Christian writers will give meaning to Bible text that is not in the texts. Danielle Bernock read **John 10:11-18, Ezekiel 34,** and conclude that "Jesus' claim to be the Good Shepherd has a meaning that is both deep and wide. Although the title, Good Shepherd, is only found in the New Testament, Jesus was intentionally reaching into the Old Testament with his words. By calling himself the good shepherd, Jesus was claiming to be the Messiah that the scriptures foretold." There are two references to the Messiah in the Old Testament and none of them is about the Good Shepherd, **Daniel 9:25-26:** "Know therefore and understand, that from the going forth of the

commandment to restore and to build Jerusalem unto the **Messiah** the Prince *shall be* seven weeks, and threescore and two weeks: the street shall be built again, and the wall, even in troublous times. **26**
And after threescore and two weeks shall **Messiah** be cut off, but not for himself: and the people of the prince that shall come shall destroy the city and the sanctuary; and the end thereof shall *be* with a flood, and unto the end of the war desolations are determined."

The Bible has 42 references to shepherd and many of them make no sense. Judge for yourself by reading John 10:11-18 below. Here is a bit of confusion to the shepherd narrative: **Mark 14:27** and **Matthew 26:31** declared, "Then said Jesus unto them, All ye shall be offended because of me this night: for it is written, I will smite the shepherd, and the sheep of the flock shall be scattered abroad."

Can you connect **John 10:11-18** to the Old Testament references to Messiah? There is no connection.

John 10:11-18. "I am the good shepherd: the good shepherd giveth
his life for the sheep. **12** But he that is a hireling, and not the shepherd, whose own the sheep are not, see the wolf coming, and leave
the sheep, and flee: and the wolf catches them, and scatters the
sheep. **13** The hireling flees, because he is a hireling, and care not
for the sheep. **14** I am the good shepherd, and know **my sheep**, and
am known of mine. **15** As the Father knoweth me, even so, know I
the Father: and I lay down my life for the sheep. **16** And other sheep
I have, which are not of this fold: them also I must bring, and they
shall hear my voice, and there shall be one fold, and one shepherd.
17 Therefore doth my Father love me, because I lay down my life,
that I might take it again. **18** No man taketh it from me, but I lay
it down of myself. I have the power to lay it down, and I have the
power to take it again. This commandment have I received of my
Father."

The Old Testament has many sheep references. There is no basis to interpret them as referring to people. Why would God repeatedly say sheep if he meant people? Why say, "know "my sheep" if he meant "know my people"? Similarly, there is no basis to regard the serpent in Genesis as being Satan. A great communicator would say exactly what he means.

Why the iconography of Jesus with a sheep over his neck?

You have read that there are stories of sixteen crucified saviours before Jesus and it's recommended that you read "The World Sixteen Crucified saviours by Kersey Graves." The stories were almost identical but they existed in different countries separated by hundreds to over a thousand years, and they had different names. Similarly, the Greeks copied gods from Egypt and gave them different names, and the same mythology could be adopted by the Romans and given a different name. Do we currently claim there is only one God, yet we give him different names in different cultures? Do we have Holy Books that are similar in content and characters? The Old Testament is the Jewish Torah. And they have characters that are in the Quran. Considering the various but different iconographies of Ram Bearers or Good Shepherds, and the habit of adopting but modifying deities, we could liken the various but different "Good Shepherds'" stories to being the result of "Chinese Whisper". A story is told and every time it's repeated it morphed into something different.

We currently claim there is only one God, yet we give him different names in different cultures.

According to Wikipedia, "The Good Shepherd is a common motif from the Catacombs of Rome (Gardner, 10, fig 54) and in sarcophagus reliefs, where **Christian and pagan symbolism are often combined, making secure identifications difficul**t. [Embolden mine]

"Kriophoros" is Greek for "ram-bearer." The epithet became associated with the **god Hermes** in connection with a story from the city of Tanagra, here **retold** by the traveller and geographer Pausanias: "There are sanctuaries of Hermes Kriophoros and of Hermes called Promachos ["champion"]. They account for the former surname by a story that Hermes averted a pestilence from the city by carrying a ram around the walls; to commemorate this, Calamis made an image of Hermes carrying a ram upon his shoulders. Whichever of the youths is judged to be the most handsome goes round the walls at the feast of Hermes, carrying a lamb on his shoulders."

Hermes Kriophoros
(The Ram Bearer)

Jesus
the Good
Shepherd

With the mythical story of Hermes and other evidence, the only conclusion we should come to is that this aspect of the Jesus story was also drawn from ancient mythical stories. This and the more ancient Egyptian Ram Bearer iconography take it away from any possibility of it being a coincidence.

Ancient Egypt Ram Bearer

Ancient Egyptian iconography

"The **Shepherd's staff**[31] sometimes pictured with Jesus "originated from the staff (known as an awet) that the Shepherds used to protect their sheep. **The crook represents the pharaoh's role as a shepherd in caring for the people of Egypt**."

In **John 10:11** it says, "I am the good shepherd: the good shepherd giveth his life for the sheep." Can you see the similarity with the Egyptian reference?

Jesus was never a shepherd in the Bible story but it claims he called himself the good shepherd. In **Ezekiel 34:11 it claims God said,** "For thus said the Lord GOD; Behold, I, even I, will both search my sheep, and seek them out." This is probably why Danielle Berdock also claimed, "By calling himself the good shepherd, Jesus was claiming to be the Almighty God." Can we assume this is in reference to people?

[31] The Crook that Shephers use while minding their sheep

So, why use references to shepherds and sheep when they are not relevant to the story since God is said to be referring to people – how would God expect us to know that sheep means people? This gives more credibility to the claims that the Jesus story was drawn from more ancient mythological stories. Here is an ancient story that links **royalty**, a **shepherd**, and a **deity**. This is probably where the story originated.

Wikipedia: "The **crook**[32] **and flail** were symbols used in ancient Egyptian society. **They were originally the attributes of the deity Osiris** that became an insignia of pharaonic authority. The shepherd's crook stood for **kingship** and the flail for the fertility of the land." See the ancient Egyptian iconography below with a shepherd Crook and a Flail:

Crook and Flail in Ancient Egypt

The Bible is a collection of many stories, mythologies, and fables that were not properly coordinated, and this is why it has so many contradictions and meaningless narratives.

[32] The Shepherd Crook and Flail stood for kingship in ancient Egypt

The mythology of the crucifixion

As stated in chapter one, history teaches us that the Bible's sixty-six books were the final result of books being voted in and out over hundreds of years until these made the final cut. These iconographies and their connection to older iconographies are more proof that man invented God and religious texts.

Since the Bible was put together by books being voted in and out over several centuries, this should eliminate any claim of supernatural[33] involvement. "The Lost Books of the Bible and the forgotten books of Eden" mentioned in chapter one has a few other books worth noting: **The gospel of the birth of Mary**, **I Infancy**, **II Infancy**, and **Adam and Eve**. Why would they remove these titles? Wouldn't Christians be interested in learning about Jesus as a child, in **II Infancy?**

[33] Beyond scientific understanding or the laws of nature

They had to remove it because it would be a lot harder to sell Christianity if it remained. Here is a short excerpt that needs no explanation, **Chapter 2**:7-**9.** "Another time Jesus went forth into the street, and a boy running by, rushed upon his shoulder. **8**. At which Jesus being angry, said to him, thou shalt go no further. **9**. And he instantly fell down dead."

Why remove the book of Mary? This book is a contrast to the marginalising of Mary in the Bible. This book venerates her, so this would be one of the reasons. The other reason would be because of the claim that **she was born from the virgin, Anna.** This is a concept that Christianity promotes as being unique to the birth of Jesus. So, they would not want this to seem like a commonplace occurrence.

The Gospel of the birth of Mary

"It was likewise from this gospel that the sect of the Collyridians, established the worship and offering of manchet bread and cracknels, or fine wafers, as sacrifices to Mary, whom they imagined to have been born of a virgin, as Christ is related in the Canonical gospel to have been born of her."

Chapter 1 verses 1-4

"The blessed and ever glorious Virgin Mary, sprung from the royal race and **family of David**, was born in the city of Nazareth, and educated in Jerusalem, in the temple of the Lord. **2.** Her father's name was **Joachim** and her mother's **Anna**. The family of her father was of Galilee and the city of Nazareth. The family of her mother was from Bethlehem. **3.** Their lives were plain and right in the sight of the Lord, pious and faultless before men, for they divided all their substances into three parts. **4.** One of which they devoted to the temple and officers of the temple, another they distributed among strangers, and persons in poor circumstances, and the third they reserved for themselves and uses of their own family."

This book is claiming Mary came from the Royal lineage of David while the Bible has Joseph and David in Jesus' genealogy. Mary and Joseph could not have the same lineage unless they were related. The Mary lineage would make more sense if it is a real story. This is because Mary gave birth to Jesus without Joseph's help, so any lineage to Jesus has to come through her. The fact that they chose to put Joseph in Jesus's lineage even though he is supposed to be God's son strengthens the point that there was an agenda to eliminate the female representation of Deity. **There is no plausible reason for Joseph to be named in Jesus's lineage instead of Mary.**

Chapter 2 An angel appears before **Joachim** and informs him that Anna shall conceive and bring forth a daughter, who shall be called **Mary**, be brought up in the temple, and while yet a virgin, in a way unparalleled, bring forth the Son of God…"

CHAPTER SIX

Obvious manmade ideas and stories masquerading as spiritual concepts

Holy wars

Only irrational thinking would accept the concept of a holy war. Since wars are usually demonstrations of our worst instinct which is using violence to solve problems, how can it also represent that which the religious regard as their highest ideal, holiness, unless holiness is compatible with mass slaughter? If this is the case, on what basis can we be punished by our "Holy Father?"

Sabbath day

We can safely assume that the religious regard the workings of Nature as the prerogative of an all-powerful God.

Exodus 31:15 states, "Six days may work be done; but in the seventh is the Sabbath of rest, holy to the LORD: whosoever doeth any work in the Sabbath day, he shall surely be put to death."

If God controls Nature, a holy or sacred day is often contradicted by the actions of God. Hurricanes, tornadoes, and volcanic eruptions, to name a few, have never shown regard for rest and worship on any day, and yet these events are regarded as "Acts of God". The reduction of, or lack of activities by adherents on "holy days", or the

Sabbath, suggests that tranquillity is relevant to such days. It's hard to feel tranquil or worship with a storm or volcanic eruption breathing down one's neck.

The useless practice of regular prayers and praise

Only an ego suffering from a deep sense of insecurity would crave never-ending praise and thanks. A human parent who requires this from their children would be regarded as suffering from a narcissistic personality disorder and this is in part characterised by a deep need for excessive attention and admiration.

Persons with this disorder need constant food to bolster their fragile sense of self-worth, so they surround themselves with people who are willing to cater to their obsessive craving for affirmation. To ascribe this desire to a being believed to be responsible for the universe and all that exists is a major contradiction, and this would relegate such a being to a low-quality human being and this would be an insult to such a being if he existed.

Everything that we require is either provided by human beings or Nature. Therefore, everything we receive requires the utilisation of energy. The oldest concept that explains how reality works is not mystical. It is the observation that there is an energy that exists in all things. We can conclude that this energy has to be intelligent because life is intelligent, and natural science is intelligent. This energy cannot be communicated with and asked for favours. This is why prayers don't work. There are no persons involved apart from us humans. Everything is an expression of this energy, and we are conscious expressions of this energy, and there are two ways we get what we want that cannot be disputed. We either have productive arrangements with each other or productive arrangements with Nature.

The absurdity of being severely punished for our thoughts and words

One of our worst motives for murder is thinking the person "looked at us with bad intention", or taking offence from their words. Yet, God, our loving parent will do worst?

Matthew 5:27-28

Ye have heard that it was said by them of old time, Thou shalt not commit adultery:

28 But I say unto you, That whosoever **look on a woman to lust** after her hath committed adultery with her already in his heart.

Matthew 5:21-22

21 Ye have heard that it was said by them of old time, Thou shalt not kill; and whosoever shall kill shall be in danger of the judgment:

22 But I say unto you, That whosoever is angry with his brother without a cause shall be in danger of the judgment: and whosoever shall say to his brother, Raca, shall be in danger of the council: but whosoever shall say, Thou fool, shall be in danger of hell fire.

Mark 3:28-29

28 Verily I say unto you, All sins shall be forgiven unto the sons of
men, and blasphemies wherewith soever they shall blaspheme: **29**
But he that shall blaspheme against the Holy Ghost hath never forgiveness, but is in danger of eternal damnation:

The impossibilities and contradictions of free will, prayers, and temptation

We can logically assume that the major practices of Christians are based on the directives of the Bible which they consider to be the word of God. Since praying and praising God is a fixture in Christianity, we can also logically assume that this is the arrangement that their God mandated as their means of communicating with him, and the nature of this would be as they practice, that is, give thanks and praise and ask for help. So, where is the definitive instruction in the Bible on prayer as it relates to current belief? The Bible's words and the lack of results they produce don't support the dominant practices of prayer in terms of expectations of help - this will be proven shortly. For the case to be made that their God's arrangement on earth requires us to pray to him he would have to have given this instruction to Adam and Eve and any number of personalities in the Old Testament. There are no such scriptures. Also, if this instruction was given, for this information to be valid in practical terms, it would include what can be prayed for, and devotees would get a response for each request either for or against but this is not the case. A considerate and loving person would not instruct us to ask him for help and then never give a response.

The most direct instruction to pray is claimed to be been given by Jesus. The wording of this entreaty lacks wisdom, therefore, it cannot come from an intelligent human much less an infinitely intelligent God, it's called the Lord's Prayer:

Matthew 6:9-13

9 After this manner, therefore, pray ye: Our Father which art in heaven, Hallowed[34] be thy name. **10** Thy kingdom come. Thy will be done in earth, as it *is* in heaven. **11** Give us this day our daily bread. **12** And forgive us our debts, as we forgive our debtors. **13** And lead us not into temptation, but deliver us from evil: For yours is the kingdom, and the power, and the glory, for ever. Amen.

Verse 10. As you will see in this book heaven doesn't have a definitive meaning, so we have no information as to what we are confirming

[34] Tell him that his name is holy. This is the sort of thing a narcissist would request.

will be done on earth. **Verse 13.** This verse is claiming that God is instructing us that when we pray to him we should ask him not to lead us into temptation. We would not ask someone not to do something unless we have reason to think they might do it. Since giving in to temptation is claimed to be punishable by God this verse makes no sense. It makes even less sense when we include the fact there is no reference in the Bible to Satan tempting humans. However, it gets stranger, here is a reference claiming God tempted one of his favourite people:

Genesis 22:1 And it came to pass after these things, that God did tempt Abraham, and said unto him, Abraham: and he said, Behold, here I am.

The above is strange and contradictory considering the following admonitions claimed to come from Jesus:

Luke 22:40 And when he was at the place, he said unto them, Pray that ye enter not into temptation.

Luke 22:46 And said unto them, Why sleep ye? Rise and pray, lest ye enter into temptation.

Mark 14:38 Watch ye and pray, lest ye enter into temptation. The spirit truly is ready, but the flesh is weak.

The following scripture gives a different take on how prayers are supposed to work. It is suggesting that it's our belief that makes prayers work, not a gift from God. This is similar to what happens in reality, when we believe in an outcome, we persistently pursued it, and we tend to achieve it. However, it tends to work irrespective of our morality.

Mark 11:24 Therefore I say unto you, What things soever ye desire, when ye pray, **believe** that ye receive them, and ye shall have them.

The following scripture contradicts the need for prayer in terms of asking for help. However, it doesn't work. Innumerable people have lived their lives according to **verse 33** instruction and have struggled, and are struggling in life currently. Perhaps how to seek the kingdom is unclear, and this would be consistent with the Bible being contradictory, and often incoherent.

Matthew 6:31-34

31 "Therefore take no thought, saying, What shall we eat? or, What shall we drink? or, Wherewithal shall we be clothed? **32** (For after all these things do the Gentiles seek:) for your heavenly Father knoweth that ye have need of all these things.

33 But seek ye first the kingdom of God, and his righteousness, and all these things shall be added unto you. **34** Take therefore no thought for the morrow: for the morrow shall take thought for the things of itself. Sufficient unto the day *is* the evil thereof." **[Take no thought for tomorrow is an instruction not to plan or set goals, and if interpreted in conjunction with verse 33 it is saying it's not necessary because our future is already taken care of. This contradicts how reality works, and it's disempowering and dangerous to hold such a belief and act on it.]**

If the Bible lacks clarity to the point where after nearly a thousand years none of the Christian denominations have figured out the correct way to seek the kingdom of God, it doesn't qualify as originating from an infinitely intelligent source. There are no Christian groups or denominations that enjoy the level of comfort and prosperity that **verse 33** promises. Surely, if this was based on reality, at least one group would have qualified for the promise by now? Christians claim they have a personal or intimate relationship with their God who speaks to them and gives them power. Some even claim to be filled with the Holy Ghost. We should expect noticeable manifestations to support such claims. This should be, at minimum, superior intelligence and wisdom, and better health than non-believers. However, their knowledge is restricted to the total of what they study, observe, and understand, just like all of us. The state of their health and death rate is dictated by their diet and lifestyle just like all of us. Also, there is no Christian group that stands out in terms of prosperity.

The rest of the temptation references that don't involve acts by Satan

1 Corinthians 10:13, No temptation has overtaken you except what is common to mankind: but **God is faithful, who will not suffer you to be tempted above that ye are able**; but when you are tempted he will make a way to escape, that ye may be able to bear it. **[Why didn't God protect Adam and Eve from temptation as stated above? An inconsistent God or inconsistent manmade dogma? Answer: God is an invention using inconsistent manmade dogma]**

In **Luke 20:23,** Jesus is claimed to ask why is he being tempted.

In **Deuteronomy 6:16,** Jesus is claimed to ask not to be tempted.

In **1 Corinthians 10:9,** someone declared they shouldn't tempt Christ.

In **Matthew 4:7,** Jesus is claimed to tell Satan not to tempt him.

Isaiah 7:12, But Ahaz said, I will not ask, neither will I tempt the LORD.

Acts 15:10, Now, therefore, why tempt thou, God, to put a yoke upon the neck of the disciples, which neither our fathers nor we were able to bear?

Malachi 3:15, And now we call the proud happy; yea, they that work wickedness are set up; yea, they that tempt God are even delivered. **[What?]**

New International Version

Malachi 3:15, But now we call the arrogant blessed. Certainly, evildoers prosper, and even when they put God to the test, they get away with it. **[What?]**

In **Acts 5:9, a** woman is accused of tempting the spirit of the Lord.

In **1 Corinthians 7:5,** there is a warning not to be tempted by Satan.

In **Exodus 17:2,** Moses is claimed to ask his people why they tempt God.

Free will – definition

"The power of acting without the constraint of necessity or faith; the ability to act at one's discretion."

If an all-powerful God has lines he doesn't want us to cross that necessitate him killing or torturing us forever according to some adherents, he would eliminate those options from our consciousness. However, the fact that we have awareness of these options, if we will be punished if we act on them this would be the opposite of free will. Free will characterises us as being opposite to animals because they are characterised as being governed and limited by instinct. Therefore, if we are prohibited from acting on free will it could be said we are not fully functioning humans. However, the human experience would be better off without the option to kill or commit murder. In the context of humans conceptualising an all-powerful God as being like a wise parent, such a parent would not give us this option because it would be tantamount to leaving a loaded gun within reach of his children and not expecting them to use it at least occasionally. For the God **they conceive** to qualify as being all-wise and all-knowing, such a god would ensure that he gets the result he wants, and therefore, he would have proceeded like in the movie, "I Robot", where robots were built with two clear dictates, they have to obey humans, and they cannot kill humans. And in our case, there would be no circuitry that would make us commit murder. A God who installs such circuitry would be responsible for it being used unless he doesn't take credit for the totality of our design and characteristics.

A religious adherent addressed the question of eliminating murder as an option of free will by suggesting that free will means unlimited options because God didn't want us to be like robots. Not being able to commit murder does not disqualify us from being human, having free will, or making us act like robots. This is obvious since most humans will live and die without acting on the option of committing murder or even killing another human being despite living in a violent world where the act of murder is well known.

In practice, free will means we are not governed by a built-in and limited uniformed action the way animals are, we can make innumerable decisions. Many of us often wish some humans didn't have bad impulses toward other humans or animals. So, in the context of the inaccurate way the religious understand reality, we would welcome "God" removing bad impulses (deliberate physical harm to others) from our possibilities. And this would remove the belief in what amounts to psychological terrorism, which is the belief that God will punish us for that which he would be the architect. In reality, we have unlimited options in terms of behaviour because no God is dictating our activities. We are self-regulated but shaped by environment, influences, ideas, and the thoughts and emotions **we cultivate.**

The belief in prayer is the irrational assumption that our plea to an invisible but listening God is causing the result of what we prayed for. However, prayer is simply the act of rolling the dice enough times that our number eventually comes up.

For God to intervene and get someone to do something for us because we prayed for it, points to the future not yet been decided because the prayer would be the trigger for the new outcome. If prayers can dictate our future, this eliminates the idea that God has a plan for us. An answered prayer would be **the person's desire for the future.** Therefore, God could not answer prayers and have his plan at the same time, unless he only answer prayers that are in line with his plan. If this is the case there is no need for prayer. Religious books encourage us to pray and give thanks. Based on the power of beliefs we cannot blame those who are indoctrinated into these useless activities. Believing that prayers are answered by an invisible being is tantamount to being locked into a perpetual state of arrested development. We can only hope that at some point they are inspired or become desperate, and break out and reach the age of reason. However, because of the often extreme intractability of beliefs, the best use of time and energy is to educate future generations so that they never get indoctrinated.

God is just an imaginary friend for grownups – Walter Crewes

The surgeon spent nine hours performing microsurgery saving a woman's life, and the first thing she said when she regained consciousness was, "Thank you, Jesus". The surgeon's name was not Jesus!

Every day billions of people thank god for foods and drinks that will injure and shorten their lives. God would require giving thanks for such things? So, when we give thanks for bad food we are thanking an imaginary being for impairing our health. Surely, if such a guardian exists he would warn us against such choices?

The evidence that prayers don't work is overwhelming.

- We are aware that for centuries and decades there has been a lack of intervention by any God to lift worshippers out of poverty and save them from oppression despite constant prayers and worship. This demonstrates that the belief that there is a God who does such things is false. No loving parent would watch their children suffer for decades and centuries, is capable of helping them but do not.
- It's impractical for a God to help humans with prosperity because such acts would contradict the principle of free will. Furthermore, the attainment of money or prosperity requires specific actions that no one can avoid, it cannot appear out of thin air like magic. The most common methods to attain money are to work; work and invest; set up a business, or sell something. Observing religions reveals the falsity of the idea that a superior all-powerful being is in the habit of bestowing prosperity to humans upon request. Whenever pastors of such organisations need money they seek it from their members who obtain it from commercial activities, but when the members need money they are encouraged to pray. Wouldn't the "holy" leaders who are thought to be highly favoured by God have greater credibility in receiving such gifts if it was possible?
- Any outcome that requires the action of other human beings cannot be attributed to God without suspending the principle of free will. An example of this is someone thanking "God" for giving them their family. How would this work in practice? Number one, this suggests that their spouse wouldn't have fallen in love with them or agreed to the union without intervention by an invisible force. And this would involve suspending the person's natural processes of thinking and feeling, and implanting others that the person wouldn't have had without intervention. Wouldn't this reduce the situation to something similar to hypnosis? If this claim is extended to crediting God for their wonderful

children, this suggests that God tailor-made their children to suit their future needs. This removes the value of how they raised and nurture their children, how they chose to respond to said nurturing, and even the sex of the children. In effect, this idea challenges the unchallengeable reality of having free will and the random nature of childbirth. It's unchallengeable that every day we make decisions based on our capacity to think and feel, and this is what produces our consistent results, and our ability to change direction.

How strange is it that billions of people are aware that billions of other people believe in different Holy Books and "The one and only true God", and yet they never question their own? They are confident and believe that they are on the right track. No doubts.

A philosophy that makes sense by Earl Nightingale

The strangest secret

Here is a situation that parallels the human mind, supposed a farmer has some land and it's good fertile land? The land gives the farmer a choice, he may plant in that land whatever he chooses, the land doesn't care, it's up to the farmer to make the decision. Now, remember, we are comparing the human mind to the land because the mind like the land doesn't care what you plant in it. It will return what you plant, but it doesn't care what you plant. Now let's say the farmer has two seeds in his hand, one is a seed of corn, and the other is nightshade a deadly poison. He digs two little holes in the earth and he plants both seeds, one corn, and the other nightshade. He covers up the holes, waters and takes care of the land, and what will happen? Invariably the land will return what's planted, as you sow so shall you reap. Remember the land doesn't care what you plant, it will return poison in wonderful abundance as it will corn. So, up come the two plants, one corn, and one poison. The human mind is far more fertile, far more incredible and mysterious than the land, but it works the same way, it doesn't care what we plant.

The story of Job – a harmful, immoral, and mind-bending story, but revered by adherents

"Is the Book of Job a true story?

The medieval Jewish scholar Maimonides declared his story a parable, and the medieval Christian Thomas Aquinas wrote a detailed commentary declaring it as true history." – Wikipedia. We can assume "God" has not intervened to clarify or explain this to anyone.

If the story is a parable as Maimonides declared, how are we supposed to know this? His conclusion should bring into question all Bible stories. Shouldn't the creation story with a talking snake be an overwhelming candidate to be a parable? How about the story of God talking as a burning bush, **Exodus 3:1-17**, or the story of the talking ass, **Numbers 22:21-38**? How can these stories be less incredulous? If a story is an analogy, an allegory, or a parable an intelligent writer would state this, especially if the entire world must understand it.

Job chapter one

"**1** There was a man in the land of Uz, whose name *was* Job; and that
man was perfect and upright, and one that feared God, and eschewed
evil. **2** And there were born unto him seven sons and three daughters.
3 His substance also was seven thousand sheep, and three thousand
camels, and five hundred yoke of oxen, and five hundred she asses,
and a very great household; so that this man was the greatest of all the
men of the east. **6** Now there was a day when the sons of God came
to present themselves before the LORD, and Satan came also among
them. **7** And the LORD said unto Satan, Whence comes thou? Then
Satan answered the LORD, and said, From going to and fro in the
earth, and from walking up and down in it. **8** And the LORD said
unto Satan, Hast thou considered my servant Job, that *there is* none

like him in the earth, a perfect and an upright man, one that fears God, and eschewed evil? **9** Then Satan answered the LORD, and said, Does Job fear God for nothing? **10** Have you not made a hedge about him, and about his house, and about all that he has on every side? Thou has blessed the work of his hands, and his substance is increased in the land. **11** But put forth thine hand now, and touch all that he has, and he will curse thee to thy face. **12** And the LORD said unto Satan, Behold, all that he hath *is* in thy power; only upon himself put not forth thine hand. So Satan went forth from the presence of the LORD."

So, in this narrative God allowed Satan to test Job's faith in him but he was not allowed to kill or harm him. These are the things Satan did in this fable:

He destroyed all his properties and killed his livestock, his servants, and his seven children. What was Job's response? **20** Then Job arose, and tore his robe, and shaved his head, and fell upon the ground, and worshipped **21** And said, Naked came I out of my mother's womb, and naked shall I return thither: the LORD gave, and the LORD hath taken away; blessed be the name of the LORD. **22** In all of this, Job sinned not, nor charged God foolishly.

What is the message in this fable to an un-indoctrinated and rational mind?

The story's harmful indoctrination of helplessness, delusion, and blind faith

- The Lord giveth and taketh is a belief that the things we achieve are given to us by external forces. This causes adherents to not acknowledge the reality of cause and effect and appreciate their skills and abilities, the help of others, and that they primarily dictate their results. It creates a false sense of reality. Believing and accepting that a loving God destroyed everything one has including one's children for no good reason would be extremely irrational and unhealthy. This cannot be overstated.

- It promotes the delusional and nonsensical idea that someone who is purely good would give us something and then destroys it for no good reason. If we attribute such behaviour to a loving, infinitely intelligent, and all-wise God, this can destroy a rational understanding of these characteristics.
- This promotes the unhealthy delusional idea that even when life is going extremely bad, this is part of a divine plan and God will eventually fix it. Out of this delusion, people accept the nonsensical idea that "God doesn't give us more than we can bear". The casualty of this belief is self-empowerment.
- Perhaps the most irrational belief that flows from believing in a God who is taking care of us is the conclusion people come to after someone survived an accident. For example, a child could be the sole survivor of a fire but suffered third-degree burns and be disabled, yet adherents will hold special services to thank God for the miracle. If God was involved and singled out the child for saving, why would this loving all-powerful God allow the child to experience the trauma, extreme pain and suffering, and permanent disfigurement before saving the child? Why not save the rest of the people in the house? Our loving parent allows some of us to die horrible deaths? The message from this is that adherents are programmed to believe in contradictions, and therefore, they will never regard anything attributed to "God" as being horrible or evil, and therefore a reason to question the legitimacy of the story. Accepting evil acts attributed to a God cannot be good for our moral compass.

In the second part of this irrational mythological story, the Devil asked God permission to further test Job's loyalty to him and he agreed.

Job Chapter 2:7 So went Satan forth from the presence of the LORD, and smote Job with sore boils from the sole of his foot unto his crown.

Accepting the irrationality and illogic that no vile act is off-limits for a loving God has to be unhealthy and harmful to the psyche, and could cause tolerance towards violence as a solution to problems or perceived problems. The violence that religion has sponsored confirms this. The end of the story that adherents regard as inspirational is: **Job 42:12-13** "So the LORD blessed the latter end of Job more than his beginning: for he had fourteen thousand sheep, and six thousand camels, and a thousand yoke of oxen, and a thousand she asses. **13** He had also seven sons and three daughters."

They celebrate this story and conveniently ignore the fact that God allowed the murder of Job's seven innocent children, his servants, and the wanton slaughter of his livestock to prove a point that an all-knowing God would have known in advance. They also inadvertently accept the callous idea that God blessed Job by causing him and his wife to have more children and a lot more livestock, and therefore he was better off than he was at the beginning of the test of his loyalty to God. So, we are like animals, our children are murdered and we have some more and everything is fine? Does this eradicate the hurt and mourning for their dead children and servants? What about their right to life?

Some of Christian writer Courtney Joseph's list of the values or lessons of the story

Because she is a believer, she invariably approached the subject with the assumption that is true. Therefore, she didn't recognise that it would be contradictory and senseless if a wise and intelligent person felt the need to prove something to his nemesis, and this would be infinitely truer if an all-wise, and infinitely intelligent God would feel the need to prove something to Satan, and allowed him to wreak death and destruction to do it. The same Satan, who supposedly represents evil incarnate, and is dedicated to destroying humanity, and his plans. Here are some of her lessons from the story:

1. "Bad things happen to good people. **2.** In the midst of suffering, we must never lose our hope in God. **3.** Even in the midst of God's silence, His presence is with us. **4.** God is with us in the midst of our storms. **5.** God is in control. **6.** Wisdom comes from fearing God and turning away from evil" She also wrote the inane comments: "One of the greatest statements of faith in all of scripture is found right in the middle of Job chapter 13. Job says: *"Though he slay me, I will hope in him."*

"Job's suffering did not come because he was bad but rather because of his unwavering faithfulness to God." **[So, the more faithful someone is to God their reward is greater suffering? It's doubtful that this would be a good advert to join]**

Sheila Miller commented on the lessons

"No, I will never lose my hope in God! He is my rock, my hope."[35]

Other inane online comments

"Job concludes that wisdom belongs to God, and all human attempts to grasp it or contain it are doomed to failure. This is Job's confession and then ultimately his salvation."

---

[35] Sheila read a story where God allowed Job's seven children and servants to be murdered for no good reason, and it didn't disturbed her moral compass. This explains the history of slaughter done in the name of God. The reason we experience less violence now is because society has evolved. Mostly, there is a separation of state from religion, so churches have less power, there are fewer adherents because societies are more educated, fewer people read the Bible, many have outgrown their Bibles – they make up some of their beliefs, and laws have been enacted to restrain our worse instincts.

"The moral of the story is that **wisdom lives with God**. To fear the scope and power of this divine wisdom is to be truly wise in a human sense. Kind of how a truly wise man knows that he knows nothing."

God with non-immortal characteristics

The Adam and Eve creation story includes the narrative that God rested on the seventh day. Without meaning to words there is no communication, so the dictionary meaning of rest has to be applied, especially because it was applied after work was done. All living beings that relax, sleep, (recover strength) can tire and every living being that can tire can get sick, and therefore die. These are all characteristics of mortal beings. This is a narrative of man inventing an imaginary being in our likeness and calling him God. The need for rest is contradictory to having immortality unless they are claiming that "God" is not immortal. Since this is not the case, the writers, thinking from a human perspective, imagine that constructing the massive aspects of our reality, earth, the universe, and galaxies would be a big job, and therefore the Creator would need to rest, especially after fast-tracking it in seven days. This type of thinking is a demonstration of some of our limitations in the interpretation of our existence.

The violence carried out in the past in the name of God based on scriptures can be attributed to there being less sophisticated populaces and the power of the churches at the time. However, do people still believe in the violent and immoral scriptures of the Bible? They do. Here is the answer to a question posed on Google:

"Is it OK to pray Psalm 109?"

"Let's also not forget that Psalm 109 (and Psalm 35, and many other imprecatory Psalms) are quoted in the New Testament. So should we pray the imprecatory Psalms as Christians? **Absolutely, as long as our prayers are in accordance with God's Word, and therefore, His will."**

Psalm 109 is imprecatory – this is defined as, invoking judgment, calamity, or curses upon one's enemies or those perceived as the enemies of God. Traditionally ascribed to King David, the Psalms have played an important role for millennia in religious ceremonies in liturgy, hymns, and private worship. Here are a few of these imprecatory to God:

6 Set thou a wicked man over him: and let Satan stand at his right hand.

7 When he shall be judged, let him be condemned: and let his prayer become sin.

8 Let his days be few, and let another take his office.

9 Let his children be fatherless, and his wife a widow.

12 Let there be none to extend mercy unto him: neither let there be any to favour his fatherless children.

What do you think unsophisticated people without restraint, and had state backing would do if they were fed on this type of narrative?

> **The sword of the church was unsheathed and plunged with a fierce and relentless ferocity into the bosoms and bowels of their neighbors and fellow Christian professors, whose only offense was that of believing and worshipping God according to the dictates of their consciences.** The Bible of Bibles – Kersey Graves 1870

Religions are inherently divisive

The more religiously diverse a society, the less integrated the human family tends to be, especially if the religiosity is fervent.

This is because the concept of good and evil as spiritual forces is an integral part of religious beliefs, and this usually translates into a philosophy that those who don't share the same belief are regarded as being on the side of evil, or at least on the wrong path – not pleasing to God. Invariably, this translates into having less human integration. This results in people being judged on their religion and not on the content of their character, and marriages and close friendships are less likely to happen or be sustained. There is even a Bible scripture that instructs its adherents not to be "unequally yoked". **2 Corinthians 6:14**

Some adherents don't vote or get involved in politics, therefore, do not lend their talents to organise our activities and solve our problems. This begs the question, how do they expect society to function without governance? The nature of being social beings and the fact that we are highly interdependent, and would not survive and thrive if we live as individuals points to the necessity of having organised societies. Some believe that "God" will set up his government in the next life. This makes their non-participation in governance nonsensical since we are better off with governments or governance, and it's definite that they do not want us to revert to a nomadic existence. In effect, even though it's not usually stated, they would recognise a theocracy. This would necessitate having an entire population who believe in their brand of Christianity.

Nonsensical hostility towards those who crucified Jesus

The hostility towards Judas, for example, is so intense, that his name is in the dictionary, and it's not a name that parents, at least in the Christian world, would burden a child with. Since adherents believe Jesus came to be killed for the "sins" of humanity, it's logical that someone had to facilitate it. Suicide, dying of old age, or climbing up the cross and crucifying himself were not options. So, after so many years, how is it that believers have not figured this out and God has not explained this to them, especially those who claim they have contact and a close relationship with God?

The macabre concept of Eucharis or Holy Communion

Why would an all-wise God desire the symbolic eating of his "flesh" and drinking his "blood" by eating bread and drinking red wine or grape juice as widely believed and practiced by Christians? Doesn't this symbolise a cannibalistic ritual? Since flesh and blood are temporary and they rot, and God is supposed to be about the spiritual, why would he want us to engage in such a meaningless ritual? How is this supposed to give us life?

John 6:53 Then Jesus said unto them, Verily, verily, I say unto you, Except ye eat the flesh of the Son of man, and drink his blood, ye have no life in you.

If we don't engage in this symbolic ritual we have no life in us? How can people grow if they believe in such a mind-bending meaningless activity? This lack of growth is demonstrated by the claim of televangelist Andrew Womack that he got rid of mildew from his house through scripture reading and rebuking it. He claimed it was a curse. He is said to be worth 15 million dollars. This suggests he has a large audience that is tolerant of such levels of ridiculous claims and therefore will believe anything he tells them. He also shamelessly tells his congregation that when they get to heaven they will kiss and thank him for taking money out of their pockets and limiting their options for unnecessary purchases. Kenneth Copeland, another televangelist who claims to be able to heal people through their television, is so confident in his congregation's lack of growth, he tells them he is being persecuted for buying two aeroplanes, one of which cost $45 million. His net worth was estimated at $760 million in 2018.

The idea that a supreme being wants us to symbolically eat his flesh and drink his blood is another example of our propensity for making up preposterous stories. Most of us, including the religious, would find such an act preposterous if it was a cultural practice of a group to honour an ancestor. Therefore, we should think it is even more preposterous for an all-wise God to require such a practice. However, religion tends to suspend natural inclinations and reasoning. The usual attitude is, "I am not qualified to question the word of God." The same attitude is often applied to those they regard as Holy men or women.

I Corinthians 11:23–25 23 For I have received of the Lord that which also I delivered unto you, that the Lord Jesus the *same* night in which he was betrayed took bread. **24** And when he had given thanks, he brakes it, and said, Take, eat: this is my body, which is broken for you: this do in remembrance of me. **25** After the same manner also *he took* the cup, when he had supped, saying, this cup is the new testament in my blood: this do ye, as oft as ye drink *it*, in remembrance of me.

The age of the earth and living forever on it

A fundamental belief in religions is that God intended humans to live forever, therefore no diseases, no killings, and no accidents. So, in such a world there would have to be no natural disasters, earthquakes, storms, hurricanes, tornadoes, or tsunamis. The natural conclusion is that natural disasters are our reality because of "original sin", and this has been said. This belief is one of the consequences of a non-biblical dogma introduced by St Augustine. So, many of us are still as superstitious as the ancient people who believed that lightning was the result of an angry god. We still regard natural disasters as "acts of God" and these damages are not always insurable.

How would finite earth sustain life if no one or nothing dies? This logical and scientific question does not interfere with their belief. They usually say it's a matter of faith.

Some Christian groups accept that the earth is billions of years old. This invalidates their claim that this earth and creation were enacted for us. This would mean as shown in chapter three that the earth and living occupants were here billions of years before we arrived. No rational thinking would claim this doesn't contradict the Bible's creation story. It is the awareness of this contradiction that some denominations claim that the earth is six thousand years old. A consequence of this belief is the rejection of dinosaurs and prehistoric animals. The scientific view is that the earth is about 4.5 billion years old and the universe about 14 billion years old. The religious dating of the earth as 6,000 years old is achieved by using Bible stories.

According to Bodie Hodge, "Where did a young-earth Worldview Come From? Simply put, it came from the Bible. Of course, the Bible doesn't say explicitly anywhere, "The earth is 6,000 years old." Good thing it doesn't; otherwise it would be out of date the following year. But we wouldn't expect an all-knowing God to make that kind of a mistake. God gave us something better. In essence, He gave us a "birth certificate." For example, using a personal birth certificate, a person can calculate how old he is at any point. It is similar to the earth. Genesis 1 says that the earth was created on the first day of creation **(Genesis 1:1-5).** From there, we can begin to calculate the age of the earth. Let's do a rough calculation to show how this works. The age of the earth can be estimated by taking the first five days of creation (from earth's creation to Adam), then following the genealogies from Adam to Abraham in **Genesis 5 and 11**, then adding in the time from Abraham to today. Adam was created on day 6, so there were five days before him. If we add up the dates from Adam to Abraham, we get about 2,000 years, using the Masoretic Hebrew text of Genesis 5 and 11.3 Whether Christian or secular, most scholars would agree that Abraham lived about 2,000 B.C. (4,000 years ago)."

This is the power of religion. It makes people apply belief to determine that which is based on science. A belief claims the earth is 6,000 years old while historical evidence declares that the earliest written language is 20,000 years old.

If an all-wise "God" wanted events to be recorded from the beginning of human life for future generations the earliest humans would be given the ability to write, and historians inspired to write it. In reality, we have pre-history, which is before writing. To interpret this period we rely on artifacts, drawings, paintings, bones, and other evidence of human activities.

Human decisions disguised as God's will

We have seen in real-time how churches arrived at decisions that the Bible attributed to God – for example, not allowing women to hold high positions of leadership in religious institutions. The men voted, and there was no mention of God paying them a spiritual visit.

In the past a king was believed to be divinely appointed – in reality this means, entirely manufactured in human minds. So, punishment for crimes against the king was severe because it was regarded as a crime against God, even though there are no such instructions from the Bible. An all-wise God would be capable of deciding what the punishment should be and dish it out himself.

Concept of a Devil

The nonsensical concept of a Devil – Is God in charge on earth or not in charge on earth? Many religious people credit the success of many of the super-rich with selling their souls to the Devil. This belief is often aimed at entertainers. So, if we apply simple logic to this belief, they inadvertently believe that if entertainers who are not devoted Christians have great success, it cannot be attributed to God. However, since the majority of the devoted are not successful and poverty tends to be more prevalent among them, then God does not reward the vast majority of his adherents. This would be some strange God to allow himself to trail in the wake of the Devil in rewarding his servants.

Evil human instincts disguised as Holy Scriptures

Ecclesiastes 3:3 A time to kill[36], and a time to heal; a time to break down, and a time to build up;

Numbers 31:17-18 Now, therefore, kill every male among the little ones, and kill every woman that hath known man by lying with him. **18** But all the **women children**, that have not known a man by lying with him, keep alive for yourselves.

2 Kings 2:23-24 And he went up from thence unto Bethel: and as he was going up by the way, there came forth little children out of the city, and mocked him, and said unto him, Go up, thou bald head; go up, thou bald head. **24** And he turned back, and looked on them, and cursed them in the name of the LORD. And there came forth two she bears out of the wood, and tare forty and two children of them.

2 Kings 2:23-24 KJV

23 And he went up from thence unto Bethel: and as he was going up by the way, there came forth little children out of the city, and

[36] What about thou shall not kill?

mocked him, and said unto him, Go up, thou bald head; go up, thou bald head. **24** And he turned back, and looked on them, and cursed them in the name of the LORD. And there came forth two she bears out of the wood, and tare forty and two children of them.

New International Version

23 From there Elisha went up to Bethel. As he was walking along the road, some boys came out of the town and jeered at him. "Get out of here, baldy!" they said. "Get out of here, baldy!" **24** He turned around, looked at them and called down a curse on them in the name of the LORD. Then two bears came out of the woods and mauled forty-two of the boys.

Luke 12:47-48

47 And that servant, which knew his lord's will, and prepared not himself, neither did according to his will, shall be beaten with many stripes. **48** But he that knew not, and did commit things worthy of stripes, shall be beaten with few stripes. For unto whomsoever much is given, of him shall be much required: and to whom men have committed much, of him, they will ask the more.

The above sounds like a manmade legal principle that states, "Ignorance of the law is no excuse". Here we have another portrayal of God as a sadistic parent, a quality that most parents don't have. Not only should we be beaten if we break one of his rules, but we should be beaten even if we didn't know his rule, albeit with fewer blows. How kind! Once again, a story that suggests human morals, and our sense of justice are greater than a God whom it's claimed is loving, and in **Psalms 136** we are encouraged to "Give thanks unto the Lord; for he is good: for his mercy endureth for ever". "His mercy endureth forever" is repeated twenty-six times in **chapter 136**! Perhaps the writer of Luke did not read **Psalms 136**, or he decided to give his personal opinion. Is it not a contradiction that someone who is infinitely merciful, and described as "God is love", would punish someone even if the transgressor unknowingly transgressed? This is one of countless proof that the God story is manmade, and should not prevail once we get to the age of reason.

A being whose mercy endureth forever could not relate to the narrative in Luke **12:47-48,** and would not perpetuate the indiscriminate mass killings in the story of Noah, and make the vile threats in **Deuteronomy 28:15-58,** just to name a few.

Deuteronomy 28:15-58 is part of the evidence that man invented God and Holy texts. If this narrative was offered as the script for an episode of "Criminal Minds" it would be rejected as being excessive and implausible. This would be on the basis that no single psychopath would have so many deranged qualities because they tend to have a small range of vile tendencies. These many sadistic tendencies would have to be divided among many different types of the criminally insane. And yet, the following actions are some of the consequences it is claimed God threatened some of his children with if they "forsake and disobey" him. Yet, in the same Bible God is described as love, and his mercy endures forever. Do these actions fit this description? No, it's a total contradiction. Not even the worse human parent would even imagine such extreme actions. These scriptures claimed God threatened his children to:

Send curses on them; cause them to be confused; strike them with body-wasting diseases; fever; inflammation. Cause them to experience scorching heat and drought, blight, and mildew. Cause them to experience nothing but cruel oppression all their days, until the sights they see drive them mad. Turn the rain of their country into dust and powder. Cause them to be defeated by their enemies; cause their dead bodies to be eaten by birds and wild animals. Cause them to experience painful boils all over their bodies that cannot be healed. Cause them to have tumours, festering sores, the itch that cannot be healed, madness, and blindness. Cause them to be oppressed, robbed, their wives raped, and children kidnapped. Cause swarms of locusts to destroy their crops, and destroy them. Cause them to experience hunger and thirst, nakedness, and dire poverty. Put an iron yoke on their necks until they are destroyed. Make them serve the enemies he sends against them. Bring a nation that has no respect for the old or pity for the young against them; this nation will steal all their food until they are ruined, and its actions will **cause them to eat their children**.

So, what was the crime his children committed to anger him to the extent that he thought they deserved these extreme punishments?

- Because of the evil you have done in forsaking him.
- Because you did not obey the LORD your God and observe the commands and decrees he gave you.
- Because you did not serve the LORD your God joyfully and gladly in the time of prosperity.

All the verses from 15 to 58 are a litany of horrific consequences of disobedience to "God". This is a shortened list for convenience. Research all if you wish. Since billions of people have not followed "all his commands and decrees", and no people on earth have had these experiences, the words are not based on reality. This is compelling proof that man invented God and Holy Scriptures. If we hear a human being utter these words we would be appalled, and think we are in the presence of a psychopath**.** If this is not enough proof that this is manmade dogma, **verse 49** should be the clincher, it says:

"The LORD will bring a nation against you, a fierce-looking nation without respect for the old or pity for the young."

Since God is supposed to be the arbiter of principles and morality this requires consistency. So, if such a God was so incensed of being **ignored**, **disobeyed**, and **not served joyfully**, that he threatened horrible consequences, why would he not have a problem with a nation that had no respect for the old or pity for the young? If he was punishing one set of humans for breaking his commandments, he would not send another set of humans who deserve said punishment, to break said commands and decrees by raining terror on another. It also doesn't make sense because he was already threatening, one should assume, the right degree of punishments, and **many of them were beyond human capabilities, therefore any nation would be incapable of fulfilling his threats.** This is the description of an out-of-control maniac and psychopath. This is a fictitious story. This story is likely a basis for the widespread belief that God is to be feared, hence the common phrase, "God-fearing man".

The concept of God is not promoted as a psychopathic being who would cause us to eat our children. He is promoted as a perfect anthropomorphic being. This is a contradiction in terms because human qualities guarantee imperfection. Considering what you have read so far about the many heinous acts of God, the most glaring contradiction of the nature of this invented anthropomorphic God is in **1 John 4:16,** "And we have known and believed the love that God hath to us. **God is love**, and he that dwell in love dwell in God, and God in him."

The contradiction gets intense when we consider Deuteronomy 6:24-25.

"And the LORD commanded us to do all these statutes, to **fear the LORD our God,** for our good always, that **he might preserve us alive**, as it is at this day.

25 And it shall be our righteousness if we observe to do all these commandments before the LORD our God, as he hath commanded us."

So, we are commanded to fear the God of love so that he will **preserve our lives**. And if we do all that he commands us to do it will make us righteous. So, what actions were commanded after Moses laid down these rules? This story is one that particularly obliterates the idea of the Bible being the word of a perfectly loving being, and its words are a moral guide. The only guide it can represent is one for wanton killing. It's only by ignoring logic and rationality that we would accept this narrative as a true story relating to a perfect supreme being who is epitomised by love and mercy. Let's break it down:

Moses lays down God's instructions to God's "holy children" to commit mass slaughter. The same Moses who supposedly received the Ten Commandment from God and one of the commandments forbids killing. These commandments are stated in **Exodus 20:3-17,** and **Deuteronomy 5:7-21**. It's also partly repeated in **Luke 18:20**, "Thou knows the commandments, Do not commit adultery, **Do not kill**, Do not steal, Do not bear false witness, Honour thy father and thy mother."

Despite this, his "Holy People" are commanded to utterly destroy a people who are also his children, as we all are, according to the Bible.

Deuteronomy 7:1-7

"When the LORD thy God shall bring thee into the land whither thou go to possess it, and hath cast out many nations before thee, the Hittites, and the Girgashites, and the Amorites, and the Canaanites, and the Perizzites, and the Hivites, and the Jebusites, seven nations greater and mightier than thou; **2** And when the LORD thy God shall deliver them before thee; **thou shalt smite** them, *and* **utterly destroy them**; thou shalt make no covenant with them, **nor show mercy unto them**: **3** Neither shalt thou make marriages with them; thy daughter thou shalt not give unto his son, nor his daughter shalt thou take unto thy son. **4** For they will turn away thy son from following me, that they may serve other gods: so will the anger of the LORD be kindled against you, and destroy thee suddenly. **5** But thus shall ye deal with them; ye shall destroy their altars, and break down their images, and cut down their groves, and burn their graven images with fire. **6** For thou *art* a holy people unto the LORD thy God: the LORD thy God hath chosen thee to be a special people unto himself, above all people that *are* upon the face of the earth. **7** The LORD did not set his love upon you, nor choose you because ye were more in number than any people; for ye were the fewest of all people."

In this horrific fable, the God of love is commanding his "Holy Children" to commit mass slaughter and take the people's land because they worshipped other gods and idols. Humans currently worship many gods and goddesses and have done so for thousands of years, but we have no record of them being destroyed. This has to be one of the scriptures where we get the idea that it's okay to have holy battles and wars. This is another invented god, like all previous gods, to suit the wants and needs of a people.

People believe the contradictory, evil, immoral, unwise, and ridiculous things the Bible says about a Creator because of the power of socialization. So, the religious accept the concept of an anthropomorphic God, that is, he has some of the same awful standards and qualities as some of us, and sometimes worse. At some point, those who believe in this concept must realise that if a Creator existed his standard would be infinitely higher than ours and nothing like what's in religious texts, a God who is worse than our worse psychopaths.

After Moses received the commandment thou shall not kill, he came down from Mount Sinai and God ordered him to kill 3,000 people for worshipping the Golden Calf. Exodus 32:228

Psychopathic God

Exodus 12:29. And it came to pass, that at midnight the Lord smote all the firstborn in the land of Egypt, from the firstborn of Pharaoh that sat on his throne unto the firstborn of the captive that was in the dungeon; **and all the firstborn of cattle.**

Psalms 137:9 Happy shall he be, that taketh and dashed thy little ones against the stones.

God of revenge, war, and murder

In the context that there have been dozens of gods of war in antiquity, including the period Christianity was installed by the Roman Empire, it shouldn't be surprising that the God of Christianity would also be in favour of wars. Here are a few of the gods of war: **Mars, Ares, Horus, Shiva, Odin, and Yahweh (originally a god of war).** You can give a god any characteristic, they are all mythological.

I Samuel 15:2-6 Thus said the LORD of hosts, I remember *that* which Amalek did to Israel, how he laid *wait* for him in the way, when he came up from Egypt. **3 Now go and smite Amalek, and utterly destroy all that they have, and spare them not; but slay both man and woman, infant and suckling, ox and sheep, camel and ass.** **4** And Saul gathered the people together and numbered them in Telaim, two hundred thousand footmen, and ten thousand men of Judah. **5** And Saul came to the city of Amalek and laid wait in the valley. **6** And Saul said unto the Kenites, Go, depart, get you down from among the Amalekites, lest I destroy you with them: for ye showed kindness to all the children of Israel when they came up out of Egypt. So the Kenites departed from among the Amalekites. **Matthew 10:34-37 Jesus said,** Think not that I am come to send peace on earth: I came not to send peace, but a sword. **35** For I am come to set a man at variance against his father, and the daughter against her mother, and the daughter-in-law against her mother in law. **36** And a man's foes *shall be* they of his own household. **37** He that loves father or mother more than me is not worthy of me: and he that loves son or daughter more than me is not worthy of me. **[This invalidates Christianity's doctrine of Jesus being Prince of Peace.]**

The Lord God of hosts or God of war

The Lord God of hosts means, Lord over earthly or heavenly armies. There are over six thousand references to the Lord of Host in the Bible. If God is Lord over heavenly or earthly armies and armies' purpose is to fight and kill, he is a God of war just like Yahweh was originally, and other gods such as Ares and Mars. Yet, even though the Bible reference Lord God of Host thousands of times, Christians don't regard their God as a God of war despite **Deuteronomy 20:2-4 stating,** And it shall be, when ye are come nigh unto the battle, that the priest shall approach and speak unto the people, **3** And shall say unto them, Hear, O Israel, ye approach this day unto battle against your enemies: let not your hearts faint, fear not, and do not tremble, neither be ye terrified because of them; **4** For the LORD your God is he that goes with you, to fight for you against your enemies, to save you. **Deuteronomy 3:22** Ye shall not fear them: for the LORD your God he shall fight for you.

Deuteronomy 1:29-30, Then I said unto you, Dread not, neither be afraid of them. **30** The LORD your God which go before you, he shall fight for you, according to all that he did for you in Egypt before your eyes. **Deuteronomy 9:3,** Understand therefore this day, that the LORD thy God *is* he which go over before thee; *as* a consuming fire he shall destroy them, and he shall bring them down before thy face: so shalt thou drive them out, and destroy them quickly, as the LORD hath said unto thee. **Exodus 15:3,** The LORD *is* a man of war: the LORD *is* his name. **Psalm 144:1,** (*A Psalm* of David.) Blessed be the LORD my strength, which teaches my hands to war, and my fingers to fight:

Exodus 32:27-29 27 And he said unto them, Thus said the LORD God of Israel, Put every man his sword by his side, and go in and out from gate to gate throughout the camp, and slay every man his brother, and every man his companion, and every man his neighbour. **28** And the children of Levi did according to the word of Moses: and there fell of the people that day about three thousand men. **29**

For Moses had said, Consecrate yourselves today to the LORD, even every man upon his son, and upon his brother; that he may bestow upon you a blessing this day.

The Bible of Bible by Kersey Graves 1870 "These injunctions to murder and slaughter have been faithfully obeyed, and the effect has been to submerge Christendom in a sea of blood. Look for proof at the war among the churches for many years about the doctrine of the Eucharist, which resulted in the destruction of three hundred thousand lives; the fight about images[37], in which fifty thousand men, women, and children were murdered; the war of a dozen churches against the sect of the Manicheans in the ninth century (A.D. 845) about some trivial doctrine of the Christian creed, and which left on the battlefield no less than a hundred thousand murdered human beings; the church schism, in the time of John Huss and Jerome of Prague, followed by the war of the Hussites, which resulted in a bloody slaughter of a hundred and fifty thousand fellow Christians; the war known as "The Holy Inquisition," established in the year 1208, made a record in its history of human butchery of two hundred thousand Christian professors, who had to atone in blood for assuming the liberty to differ from the popular creed; and finally, the thirty Years' war which strewed the earth with bloody corpses to the frightful number of five millions of human beings. **The whole makes a sum total of eighteen million**, a large portion of which were Christian professors – all the work of Christian hands and Christian churches, professed followers of the "Prince of peace."

How can scriptures such as these not have an immoral effect on the minds of adherents to a varying degree throughout history? Is it an accident that the religious world has a long history of violence?

---

[37] This is likely to do with **Iconoclastic Controversy**, a dispute over the use of religious images (icons) in the Byzantine Empire in the 8th and 9th centuries.

A few scriptures on Lord of hosts

Zechariah 8:14 For thus said the LORD of hosts; As I thought to punish you, when your fathers provoked me to wrath, said the LORD of hosts, and I repented not: **Jeremiah 46:10** For this *is* the day of the Lord GOD of hosts, a day of vengeance, that he may avenge him of his adversaries: and the sword shall devour, and it shall be satiate and made drunk with their blood: for the Lord GOD of hosts hath a sacrifice in the north country by the river Euphrates. **Isaiah 51:15** But I *am* the LORD thy God, that divided the sea, whose waves roared: The LORD of hosts *is* his name. **Isaiah 1:24** Therefore said the Lord, the LORD of hosts, the mighty One of Israel, Ah, I will ease me of mine adversaries, and avenge me of mine enemies:

The Bible is not a moral Guide

Would someone qualify as a mentor if they advocate good precepts and evil precepts at the same time? The obvious answer is no. Would you allow such a person to guide your children? The answer is no, and therefore this should disqualify the Bible as a moral guide.

To accept that the following scriptures are suited to be in a book that is supposed to be a moral guide and attributed to an infinitely intelligent, rational, merciful, kind, and loving God, (our divine parent), requires ignoring our understanding of these words. This is especially true if we attribute them to a Holy Father. If the Bible was written by an author in the current time, no publisher would be interested because of its poor standard. However, because it's believed to come from a divine source, its often unintelligibility, nonsensicality, and silliness are ignored and tolerated – a truly astonishing phenomenon. The following is just a smidgen of the hundreds of errors, silly stories, contradictions, and immoralities that are in the Bible. An extensive list and explanation of this can be found in, The Bible of Bibles, by Kersey Graves.

Revelation 17:15 And he said unto me, The waters which thou saw, where the whore sits, are peoples, and multitudes, and nations, and tongues.

Jeremiah 3:3 Therefore the showers have been withholding, and there hath been no latter rain, and thou has a whore's forehead, thou refuses to be ashamed.

Why are these scriptures in a Holy Book?

Since the Bible is regarded as the word of God and its purpose is to guide humanity, all its scriptures should serve this purpose. So, any story that believers are not advised to treat as a warning, and to avoid such actions because God disapproves, the reader would have no reason not to accept it as morally correct. This is especially true if the actions are attributed to God or Jesus. This is why whenever any scripture is criticised, the devotee's response is usually, "Who am I to question God."

Jesus restores two Demon-Possessed men – an immoral story NIV

Matthew 8:28-34 When he arrived at the other side in the region of the Gadarenes, two demon-possessed men coming from the tombs met him. They were so violent that no one could pass that way. **29** "What do you want with us, Son of God?" they shouted. "Have you come here to torture us before the appointed time?" **30** Some distance from them a large herd of pigs was feeding. **31 The demons begged Jesus, "If you drive us out, send us into the herd of pigs."** **32** He said to them, "Go!" So they came out and went into the pigs, and the whole herd rushed down the steep bank into the lake and died in the water. **33** Those tending the pigs ran off, went into the town, and reported all this, including what had happened to the demon-possessed men. **34** Then the whole town went out to meet Jesus. And when they saw him, they pleaded with him to leave their region. [**It should not be possible to glean morality from this story but believers don't see immorality in any action attributed to their God or his son. Jesus granted the wishes of the demons and enabled them to kill a herd of pigs when he should be able to destroy demons. This story makes no sense**]

Mark 12:19 Master, Moses wrote unto us, If a man's brother dies, and leave his wife behind him, and leave no children, that his brother should take his wife, and raise up seed unto his brother.

Genesis 38:8-10 And Judah said unto Onan, Go in unto thy brother's wife, and marry her, and raise up seed to thy brother. **9** And Onan knew that the seed should not be his; and it came to pass, when he went in unto his brother's wife, that he spilled *it* on the ground, lest that he should give seed to his brother.

10 And the thing which he did displease the LORD: wherefore he slew him also.

There is no ambiguity in the above scripture because God took decisive action to finalise it. The message is clear, a man is obligated to marry and impregnate his brother's widow if they had no children, and if he practiced safe sex God will kill him. Accepting this story as being true can do damage to a person's rational and moral compass, and affect growth and development.

Leviticus 20:15-16 And if a man lies with a beast, he shall surely be put to death: and ye shall slay the beast. **16** And if a woman approaches unto any beast, and lie down thereto, thou shalt kill the woman, and the beast: they shall surely be put to death; their blood shall be upon them.

Even if we accept the ridiculous idea that even minor things that are regarded as "sin" can result in death, it makes no sense that an all-wise infinitely intelligent God would want the innocent beasts killed.

Exodus 4:21-26

21 The LORD said to Moses, "When you return to Egypt, see that you perform before Pharaoh all the wonders I have given you the power to do. But I will harden his heart so that he will not let the people go. **22** Then say to Pharaoh, 'This is what the LORD says: Israel is my firstborn son, **23** and I told you, "Let my son go, so he may worship me." But you refused to let him go; so I will kill your firstborn son.'" **24** At a lodging place on the way, the LORD met Moses and was about to kill him. **25** But Zipporah took a flint knife, cut off her son's foreskin, and touched Moses' feet with it. "Surely you are a bridegroom of blood to me," she said. **26** So the LORD let him alone. (At that time she said "bridegroom of blood," referring to circumcision.)

The above scriptures defy all logic and reason. The most astonishing thing is that people read this story and accept it as inspired by an infinitely intelligent being when it should not qualify as a real story. It claims God wanted Moses to ask Pharaoh to let his children go. However, he hardened Pharaoh's heart so that he refused. Moses should then tell Pharaoh God will kill his firstborn son because he refused. God then wanted to kill Moses for an unknown reason. This could legitimise wanton killing since God had an impulse to kill without reason. And as is common in Bible texts, the story degenerates into gobbledygook in verses 25 and 26.

Examples of other nonsensical scriptures

Matthew 8:21-22

New International Version

21 Another disciple said to him, "Lord, first let me go and bury my father." **22** But Jesus told him, "Follow me and let the dead bury their own dead." **Romans 8:38-39** "For I am convinced that neither death nor life, neither angels nor demons, neither the present nor the future, nor any powers, neither height nor depth, nor anything else in all creation, will be able to separate us from the love of God that is in Christ Jesus our Lord." **Based on this we can all relax and fear nothing, right?**

Because of the belief that the Bible is from a divine source, the suspension of reasoning and reasonableness is quite common when believers feel compelled to justify scriptures that don't make sense. For example, a man was told the story in the above **Matthew 8:21-22** which is a philosophy observed in our time by people who didn't believe in attending funerals. He was asked repeatedly if it makes sense, and he repeatedly said "No, the dead cannot bury the dead." The moment he was told that Jesus said it originally, in a Nanosecond he was attempting to apply meaning to it.

Even though it's mind-bending that an infinitely intelligent being who created all things welcomes the sacrifices of his animal creations, it deteriorates even more. Based on the following scripture God likes salt with his "offerings"

KJV Leviticus 2:13 And every oblation of thy meat offering shalt thou season with salt; neither shalt thou suffer the salt of the covenant of thy God to be lacking from thy meat offering: with all thine offerings thou shalt offer salt.

Silly customs and a few of many Bible contradictions

Should we grow our hair? 1 Corinthians, 11:14 doth not even nature teach you, that, if a man has long hair, it is a shame unto him? **Leviticus 21:5** KJV – They shall not make baldness upon their head, neither shall they shave off the corner of their beard, nor make any cuttings in their flesh. **Ezekiel 44:20** KJV – Neither shall they shave their heads nor suffer their locks to grow long; they shall only poll their heads. **[What?] Numbers 6:5** All the days of the vow of his separation there shall no razor come upon his head: until the days be fulfilled, in the which he separates *himself* unto the LORD, he shall be holy, *and* shall let the locks of the hair of his head grow. [A man is holy if he let his locks grow] **1 Corinthians 11:14-15 Does not even nature itself teach you, that, if a man has long hair, it is a shame unto him**? **15** But if a woman has long hair, it is a glory to her: for *her* hair is given her for a covering. **New International Version Leviticus 21:5** Priests must not shave their heads or shave off the edges of their beards or cut their bodies.

Is laughter good?

Ecclesiastes 3:4 Yes. A time to weep, and **a time to laugh**; a time to mourn, and a time to dance; **5** A time to cast away stones, and a time to gather stones together; a time to embrace, and a time to refrain from embracing; **Ecclesiastes 8:15. Yes.** Then I commended mirth, because a man hath no better thing under the sun than to eat, and to drink, and to be merry: for that shall abide with him of his labour the days of his life, which God giveth him under the sun. **Ecclesiastes 7:3-4. No.** Sorrow *is* better than laughter: for by the sadness of the countenance the heart is made better. **4** The heart of the wise is in the house of mourning, but the heart of fools is in the house of mirth.

Is hatred good?

No. 1 John 3:15 Whosoever hates his brother is a murderer: and ye know that no murderer hath eternal life abiding in him.

Yes. Luke 14:26 If any man comes to me, and hate not his father, and mother, and wife, and children, and brethren, and sisters, yea, and his own life also, he cannot be my disciple. [There is nothing ambiguous about this scripture but adherents have spin doctored it for it to be acceptable by claiming it's a metaphor. An all-wise God chose not to use plain language but say the opposite of what he meant?]

Is anger recommended?

Yes. Ephesians 4:26-27 Be ye angry, and sin not: let not the sun go down upon your wrath: **27** Neither give place to the devil.

No. Ecclesiastes 7:9 Be not hasty in thy spirit to be angry: for anger rests in the bosom of fools.

Shall the righteous and just be happy?

Yes. Proverbs 12:21 There shall no evil happen to the just: but the wicked shall be filled with mischief.

No. Acts 14:22 Confirming the souls of the disciples and exhorts them to continue in the faith, and that we must through **much tribulation enter into the kingdom of God.**

Shall the righteous flourish or perish?

Psalm 92:12 The righteous shall flourish like the palm tree: he shall grow like a cedar in Lebanon.

Isaiah 57:1 The righteous perish, and no man lays *it* to heart: and merciful men *are* taken away, none considering that the righteous is taken away from the evil *to come.*

Romans 3:10 As it is written, **There is none righteous**, no, not one:

Exodus 23:7 Keep thee far from a false matter; and **the innocent and righteous slay thou not**: for I will not justify the wicked.

The immoral God - Endorsement of slavery – 3 translations but scripture no less immoral

King James Version – 1 Corinthians 7:22 For he that is called in the Lord, being a servant, is the Lord's freeman: likewise, also he that is called, being free, is Christ's servant.

New International Version For the one who was a slave when called to faith in the Lord is the Lord's freed person; similarly, the one who was free when called is Christ's slave.

New Living Translation And remember, if you were a slave when the Lord called you, you are now free in the Lord. And if you were free when the Lord called you, you are now a slave of Christ.

King James Version Exodus 21:20-21

20. And if a man smites his servant, or his maid, with a rod, and he dies under his hand; he shall be surely punished. **21.** Notwithstanding, if he continues a day or two, he shall not be punished: for he is his money

New World Translation

20. And in case a man strikes his slave man or his slave girl with a stick and that one actually dies under his hand, that one is to be avenged without fail **21.** However, if he lingers for a day or two days, he is not to be avenged, because he is his money.

New International Version

20. Anyone who beats their male or female slave with a rod must be punished if the slave dies as a direct result, **21** but they are not to be punished if the slave recovers after a day or two since the slave is their property. . **[If the person survives a day or two there will be no punishment? The awfulness of this is hard to put into words]**

Jesus promotes the idea that Demons cause diseases

Matthew 17:14-20

14 When they came to the crowd, a man approached Jesus and knelt before him. **15** "Lord, have mercy on my son," he said. "He has seizures and is suffering greatly. He often falls into the fire or into the water. **16** I brought him to your disciples, but they could not heal him." **17** "You unbelieving and perverse generation," Jesus replied, "How long shall I stay with you? How long shall I put up with you? Bring the

boy here to me." **18** Jesus rebuked the demon, and it came out of the
boy, and he was healed at that moment. **19** Then the disciples came
to Jesus in private and asked, "Why couldn't we drive it out?" **20** He
replied, "Because you have so little faith. Truly I tell you, if you have faith as small as a mustard seed, you can say to this mountain, 'Move from here to there,' and it will move. Nothing will be impossible for you." [Many still believe in demons and that they can cause diseases. So, scriptures like these do not lift our growth and development]

Matthew 10:5-8

5 These twelve Jesus sent out with the following instructions: "Do
not go among the Gentiles or enter any town of the Samaritans. **6** Go
rather to the lost sheep of Israel. **7** As you go, proclaim this message:
'The kingdom of heaven has come near. **8** Heal the sick, raise the
dead, cleanse those who have leprosy, and drive out demons. Freely you have received; freely give. **[What?]**

The Bible's Unfulfilled promise

Luke 12:28-32 28 If then God so clothes the grass, which is today in
the field, and tomorrow is cast into the oven; how much more will he
clothe you, O ye of little faith? **29** And seek not ye what ye shall eat,
or what ye shall drink, neither be ye of doubtful mind. **30** For all these
things do the nations of the world seek after: and your Father knoweth
that ye have need of these things. **31** But rather seek ye the kingdom
of God, and all these things shall be added unto you. **32** Fear not, little flock; for it is your Father's good pleasure to give you the kingdom.

A brief synopsis of an anthropomorphic God with our worst deficiencies magnified

God is claimed to be so emotionally driven that he:

Impulsively kills for no apparent reason or a reason not applied to anyone else.

Exodus 4:24 At a lodging place on the way, the LORD met Moses and was about to kill him.

Chronicles 2:3 claims: "And Er, the firstborn of Judah, was evil in the sight of the LORD; and he slew him" [Lots of evil people live long lives]

Can be extremely jealous A people cannot grow to maximum capacity if they believe the force behind the universe is the same or of a lower standard than we are.

Three characteristics of Jealousy – an unrealistic expectation about a relationship, low self-esteem, and strong feelings of unhappiness when feeling betrayed.

Exodus 34:14, "For thou shalt worship no other god: for the Lord, whose name is Jealous, is a jealous God." So, how does the Bible claims God reacts when he is jealous?

Exodus 32:7-10

And the LORD said unto Moses, Go, get thee down; for thy people, which thou brought out of the land of Egypt, have corrupted
themselves: **8** They have turned aside quickly out of the way which I
commanded them: **they have made them a molten calf, and have
worshipped it**, and have sacrificed thereunto, and said, These be thy
gods, O Israel, which have brought thee up out of the land of Egypt.
9 And the LORD said unto Moses, I have seen these people, and,
behold, it is a stiffnecked people: **10** Now, therefore, let me alone,
that my wrath may wax hot against them, and that I may consume
them: and I will make of thee a great nation.

This anger and unhappiness led to:

Exodus 32:26-28

Then Moses stood at the gate of the camp, and said, Who is on the LORD'S side? Let him come unto me. And all the sons of Levi gathered themselves together unto him. **27** And he said unto them, Thus said the LORD God of Israel, Put every man his sword by his side, *and* go in and out from gate to gate throughout the camp, and slay every man his brother, and every man his companion, and every man his neighbour. **28** And the children of Levi did according to the word of Moses: and there fell of the people that day about **three thousand men.**

Is there any human being who would order the killing of 3,000 men because of jealousy, unless they were mentally challenged?

The religious believe the force behind life and the universe is so emotionally charged and intolerant, and yet do not have the urge to talk to humanity for the past 2000 years even though there are so many things we do that he hates?

CHAPTER SEVEN

Final thoughts – God does nothing for humanity

After getting to the age of reason and realising the obvious fallacy of religion, there is a question that has been asked of a few religious adherents, and no definitive answer has been given. The question is, what role does God play in their daily lives? They were then asked to provide a list. The rationale is that, since they are inviting others to join, there should be some benefits that are not based on something they can't prove, such as a belief in events after we die.

Even though no list of benefits has been provided, ever so often people make claims that they attributed to God. These claims suggest that they have not applied a great deal of reasoning to what they believe. For example, they suggest that we should give God thanks for waking up in the morning. They are inadvertently claiming that God decides whether we wake up or not, which is the same as saying God decides whether we live or die, therefore, on occasion, he kills some of us, or circumvents the Law of Cause and Effect, and make us not die. Since a lot of evil people wake up every morning and some good people don't, how would they rationalise this?

Let's say it is a reality that a person can have a personal relationship with someone they call God, the most powerful force in the universe; if this person was endangering their life by eating harmful foods; would you not expect this God to alert them to this danger? In reality, in the main, religious people die because of eating-related diseases as much as those who are not religious. What does this tell us?

If there is a God who speaks to humanity, one would not expect it to be a trivial conversation that we often have with others to pass the time. We would expect that definitive information about the major issues that affect our lives would be imparted. Definitive information on how to be healthy, happy, have good relationships, and be successful would be communicated. However, in the context of the belief that God is the parent of humanity, it makes no sense that God would talk to just one person, or a few because they claim the Bible is a divine revelation to all people. So, God would talk to all of us, not just a few persons, and leave the rest of us wondering if they are lying or having mental issues.

The requirement of shaping our own lives has proved too much for many, because they have been trained not to accept responsibility for life's events, and because there is a dominant religious philosophy that teaches that we do not control our destinies. We have not been indoctrinated to view the peaks and troughs of life as necessary for us to grow and develop, and we control how we respond to these experiences. Consequently, this belief in a lack of control has driven many to despair. The placing in the consciousness of a belief in separate forces called 'good' and 'evil' has proven onerous to many of us growth and development because this is a contradicting philosophy. On one hand, we have desires to be happy, healthy, and successful and we know that we have to physically work to make it happen; on the other hand, we're taught that our destinies are at best 'influenced' by these external forces of 'good' and 'evil'. At worse, we are taught that *everything* is in the 'hands' of 'God' or controlled by the 'Devil' and not in our control. With such contradicting philosophies, it's no wonder the world has so many confused and disempowered people, and many live lives of quiet desperation. A contradicting understanding of how life works is disempowering and cannot foster successful living

Thoughts can heal our bodies. It can make us sick and it makes us happy or sad. It is everything! This is the glory of *thought,* so let nobody tell you not to think. The best kind of *thought* is free-thinking; not conditioned beliefs. Reject all philosophies that encourage blind submission to any creed. Listen to everybody but do your own thinking and arrive at your own conclusions. Your actions should be the end product of the contemplation of all the teachings, observations, life experiences, and intuition. This should never be your philosophy: "Someone said to believe or do X therefore I will believe and do X".

Just as there are predators in the wild, the human world has many who wish to control and live off the resources of others. We all have the choice of either being controlled and led by others or living on a co-operative equal basis with everybody.

Our mind is what makes us human and this is inherited almost incomplete. We have to learn to do almost everything such as, eat, walk and talk, but the most complex is that we have to learn how to think and how to think is a skill we'll never completely master. There is analytical thinking, deductive thinking, and inductive thinking, and the most difficult are creative thinking and wisdom. No one knows the limit of the mind. It seems that this 'mind substance' called thinking is something we can 'mould' in any way we choose. It seems to be like electricity which is part of the *unlimited* fabric of *Nature*. It's never in limited supply and once we have learned how to think our minds will never be the same as at birth. However, we're all aware of people losing this faculty in the form of senility or other neurological defects. From our experience we learn that the mind needs exercise; it has to be stimulated into action. The disparity between humans is partly due to the quality of the mental food that the mind is fed. The food of the mind is words and ideas. If the mind is inadequately fed it tends to shrink and our emotions will then take centre stage. We have all seen the consequences of unchecked emotions. The one thing we can be sure of is that whether it is healthy or unhealthy, the mind will produce something. This is in harmony with the universe as nothing ever stands still, and in the case of the mind, an absence of knowledge will be filled with impressions that are translated into feelings. Feelings are inadequate for complex matters.

A child who is not adequately stimulated will never properly develop. We need mental food. However, poor nutrition can affect the function of the mind as we're holistic beings; the mind, body, and spirit (life energy) work best when they work in harmony.

Because we live in a universe that is based on precise natural laws and there is an absence of vagueness, it is beneficial if we train our minds to think with precision as is the order of the universe. Since everything about our natural world is precise, then the *fabric of us is* of the same characteristic. So the more we train our minds to harmonise with the Intelligent Universe, the more we will be as one with the *energy that sustains us.* Therefore, let's seek clarity on this most important subject; our quest to be in harmony with that which is real. Here are some questions for the undecided to ponder, and help fresh minds to understand how reality works:

- Does 'God' keep us healthy?
- Does 'God' make us successful?
- Does 'God' protect us?
- Does 'God' make us happy?

The informed would know that life is governed by the universal law of cause and effect. So, good health is the result of learning and practicing the causes of health – both mind and body. They would also know that success is also governed by the principle of cause and effect, identifying the factors that lead to success, and setting them in motion – like the basics of having a plan and setting goals. We can easily scratch the idea of protection from a Deity because we have observed innumerable killings of babies and children and even the religious in their place of worship.

We can disregard many of the instructions or admonitions in religious books and sufferer no consequence in our lifetime. However if we disregard the sciences and principles that govern our existence we are guaranteed to suffer consequences in our lifetime. For example, if we disregard gravity and step off a high place, the result is uncompromising and immediate. If we disregard the science of our body and consistently put the wrong things in it there will be negative consequences.

Happiness is an internal affair, that is, it is largely based on our interpretation of life and our experiences. Enduring happiness grows after designing a life from our capacity to paint a mental picture of a future that we look forward to with anticipation, a lifestyle we are moving towards, and have the confidence that we can attain it – a future we can be happy about. The process of taking action to bring this vision of the future into reality excites our senses.

And finally, how fortunate we are that Governments and our courts don't believe in the Bible. Leaders swear on it to take up office, and the public swears on it to testify in court. Yet, its fundamental message, a belief in God and the Devil is not recognised as a basis for a crime. If a person went to court and claim that God or the Devil made them do it, they would be locked up with the criminally insane. At most, one can claim diminished responsibility. Politicians passed these laws. So, if they thought God and the Devil were viable causes of crimes, they would put it in the law. We should be grateful that law enforcement does not have the unenviable task of tracking down evil spirits for crimes. This is a contradiction we should welcome, they swear on the Bible, lock you up if you lied after swearing on it, but do not take its significance or contents any further.

Nature cannot be separated from whatever is responsible for existence. It has to be in harmony with it, just like everything that exists is. Nature and everything else has to operate in harmony with the source and cause of existence. So, if nature doesn't agree with our concept of reality it's not valid. We are the only creatures that can imagine that which does not exist. When we create things we first imagine them. However, we cannot imagine or will an infinitely intelligent being into existence. If we could, we would be physically acquainted with such a being already, and would not need to believe, we would know. Over centuries, we have imagined thousands or perhaps millions of such beings but none have ever materialised, and we call those old gods, myths.

The universe and nature do not have manmade moral codes like Christianity, Hinduism, Islam, etc. They simply reward those who follow their rules. The universal rule is cause and effect. We set in motion through our thoughts and actions our outcomes, good, bad, or indifferent.

Some of what we call sins are ideas in our minds and not recognised by the rules or laws we choose to live by. Claimed moral issues, such as having sex before marriage and envy, are not laws the universe has shown any response to. These are imaginary infractions we invented. We have built-in aversions against stealing, murder, and being accused wrongfully because we do not want these things to happen to us. So, we create laws to punish them.

Believing in an invisible being can cause us to become lazy and give up our responsibility to take control of our lives, and blame the imaginary Satan when we fail. The philosopher, Jim Rohn, suggested that the story of Adam and Eve taught us not to take responsibility for our actions. God blamed the man, the man blamed the woman, and the woman blamed the serpent.

ADDENDUM

Bible references to Hell

Mark 9:47 And if thine eye offend thee, pluck it out: it is better for thee to enter into the kingdom of God with one eye, than having two eyes to be **cast into hell fire: [What is the offence?]**

Matthew 5:22 But I say unto you, that whosoever is angry with his brother without a cause shall be in danger of the judgment[38]: and whosoever shall say to his brother, Raca, shall be in danger of the council: but whosoever shall say, Thou fool, shall be in danger of hell fire.

Matthew 10:28 And fear not them which kill the body, but are not able to kill the soul: but rather fear him which is able to destroy both soul and body in hell. **[Seems to be the same as Luke 12:5.** The **body** will be in hell and destroyed by God?]

Matthew 5:29 And if thy right eye offend thee, pluck it out, and cast it from thee: for it is profitable for thee that one of thy members should perish, and not that thy whole body should be cast into hell. **[What?]**

Matthew 11:23 And thou, Capernaum, which art exalted unto heaven, shalt be brought down to hell: for if the mighty works, which have been done in thee, had been done in Sodom, it would

[38] So, Jesus is introducing the thought "crime" of being angry with a brother without a cause, and the punishment will be hell fire.

have remained until this day. **[What? Another example of a poorly written book that could not have been written by an intelligent author much less an infinitely intelligent being]**

Matthew 16:18 And I say also unto thee, That thou art Peter, and upon this rock I will build my church; and the gates of hell shall not prevail against it. **[What? Hell shall not survive the church?]**

Matthew 23:15 Woe unto you, scribes and Pharisees, hypocrites! for ye compass sea and land to make one proselyte, and when he is made, ye make him twofold more **the child of hell** than yourselves. **[What?]**

Matthew 23:33 Ye serpents, ye generation of vipers, how can ye escape the damnation of hell?

Mark 9:45 And if thy foot offend thee, cut it off: it is better for thee to enter halt into life, than having two feet to be cast into hell, into the fire that never shall be quenched: **[What is the offence?]**

Isaiah 14:15 Yet thou shalt be brought down to hell, to the sides of the pit

Deuteronomy 32:22 For a fire is kindled in mine anger, and shall burn unto the lowest hell, and shall consume the earth with her increase, and set on fire the foundations of the mountains. **[What?]**

Luke 10:15 And thou, Capernaum, which art exalted to heaven, shalt be thrust down to hell.

Proverbs 5:5 Her feet go down to death; her steps take hold on hell. **[What?]**

Psalms 18:5 The sorrows of hell compassed me about: the snares of death prevented me. **[What?]**

Proverbs 7:27 Her house is the way to hell, going down to the chambers of death. **[What?]**

Proverbs 15:24 The way of life is above to the wise, that he may depart from hell beneath. **[What? How can one depart from hell if it's the consequence of the final judgement, and this hasn't happened yet?]**

Proverbs 15:11 Hell and destruction are before the LORD: how much more than the hearts of the children of men? **[What?]**

Proverbs 27:20 Hell and destruction are never full; so the eyes of man are never satisfied**. [What?]**

Psalms 116:3 The sorrows of death compassed me, and **the pains of hell** got hold upon me: I found trouble and sorrow. [**This is a living person, a dead person doesn't have trouble and sorrow, and the myth of judgment day is a future event**]

2 Peter 2:4 For if God spared not the angels that sinned, but cast them down to hell, and delivered them into chains of darkness, to be reserved unto judgment; **[A contradiction? Punishment before judgement?]**

Psalms 139:8 If I ascend up into heaven, thou art there: if I make my bed in hell, behold, thou art there**. [What?]**

Amos 9:2 Though they **dig into hell**, thence shall mine hand take them; though they climb up to heaven, thence will I bring them down: **[What**]

Isaiah 5:14 Therefore hell hath enlarged herself, and opened her mouth without measure: and their glory, and their multitude, and their pomp, and he that rejoiced, shall descend into it**. [What?]**

Luke 12:5 But I will forewarn you whom ye shall fear: Fear him, which **after he hath killed hath power to cast into hell;** yea, I say unto you, Fear him. **[Someone who has killed gain power to cast into hell, who?]**

Isaiah 28:18 And your covenant with death shall be disannulled, and your agreement with hell shall not stand; when the overflowing scourge shall pass through, then ye shall be trodden down by it. **[What? Someone can have an agreement with hell?]**

Habakkuk 2:5 Yea also, because he transgressed by wine, he is a proud man, neither kept at home, who enlarges his desire as hell, and is as death, and cannot be satisfied, but gathered unto him all nations, and heaped unto him all people: **[What?]**

James 3:6 And the tongue is a fire, a world of iniquity: so is the tongue among our members, that it defiles the whole body, and set on fire the course of nature; and it is set on fire of hell. **[What?]**

Ezekiel 31:17 They also went down into hell with him unto them that be slain with the sword; and they that were his arm, that dwelt under his shadow in the midst of the heathen. **[What?]**

Isaiah 28:15 Because ye have said, We have made a covenant with death, **and with hell are we at agreement**; when the overflowing scourge shall pass through, it shall not come unto us: for we have made lies our refuge, and under falsehood have we hid ourselves: **[What?]**

Ezekiel 31:16 I made the nations to shake at the sound of his fall, when I cast him down to hell with them that descend into the pit: and all the trees of Eden, the choice and best of Lebanon, all that drink water, shall be comforted in the nether parts of the earth. **[What?]**

Revelation 20:13 And the sea gave up the dead which was in it; and death and hell delivered up the dead which was in them: and they were judged every man according to their works. **[What? They were in hell before judgement? This must be on earth]**

Revelation 6:8 And I looked, and behold a pale horse: and his name that sat on him was Death, and Hell followed with him. And power was given unto them over the fourth part of the earth, to kill with sword, and with hunger, and with death, and with the beasts of the earth. **[To kill with death? What?]**

Ezekiel 32:27 And they shall not lie with the mighty that are fallen of the uncircumcised, which are gone down to hell with their weapons of war: and they have laid their swords under their heads, but their iniquities shall be upon their bones, though they were the terror of the mighty in the land of the living. **[What?]**

Psalms 86:13 For great *is* thy mercy toward me: and thou hast delivered my soul from the lowest hell. [What? This is a living person. Religious dogma claims hell happens after Judgment day]

The scriptural basis of "God moves in mysterious ways."

Romans 11:33

O the depth of the riches both of the wisdom and knowledge of God! How unsearchable are his judgements, and his ways past finding out!

Isiah 40:28

Has thou not known? Has thou not heard, that the everlasting God, the Lord, the Creator of the ends of the earth, fainted not, neither is weary? There is no searching of his understanding.

Isiah 55:8-9

For my thoughts are not your thoughts, neither are your ways my ways, said the Lord. 9. For as the heavens are higher than the earth, so are my ways higher than your ways, and my thoughts than your thoughts.

Ephesians 3:4 Whereby, when ye read, ye may understand my knowledge in the mystery of Christ (We may understand?)

Ephesians 5:32 This is a great mystery: but I speak concerning Christ and the church.

1 Timothy 3:9 Holding the mystery of the faith in a pure conscience.

Colossians 4:3 Withal praying also for us, that God would open unto us a door of utterance, to speak the mystery of Christ, for which I am also in bonds:

Revelation 10:7 But in the days of the voice of the seventh angel, when he shall begin to sound, the mystery of God should be finished, as he hath declared to his servants the prophets. (God is a mystery?)

Ephesians 6:19 And for me, that utterance may be given unto me, that I may open my mouth boldly, to make known the mystery of the gospel. (So, the Gospel was written as a mystery, why?)

1 Corinthians 2:7 But we speak the wisdom of God in a mystery, even the hidden wisdom, which God ordained before the world unto our glory:

Colossians 2:2 That their hearts might be comforted, being knit together in love, and unto all riches of the full assurance of understanding, to the acknowledgement of the mystery of God, and of the Father, and of Christ; (How would being mysterious edify us?)

Mark 4:11 And he said unto them, Unto you it is given to know the mystery of the kingdom of God: but unto them that are without, all these things are done in parables: (For the masses it's in parables?)

Claims of God speaking to us in various ways

Genesis 26:5 Because that Abraham obeyed my voice, and kept my charge, my commandments, my statutes, and my laws.

Exodus 19:5 Now therefore, if ye will obey my voice indeed, and keep my covenant, then ye shall be a peculiar treasure unto me above all people: for all the earth is mine:

Joel 3:16 The LORD also shall roar out of Zion, and utter his voice from Jerusalem; and the heavens and the earth shall shake: but the LORD will be the hope of his people, and the strength of the children of Israel.

Joel 2:11 And the LORD shall utter his voice before his army: for his camp is very great: for he is strong that executes his word: for the day of the LORD is great and very terrible; and who can abide it?

Exodus 3:4-8

4 And when the LORD saw that he turned aside to see, God called unto him out of the midst of the bush, and said, Moses, Moses. And he said, Here *am* I.

5 And he said, Draw not nigh hither: put off thy shoes from off thy feet, for the place whereon thou stands *is* holy ground.

6 Moreover he said, I *am* the God of thy father, the God of Abraham, the God of Isaac, and the God of Jacob. And Moses hid his face; for he was afraid to look upon God.

7 And the LORD said, I have surely seen the affliction of my people which *are* in Egypt, and have heard their cry by reason of their taskmasters; for I know their sorrows;

8 And I am come down to deliver them out of the hand of the Egyptians, and to bring them up out of that land unto a good land and a large, unto a land flowing with milk and honey; unto the place of the Canaanites, and the Hittites, and the Amorites, and the Perizzites, and the Hivites, and the Jebusites.

Bible characters, tradition, historical or spurious claims?

A real story endorsed and established by the powerful Roman Empire would not be filled with characters based on tradition, and not history. As you will see in the narratives below, the characters closely related to the Jesus story are either accredited to tradition, scriptures, or "spurious" claims. There are no firm historical claims. Here are the twelve disciples and others:

1. first, Simon, who is called Peter,
2. and Andrew his brother;
3. James the son of Zebedee,
4. and John his brother;
5. Philip and
6. Bartholomew;
7. Thomas and
8. Matthew the tax collector;
9. James the son of Alphaeus, and
10. Thaddaeus;
11. Simon the Zealot, and
12. Judas Iscariot, who betrayed him.

Note with interest that all the disciples and others named in the Jesus story are now Saints in the founding Catholic Church, and yet they are not recorded as historical figures. They are not known outside of biblical accounts; the account is sketchy, and sometimes regarded as spurious.

Wikipedia

Alphaeus is a man mentioned in the *New Testament* as the father of two of the Twelve Apostles, namely: Matthew the Evangelist and James, son of Alphaeus. He is implied to be the father of: Joseph or Joses, and in Church **tradition**, he is the father of: Abercius and Helena

Usually, in the Western **Catholic tradition**, there are believed to be two men named Alphaeus. One of them was the father of the apostle James and the other the father of Matthew (Levi). Though both Matthew and James are described as being the "son of Alphaeus," there is no Biblical account of the two being called brothers, even in the same context where John and James or Peter and Andrew are described as being brothers. Despite this, Eastern Church tradition typically states that Matthew and James were brothers.

Encyclopedia Britannica

Judas Iscariot, (died *c.* AD 30), one of the Twelve Apostles, was notorious for betraying Jesus. Judas' surname is more probably a corruption of the Latin *sicarius* ("murderer" or "assassin") than an indication of family origin, suggesting that he would have belonged to the Sicarii, the most radical Jewish group, some of whom were terrorists. Other than his apostleship, his betrayal, and his death, **little else is revealed about Judas in the gospels.**

Encyclopedia Britannica

Judas Thaddaeus

St. Jude is distinguished in John 14:22 as Judas but "not Iscariot" to avoid identification with the betrayer of Jesus, Judas Iscariot. Indeed, the **tradition** of calling him "Jude" rather than the Scriptural "Judas" likely started to avoid such confusion. He is listed in Luke 6:16 and Acts 1:13 as "Judas of James," and, depending on the Bible consulted, he is probably the son (Revised Standard and New English) or brother (Authorized and Douay) of St. James the Less, son of Alphaeus.

Wikipedia

Judas Thaddaeus

Jude (Judas Thaddaeus) was one of the Twelve Apostles of Jesus according to the New Testament. He is generally identified with Thaddeus (and is also variously called Jude of James, Jude Thaddaeus, Judas Thaddaeus, or Lebbaeus. He is sometimes identified with **Jude, the brother of Jesus.**

Encyclopedia Britannica

Simon the Zealot

In the Gospels of Mark and Matthew, he bears the epithet *Kananaios*, or the Cananaean, often wrongly interpreted to mean "from Cana" or "from Canaan." *Kananaios* is the Greek transliteration of an Aramaic word, *qan*ʾ *anaya*, meaning "the Zealot," the title given him by Luke in his Gospel_and in Acts. It is uncertain whether he was one of the group of Zealots, the Jewish nationalistic party before AD 70. Apparently, the titles may have been an attempt to distinguish him from the apostle St. Simon Peter.

Nothing further is known about him from the New Testament. He supposedly preached the Gospel in Egypt and then joined the apostle St. Judas (Thaddaeus) in Persia, where, according to the apocryphal Acts of Simon and Judas, he was martyred by being cut in half with a saw, one of his chief iconographic symbols (another being a book). According to St. Basil the Great, the 4th-century Cappadocian Father, Simon died peacefully at Edessa.

Wikipedia

Simon the Zealot (Acts 1:13, Luke 6:15) or **Simon the Canaanite** or **Simon the Canaanean** (Matthew 10:4, Mark 3:18; Greek. was one of the most obscure among the apostles of Jesus. A few **pseudepigraphical writings** were connected to him, but Saint Jerome does not include him in De viris illustribus[39] written between 392 and 393 AD.

The name Simon occurs in all of the Synoptic Gospels and the Book of Acts each time there is a list of apostles, without further details.

Encyclopedia Britannica

Saint James

St. James the Less, also called **James, son of Alphaeus,** or **James the Younger**, (flourished 1st century CE; Western feast day May 3; Eastern feast day October 9), one of the Twelve Apostles of Jesus.

James may be he whose mother, Mary (not the mother of Jesus), is mentioned among the women at Jesus' crucifixion and tomb (Mark 15:40, 16:1; Matthew 27:56). He is not to be confused with the apostle St. James the Greater, son of Zebedee, or St. James, the Lord's brother, who was not one of the Twelve. Depending upon the Bible consulted, he is probably the father (Revised Standard and New English) or brother (Authorized and Douay) of the apostle St. Jude

[39] This is significant because **Saint Jerome** was a Christian priest, confessor, theologian, and **historian**. He is best known for his translation of most of the Bible into Latin and he wrote *De viris illustribus* which is a short collection of biographies of 135 authors but it didn't include any work by Thomas. Hence, the justification for suggesting that writings attributed to Simon was pseudepigraphical. A Christian priest and historian would not ignore the work of such a writer.

(Judas, not Iscariot). Nothing further is known of him, and a late legend of his martyrdom in Persia is spurious[40].

Encyclopedia Britannica

Saint Matthew

Other than naming Matthew in the list of Apostles, usually pairing him with St. Thomas, the New Testament offers scant and uncertain information about him. Outside the New Testament, a statement of importance about him is the passage from the Apostolic Father Papias of Hierapolis preserved by Bishop Eusebius of Caesarea: "So then Matthew composed the Oracles in the Hebrew language, and each one interpreted them as he could." The Gospel According to Matthew was certainly written for a Jewish-Christian church in a strongly Jewish environment, but that this Matthew is definitely the Synoptic author is seriously doubted.

Encyclopedia Britannica

Saint Thomas

Thomas's character is outlined in The Gospel According to John. His devotion to Jesus is clearly expressed in John 11:5–16: when Jesus planned to return to Judaea, the disciples warned him of the Jews' animosity ("now seeking to stone you"), to which Thomas soon replied, "Let us also go, that we may die with him." At the Last Supper (John 14:1–7) Thomas could not comprehend what Jesus meant when he said, "I will come again and will take you to myself, that where I am you may be also. And you know the way where I am going." Thomas's question "How can we know the way?" caused Jesus to answer, "I am the way, and the truth, and the life."

---

[40] Not being what it purports to be; false or fake

Perhaps the best-known event in his life is the one from which the phrase "doubting Thomas" developed. In John 20:19–29 he was not among those disciples to whom the risen Christ first appeared, and, when they told the incredulous Thomas, he requested physical proof of the Resurrection, fulfilled when Christ reappeared and specifically asked Thomas to touch his wounds. ***[The Bible claims Thomas was devoted to Jesus, and yet he doubted his resurrection? This suggests that this devoted disciple wasn't told that he was the son of God and he came to die for the sins of mankind, and yet other disciples called him the Son of God – doesn't make any sense. What would be the point of this being a secret? In the context of humanity worshipping many gods and goddesses at the time, it makes no sense for God to send his son to earth and his main strategy wasn't to convince humanity that he represented the one and only true God, as he is currently regarded by Christians.]***

Encyclopedia Britannica

Saint Bartholomew, (flourished 1st century AD—died unknown date, **traditionally** Albanopolis, Armenia; Western feast day August 24; date varies in Eastern churches), one of the Twelve Apostles.

Apart from the mentions of him in four of the Apostle lists (Mark 3:18, Matt. 10:3, Luke 6:14, and Acts 1:13), nothing is known about him from the New Testament. Bartholomew is a family name meaning "son of [Hebrew: *bar*] Tolmai, or Talmai," so he may have had another personal name.

Encyclopedia Britannica

Saint Philip the Apostle, (born, Bethsaida of Galilee—died 1st century; Western feast day May 3, Eastern feast day November 14), one of the Twelve Apostles. Mentioned only by name in the Apostle lists of the Synoptic Gospels, he is ***a frequent character in the Gospel According to John***, according to which (1:43–51) he came from Bethsaida, answered Jesus' call ("Follow me")

Encyclopedia Britannica

St. Andrew, also called **Saint Andrew the Apostle**, (died 60/70 CE, Patras, Achaia [Greece]; feast day November 30), one of the Twelve Apostles of Jesus and the brother of St. Peter. He is the patron saint of Scotland and of Russia. In the Synoptic Gospels (Matthew, Mark, and Luke), Peter and Andrew—whose Greek name means "manly"—were called from their fishing by Jesus to follow him, promising that he would make them "fishers of men." With Saints Peter, James, and John, Andrew asked Jesus on the Mount of Olives for signs of the earth's end, which inspired the eschatological discourse in Mark 13. In The Gospel According to John, Andrew is the first Apostle named, and he was a disciple of St. John the Baptist before Jesus' call.

Encyclopedia Britannica

St. John the Apostle, also called Saint John the Evangelist or Saint John the Divine**,** (flourished 1st century CE; Western feast day December 27; Eastern feast days May 8 and September 26), one of the Twelve Apostles of Jesus and **traditionally** believed to be the author of the three Letters of John, the Fourth Gospel, and possibly the Revelation to John in the New Testament. He played a leading role in the early church in Jerusalem.

John was the son of Zebedee, a Galilean fisherman, and Salome. John and his brother St. James were among the first disciples called by Jesus. In the Gospel According to Mark, he is always mentioned after James and was no doubt the younger brother. His mother was among those women who ministered to the circle of disciples. James and John were called Boanerges, or "sons of thunder," by Jesus, perhaps because of some character trait such as the zeal exemplified in Mark 9:38 and Luke 9:54, when John and James wanted to call down fire from heaven to punish the Samaritan towns that did not accept Jesus. John and his brother, together with St. Peter, formed an inner nucleus of intimate disciples. In the Fourth Gospel, ascribed by early tradition to John and known formally as the Gospel According to John, the sons of Zebedee are mentioned only once, as being at the shores of the Sea of Tiberias when the risen Lord appeared. Whether the "disciple whom Jesus loved" (who is never named) mentioned in this Gospel is to be identified with John (also not named) is not clear from the text.

Encyclopedia Britannica

St. James, also called **James, son of Zebedee**, or **James the Greater**, (born, Galilee, Palestine—died 44 CE, Jerusalem; feast day July 25), one of the Twelve Apostles, distinguished as being in Jesus' innermost circle and the only apostle whose martyrdom is recorded in the New Testament (Acts 12:2).

In **The Gospel According to John,** Andrew is the first Apostle named, and he was a disciple of St. John the Baptist before Jesus' call.

Encyclopedia Britannica

Saint Peter

The sources of information concerning the life of Peter are limited to the New Testament: the four Gospels, Acts, the letters of Paul, and the two letters that bear the name of Peter. He probably was known originally by the Hebrew name Simeon or the Greek form of that name, Simon.

Encyclopedia Britannica

Mary, also called **St. Mary** or **the Virgin Mary**, (flourished beginning of the Christian era), the mother of Jesus, was venerated in the Christian church since the apostolic age and a favourite subject in Western art, music, and literature. Mary is known from biblical references, which are, however, too sparse to construct a coherent biography.

Encyclopedia Britannica

David, (flourished c. 1000 BCE), second king of ancient Israel. He founded the Judaean dynasty and united all the tribes of Israel under a single monarch. His son Solomon expanded the empire that David built. David is an important figure in Judaism, Christianity, and Islam.

The primary evidence for David's career consists of several chapters in the books 1 and 2 Samuel in the Hebrew Bible (Old Testament). The Psalms are also attributed to him, a tribute to his legendary skill as a poet and hymnodist. **Material evidence for his reign, while a matter of intense debate among scholars, is scant.**

Encyclopedia Britannica

St. Joseph, (flourished 1st century CE, Nazareth, Galilee, region of Palestine; principal feast day March 19, Feast of St. Joseph the Worker May 1), in the New Testament, Jesus' earthly father and the Virgin Mary's husband. St. Joseph is the patron of the universal church in Roman Catholicism, and his life is recorded in the Gospels, particularly Matthew and Luke. Joseph was a descendant of the house of King David.

Wikipedia

Joseph (Hebrew, romanized: *Yosef*; Greek) was a 1st-century Jewish man of Nazareth who, according to the canonical Gospels, was married to Mary, the mother of Jesus, and was the legal father of Jesus. **In Catholic traditions**, Joseph is regarded as the patron saint of workers and is associated with various feast days.

Old Testament references to Satan

1 Chronicles 21:1 And Satan stood up against Israel, and provoked David to number Israel. **[What?]**

Job 1:6 Now there was a day when the sons of God came to present themselves before the LORD, and Satan came also among them.

Job 1:7 And the LORD said unto Satan, Whence comes thou? Then Satan answered the LORD, and said, From going to and fro in the earth, and from walking up and down in it.

Job 1:8 And the LORD said unto Satan, Hast thou considered my servant Job, that there is none like him in the earth, a perfect and an upright man, one that fears God, and eschewed evil?

Job 1:12 And the LORD said unto Satan, Behold, all that he hath is in thy power; only upon himself put not forth thine hand. So Satan went forth from the presence of the LORD.

Job 2:3 And the LORD said unto Satan, Hast thou considered my servant Job, that there is none like him in the earth, a perfect and an upright man, one that fears God, and eschewed evil? And still he holds fast his integrity, although thou moved me against him, to destroy him without cause.

Job 2:4 And Satan answered the LORD, and said, Skin for skin, yea, all that a man hath will he give for his life.

Job 2:7 So went Satan forth from the presence of the LORD, and smote Job with sore boils from the sole of his foot unto his crown.

Psalms 109:6 Set thou a wicked man over him: and let Satan stand at his right hand.

Zechariah 3:1 And he shewed me Joshua the high priest standing before the angel of the LORD, and Satan standing at his right hand to resist him.

Zechariah 3:2 And the LORD said unto Satan, The LORD rebuke thee, O Satan; even the LORD that hath chosen Jerusalem rebuke thee: is not this a brand plucked out of the fire? (What?)

New Testament references to Satan

Matthew 4:10 Then said Jesus unto him, Get thee hence, Satan: for it is written, Thou shalt worship the Lord thy God, and him only shalt thou serve.

Matthew 12:26 And if Satan cast out Satan, he is divided against himself; how shall then his kingdom stand?

Matthew 16:23 But he turned, and said unto Peter, Get thee behind me, Satan: thou art an offence unto me: for thou savours not the things that be of God, but those that be of men

Mark 1:13 And he was there in the wilderness forty days, tempted of Satan; and was with the wild beasts; and the angels ministered unto him

Mark 3:23 And he called them unto him, and said unto them in parables, How can Satan cast out Satan?

Mark 3:26 And if Satan rise up against himself, and be divided, he cannot stand, but hath an end.

Mark 4:15 And these are they by the way side, where the word is sown; but when they have heard, Satan cometh immediately, and taketh away the word that was sown in their hearts.

Mark 8:33 But when he had turned about and looked on his disciples, he rebuked Peter, saying, Get thee behind me, Satan: for thou savours not the things that be of God, but the things that be of men. [Jesus called Peter Satan, so, is it a being or a behaviour?]

Luke 4:8 And Jesus answered and said unto him, Get thee behind me, Satan: for it is written, Thou shalt worship the Lord thy God, and him only shalt thou serve.

Luke 10:18 And he said unto them, I beheld Satan as lightning fall from heaven.

Luke 11:18 If Satan also be divided against himself, how shall his kingdom stand? because ye say that I cast out devils through Beelzebub. **[What? How can Satan be divided against himself?]**

Luke 13:16 And ought not this woman, being a daughter of Abraham, whom Satan hath bound, lo, these eighteen years, be loosed from this bond on the Sabbath day? **[What?]**

Luke 22:3 Then entered Satan into Judas surnamed Iscariot, being of the number of the twelve.

Luke 22:31 And the Lord said, Simon, Simon, behold, Satan hath desired to have you, that he may sift you as wheat: **[What?]**

Acts 5:3 But Peter said, Ananias, why hath Satan filled thine heart to lie to the Holy Ghost, and to keep back part of the price of the land?

Acts 26:18 To open their eyes, and to turn them from darkness to light, and from the power of Satan unto God, that they may receive forgiveness of sins, and inheritance among them which are sanctified by faith that is in me.

Romans 16:20 And the God of peace shall bruise Satan under your feet shortly. The grace of our Lord Jesus Christ be with you. Amen. **[What?]**

1 Corinthians 5:5 To deliver such an one unto Satan for the destruction of the flesh, that the spirit may be saved in the day of the Lord Jesus. **[What?]**

1 Corinthians 7:5 Defraud ye not one the other, except it be with consent for a time, that ye may give yourselves to fasting and prayer; and come together again, that Satan tempt you not for your incontinency.

2 Corinthians 2:11 Lest Satan should get an advantage of us: for we are not ignorant of his devices.

2 Corinthians 11:14 And no marvel; for Satan himself is transformed into an angel of light.

2 Corinthians 12:7 And lest I should be exalted above measure through the abundance of the revelations, there was given to me a thorn in the flesh, the messenger of Satan to buffet me, lest I should be exalted above measure.

1 Timothy 1:20 Of whom is Hymenaeus and Alexander; whom I have delivered unto Satan, that they may learn not to blaspheme.

1 Timothy 5:15 For some are already turned aside after Satan.

1 Thessalonians 2:18 Wherefore we would have come unto you, even I Paul, once and again; but Satan hindered us.

2 Thessalonians 2:9 Even him, whose coming is after the working of Satan with all power and signs and lying wonders,

Revelation 2:9 I know thy works, and tribulation, and poverty, (but thou art rich) and I know the blasphemy of them which say they are Jews, and are not, but are the synagogue of Satan.

Revelation 2:13 I know thy works, and where thou dwells, even where Satan's seat is: and thou holds fast my name, and hast not denied my faith, even in those days wherein Antipas was my faithful martyr, who was slain among you, where Satan dwells.

Revelation 2:24 But unto you I say, and unto the rest in Thyatira, as many as have not this doctrine, and which have not known the depths of Satan, as they speak; I will put upon you none other burden.

Revelation 3:9 Behold, I will make them of the synagogue of Satan, which say they are Jews, and are not, but do lie; behold, I will make them to come and worship before thy feet, and to know that I have loved thee.

Revelation 12:9 And the great dragon was cast out, that old serpent, called the **Devil**, and Satan, which deceived the whole world: he was cast out into the earth, and his angels were cast out with him.

Revelation 20:7 And when the thousand years are expired, Satan shall be loosed out of his prison,

Revelation 20:2 And he laid hold on the dragon, that old serpent, which is the **Devil**, and Satan, and bound him a thousand years,

As is the norm, every subject in the Bible is filled with contradictions. In contrast to the word "Satan" which is always written with a capital 'S', the 57 references of the word "devil" only has two references using a capital 'D', and it has a far less definitive meaning than the word Satan. The two capitol 'D's' are above, Revelation 12:9 and Revelation 20:2.

1 John 3:8 He that committed sin is of **the devil;** for the devil sinned from the beginning. For this purpose the Son of God was manifested, that he might destroy the works of the devil.

John 10:21 Others said, These are not the words of him that have **a devil**. Can a devil open the eyes of the blind?

Luke 11:14 And he was casting out a devil, and it was dumb. And it came to pass, when the devil was gone out, the dumb spake; and the people wondered.

Matthew 15:22 And, behold, a woman of Canaan came out of the same coasts, and cried unto him, saying, Have mercy on me, O Lord, thou Son of David; my daughter is grievously vexed with **a devil**.

www.ingramcontent.com/pod-product-compliance
Ingram Content Group UK Ltd.
Pitfield, Milton Keynes, MK11 3LW, UK
UKHW020144250726
13967UKWH00002B/860

9 781513 698052